THE SMART GUIDE TO

Starting Your Own Business

OPEN
FOR
BUSINESS

BY BARRY THOMSEN

SECOND EDITION

The Smart Guide To Starting Your Own Business - Second Edition

Published by

Smart Guide Publications, Inc.
2517 Deer Chase Drive
Norman, OK 73071
www.smartguidepublications.com

For information, address: Smart Guide Publications, Inc. 2517 Deer Creek Drive, Norman, OK 73071

SMART GUIDE and Design are registered trademarks licensed to Smart Guide Publications, Inc.

International Standard Book Number: 978-1-937636-11-1

Library of Congress Catalog Card Number:
11 12 13 14 15   10 9 8 7 6 5 4 3 2 1

Printed in the United States of America

Cover design: Lorna Llewellyn
Back cover design: Joel Friedlander, Eric Gelb, Deon Seifert
Back cover copy: Eric Gelb, Deon Seifert
Illustrations: James Balkovek
Production: Zoë Lonergan
Indexer: Cory Emberson
V.P./Business Manager: Cathy Barker

ACKNOWLEDGEMENTS

Without all the customers, suppliers, bankers, accountants, attorneys and loyal employees I have had over 30 years and 20 businesses this book could not be possible. The ideas and knowledge I received from all of them taught me many lessons that I am able to share in this book. Thanks to those who kept my spirits up when things got tough. Thanks to the instructors at DeVry University for pushing me to my limits in learning the logic of math, science and business. I most want to thank my Pastor and golf friend Bill Gamble for the spiritual guidance to keep writing when I felt like I hit a brick wall.

Thanks to my agent May Sue Seymour for encouraging me to write this book because of all the past experience I have had starting businesses. Thank you to my illustrator Lorna Llewellyn who put the personal touch to all the pages and made the book easy to read. Thanks to my publisher for sending the manuscript back to me several times until it was just right.

My wish is for all the aspiring entrepreneurs that read this book and use it's ideas to achieve great success in owning and building their own business!

TABLE OF CONTENTS

INTRODUCTION xv

   The First Step xv
     Do Your Research xv
     Marketing Your Business xvi
     Inside the Book xvi

1 Making the Commitment 1

   Why Bother? 1
     Your Goals 2
     Case Study 3
   Know Your Industry 4
     Work in the Industry 5
     Watch How the Business Works 6
   Learn How a Business Works 7
     Continuing Education 7
     Read and Listen 8
   Get Business Assistance 10
     SCORE 10
   Ask Yourself 11
   Your Business Plan 14
   Your Mission Statement 15

2 Your Business Structure 17

   Sole Proprietorship 18
     Pros and Cons of a Sole Proprietorship 18
   General Partnership 19
     Pros and Cons of a General Partnership 20
   C Corporation 21
     Pros and Cons of a C Corporation 22
   S Corporation 23
     Pros and Cons of an S Corporation 24
   Limited Liability Company (LLC) 24
     Pros and Cons of an LLC 24
   Naming Your Business 26
     Make the Name Unique 26
     Naming Dos and Don'ts 27
   Protect Your Business Name 28

3 Start-Up Capital 31

The First Hurdle 31
Friends, Relatives, and Angels 32
   Friends 32
   Relatives 33
   Angels. 33
Bank and Credit Union Loans 34
   Questions Your Banker Will Ask 34
   Reasons for Rejection 35
Credit Cards and Lines of Credit 36
   Lines of Credit are Best 37
Home Equity Financing 37
   It May Be Tax Deductible 38
Other Sources of Start-Up Capital 38
   Business Incubators 39
   Venture Capital Firms. 39
   Bootstrapping 39
   Grants 40

4 Accountants, Lawyers, and Bankers 41

Why Do I Need Them? 41
Your Accountant 42
   The Relationship. 43
   Who Works on Your Business? 43
   What to Expect from Your Accountant 44
   If It Doesn't Work Out. 45
Your Lawyer 46
   Finding a Good Lawyer 47
   Ask, But You Will Pay. 48
Your Banker. 49
   Select a Bank You Can Visit 49
When it's Time to Change 50

5 Location—Does It Matter? 51

Home-Based Business Setup 52
   Check Local and County Laws 54
   Deliveries. 54
Distribution or Industrial Space 54
   Considerations. 55
Retail Space 55

Selecting Your Store and Location 57
Before You Decide 57
Your Friendly Shopping Mall 58
Internet Business 60
Leases and Options 60
Lease Dos and Don'ts 61

6 Franchises 63

Do You Have the Expertise? 63
If You're Not Sure 64
Is a Franchise Right for You? 65
Where to Find a Franchise 66
Finding All the Choices 66
Do Your Due Diligence 68
Are You On Your Own? 69
Franchise Dos and Don'ts 70

7 Buying a Business 73

Why Buy an Existing Business? 73
Where to Find an Existing Business 74
Advertisements 74
Business Brokers 75
Referrals 75
What to Look For 76
What About Leases? 79
The Employees and Training 79
Training the New Owner 80
Retraining the Employees 80
Seller Financing 81
How It Works 82

8 Defining Your Target Market 85

Target Markets 85
Who Will Be Your Customers? 86
What You Need to Know 86
Why Will Anyone Buy from You? 87
What You Need to Offer 88
Your Competitors 89
Where Will You Find Customers? 92
Business Customers 92

Retail Customers. 92
Online Customers 93
Jump-Start Your New Business 93

9 Setting Up Suppliers 99

Who Will Make or Supply Your Products? 99
Get Samples or Testimonials 100
Become Partners with Suppliers 101
Free Sales Literature 101
Supplier Loyalty 102
Quantity Pricing and Shipping Costs .103
Establish Credit with Suppliers 104
What Can You Outsource? 105
Where Do You Find Outsourcers? 105
Keep Checking on Outsourcers 106

10 Accepting Credit Cards and Giving Credit 107

Choosing Your Merchant Service Provider 107
The Application 107
Getting a Credit Card Machine. 109
Processing Software 109
PayPal and Others 110
How It Works 111
Scams and Excessive Fees 111
Watch Out 112
Giving Customers Credit 113
Selling For Resale 115

11 Setting Up Your Website and Blog 117

Purpose of Your Site 117
Make Changes Later. 118
Make it Easy for Everyone. 119
Decide How Your Site Should Be Used. 121
Make Changes Regularly 121
Free E-mail Stuff. 121
Suggestion Box Link 122
Get the Word Out 123
Affiliate Marketing 124
Blogs Create Interest 124
Starting Your Blog 125
Making Your Blog Interesting. 126

12 Your First Employees 127

Adding Employees to Your Business .127
Interview with Care 128
    Hiring Hourly Employees 128
    Hiring Telemarketing Employees .130
    The Right In-Store Sales People .131
    Part-Time Outside Sales People .132
    Some Good Interview Questions .133
Train, Retrain, and Cross Train 134
    What Is Cross Training? 135
Supervise, Mentor, and Delegate 135
    Employees Must Be an Asset 136
    Delegate and Oversee 137
    Open-Door Policy 138
    Frontline Authority 139
    Ways to Make Employees Team Players 140
    Bully Employees 141
Superstars and Trust 142
    Superstar Employees 142
Building Trust 144

13 The Retail Jungle 145

Finding Retail Employees 145
Training New Hires 147
    Superstar Employees 147
The Customer Experience 147
    Wear Your Customers' Shoes 147
    Customers Want to Trust You 148
    Create Loyalty 149
    Reasons Customers Will Pay More 150
    Listen to Customers & Clients .150
    The Unfriendly Customer 151
    Customer and Client Rights 151
Having A Retail Sale 152
Shopping At A Small Store 153
Small Retailer Holiday Ideas 154
Retail Is Not For Everyone 154
    Why You Might Lose a Customer 154

14 Planning Your Grand Opening 157

Planning for Opening Day 157

Jump-Start Your New Business 158
   Promotions Help. 160
   Do It Now 160
Giveaways and Deals. 161
   Give Them Something. 161
   Surprise Customers 162
Partner with Other Businesses 162
   Cross Promotions 162
Use the Media 164
   Write Articles and Be an Expert 165
On-the-Air Publicity. 165
Other Events and Celebrations 166
   When Is Your Birthday?. 167
   First Anniversary 167

15 Products, Services, Guarantees 168

One-Stop Shop 169
Stand Behind All Sales. 170
A Little About Pricing 171
   Competitors, Price, and Value .171
   Pricing Headaches 172
State-of-the-Art Products 173
   Twist and Shout!. 173
   Offer Silver, Gold, and Platinum Levels 174
Follow Up on Large Sales 174
   What to Call About 175
Check Supplier Deals 175
   Overstocks, Deals, and Consignments 176
New Products and Services 176

16 Customer Service is King 179

The Importance of Customer Service .179
Be Available for Customer Consultation. 180
   Customer-Friendly Hours. 180
   Breaking Promises 182
Watch the Competition 183
   Questions about Competitors 183
Outsource and Monitor 185
Make Your Service Outstanding 185
   Make Them Say Wow! 186

Use the Telephone 186
Great Customer Service Rules 188
Create Loyalty 188
The Unresponsive Customer 189

17 Marketing and Publicity 191

Cheap Marketing Ideas 192
Free Publicity 193
Advertise or Not? 195
   Advertise to Four Levels 195
   Phrases Not to Use in Advertising .196
Direct Mail Works 197
   Why Direct Mail? 198
   Postcard Mailings 199
   E-Mail Marketing 200
Using New Promotion Ideas 201
Eleven Marketing Mistakes 201

18 Promotions Work 203

Ideas for Promotions 203
   Time for a Sale 204
   Gift Cards 206
   Do Something Outrageous 207
Retail Promotion Ideas 207

19 First-Year Problems 209

The Unpredictable 209
   The Unexpected 210
Owner Attitude and Burnout 211
   First-Year Burnout 211
Overspending 212
First-Year Pitfalls 213
   A Bad Publicity Story 215

20 Trade Shows, Conventions & Conferences 219

General Sessions & Keynotes 219
   Special Dinners & Luncheons 220
Attending Shows and Conferences 220
   Getting the Most Out Of Attending .221

Exhibiting At Trade Shows and Expos 221
   Tradeshow Exhibiting Expenses 222
   Working Your Exhibit Booth 223
   After the Show 224
   8Seminar 224
   Seminars by Others 224
   Seminars By You 225
Finding The Right Shows 225

21 New Business Tips and Ideas 227

Business Slowdowns 227
   Temporary Slow Periods 228
   A Serious Slowdown 229
   Unnecessary Personnel 230
Buy Your Umbrella When the Sun Is Shining .231
Being Small 232
   Small Can Be Great 232
   Small Business Can Mean Big Business 234
Join Up! 235
   Join the Chamber of Commerce 235
   Toastmasters 236
Other Ideas 237
   Where Are Your Business Cards? 238
   Give Discounts Cordially 239
   Home Business Meetings 239
   High Rollers 241
   Be a Radio Guest 242
   Obsolete Products 243

22 Sell Out or Bail Out 245

Are You Getting Too Big? 245
   Too Many Nuisance Sales 246
Stress and Long Hours 247
   Long Working Hours 248
Retire or Move On 248
   Selling the Business 248
   Giving the Business to a Family Member 249
   Close the Business 250
Financially Unstable 251

Index 253

INTRODUCTION

You want to start a business of your very own and be a huge success. You feel you have considered it thoroughly, and you can't miss with all your drive and determination. You know (or do you?) there's a lot to do in the beginning, and you're mentally prepared for it. It's time to get started, but you need some guidelines on what to do, the order in which they should be done, and when to do them—steps that are important to any business, especially a new one, to assure a successful venture. *The Smart Guide for Starting Your Own Business* will point you in the right direction, guiding you to prosperity and success.

Most of us will never achieve number one status in our field, but we don't really have to be number one. Operating our own challenging, satisfying, and profitable business is really what it's all about. If you're happy with your level of success, you have already accomplished more than most people.

The First Step

Just starting a business like all the others won't give many customers any reason to buy from you. There needs to be some stimulus to make people spend their money with your new company. And if you're not offering something better than they have now, why should they even bother? Before doing anything else, you need to have an idea of the type of business you want to run.

Start by making a list of everything in your area of interest that would be a better product or service. Put it on your list whether it's possible to supply it or not. You need to have a lot of items on your list, not just one or two, so write every idea down, even if it seems trivial. Then go back over every item you have written down and decide which ones you can provide profitably. There should be several, not just one, to offer customers and prospects. One new idea has less of a chance of catching on than several. You want to appeal to as many buyers and purchasers as possible.

Do Your Research

Remember, you have no experience and no track record, so the first purchase from you has some risk connected to it. If you can't make that risk worthwhile, however small it is, there is no reason to buy from you. In plain English, you need to determine why anyone would buy from you and who these customers would be. What type of person or business is your target market? You must know that answer to direct your marketing correctly because if your target market is not well defined, you're just wasting money going in the wrong direction.

Do some research and visit future competitors to see what's missing. Check their websites and, if possible, talk to some of their customers. The more information you can collect, the better chance you have to attract patrons when you open.

If you're going to start a local business, appealing to local customers, then all other similar businesses in the area will be your competitors. To learn and ask questions of others in your industry, you may need to take a trip out of town.

Go to a city about the size of yours but at least 100 miles away to visit similar businesses. You can either make an appointment or just walk in and ask for the owner or manager. Explain what you are planning to do and ask for their advice and suggestions. Once they know that you won't be a competitor of theirs, the walls should come down.

Most people enjoy helping other people and are even flattered when asked for their opinion. You might even ask if you can spend a few hours watching their business in action to get some firsthand experience. Be sure to offer to buy them dinner or give a small gift for their time.

You need to consider whether your new idea could expand the current market or open up a new one. Will your way of doing business open some new doors and entice a new group of purchasers? How will competitors react to your new idea once they see it working? Can you keep one step ahead of them? Will your new idea be protected in any way, or isn't that possible?

Marketing Your Business

Starting a business is easy, but making it successful and long-lasting is another thing. Don't just assume that people will flock to your door just because you are open. In fact, it may be exactly the opposite. You will have to go out and get them using all the marketing tools you can afford to use. Just running an ad or sending a flyer is not going to get everyone. You need a mix of several marketing methods to reach all the possible customers you can. If you monitor where your best responses are coming from, you will soon learn what is working for you. You'll learn in this book how to get the word out and how to treat customers so they will come back again and again.

Inside the Book

The Smart Guide to Starting Your Own Business was written for the average person who is serious about opening his or her own business. The advice in this book is easy to understand; you don't need a master's degree to use the ideas and methods that are offered here. You may want to take a few courses in computer basics, accounting, and general business to enhance your chances of success. I've even seen a few small-business courses being offered. Anything you can put in your personal arsenal before you start gives you a better chance of success. Remember, a horse who wins a race by a nose is still the winner.

So, you may ask, why am I qualified to write this book, and why should I expect you to buy my book and use my ideas? Well, over the past thirty-five years, I've opened many small businesses and helped others start theirs. I've had my ups and downs, successes and failures, and now you can benefit from my experiences and the knowledge I've gained.

I have had businesses in several different industries and had to learn and adapt to each one. I've also seen people go into business without a plan and no knowledge of what should be done. They didn't do what's necessary to be successful and were soon closed and their investment lost. One thing I have learned is you should listen to as much advice as you can get, and then sort out what will work for you. This book is here to assist you. Read it, highlight passages, refer back to it often, and go grab success in your own business.

CHAPTER 1

Making the Commitment

In This Chapter

➤ Are you ready to start a business?

➤ Learn your industry

➤ How a business works

➤ Business plan and mission statement

In this chapter you will learn what it takes to reach success in a small business. You will learn how to get your business plan and mission statement on paper before you take the plunge. You'll also learn if you have the knowledge to start a business and where to get help if you need it.

Before you even start or make any investment in a new business, a total commitment must be present in your mind and in your heart. You're not going to try to open a new business; you're going to succeed in a new business. If you don't feel that way up front, you may not be ready yet, and you may need to do more soul searching. Without a commitment, you would have a better chance at making profits by putting your money in a mutual fund or another investment and keeping your day job. But if that total commitment is there and you are willing to learn, invest the time, and make a 110 percent effort, you're ready to begin on that journey to success.

Why Bother?

You want to quit your job and open a small business—are you crazy? All those years at your current company building tenure and loyalty will go down the drain. What about your retirement plan or pension (do they still offer these?) and all your benefits? Will your family, relatives, and friends try to get you committed to a mental institution? Why would anyone with a sane mind give up security and take a chance on failure? It's like a casino saying that the players can be the house, or buying a lottery ticket for Saturday's drawing and ordering a new sports car and speedboat Friday on credit. Some things are just too wild and risky to even consider. Why would you put so much on the line when the outcome is so uncertain?

Business Vocab

A commitment is a promise, guarantee, or pledge to do something to the best of your abilities.

Why? Because you have that inner drive that just won't go away and won't let you stay in your comfortable, stable, and dead-end position. When you try to suppress all those thoughts about opening a business, they always seem to creep back. The idea keeps gnawing at you; do it now or soon because you're not getting any younger.

But should you take the risk and how big of a risk is it anyway? What happens if you fail, can you ever face your family and friends again? Life-changing decisions can be the most difficult to make, and the answers don't come easy. But, hey, if you're even reading this book, you must have some inclination to go ahead and take the plunge, so read on.

Your Goals

Starting a business doesn't have to be as scary and risky as it sounds. And you are certainly not alone; there are over a million new businesses that open every year. Some of these are home based and others are just part-time, but they all needed investment and desire to be successful. Of course, just wanting success is not enough—you have to work hard to achieve it.

Ask Yourself

Are you ready to make the total commitment to starting a business? Have you discussed your idea with your family and do they support you? Starting a small business is more than a full-time job; your family needs to be behind you.

You can't just wait for a beautiful, delicious-looking ripe apple on a tree branch 20 feet high to fall in your lap; you have to climb up the tree to get it. And this might not be as easy as you think, so you need to have a plan. Opening a new business is the same; you don't just turn on your open sign and get ready for the customer stampede.

You need to plan how you will start and operate your business in advance if you want to avoid being part of the business failure statistic. And if you don't know how to plan, you will have to learn before you start.

Regardless of what industry you will be going into, a business plan is a necessity. If this sounds like being in school, it is, but there is a lot more at stake here. This is the assignment you want to get an A+ on, and you want to be top of your class. Your class will be the other million would-be entrepreneurs that are also starting a business this year. There will be no extracurricular activities, just classwork, homework, special projects, and maybe even a term paper. Does this all sound a little far-fetched and overblown? Well it isn't, and you should always take your decision to open a business seriously, especially if it's your first one.

Business Facts

Of the million-plus businesses that start every year, less than 50 percent of them survive five years and less than 30 percent last ten years. There are some that don't even last the first year. The biggest reason for failure that I see is lack of commitment and focus.

Case Study

I still remember when I opened my first business in the Chicago area. I was working at a computer employment agency and got a commission for everyone I placed in a position. I was newly married with our first child on the way. I had reached the position of number two producer out of forty people and was making a decent income. But every time I came up with a new idea or wanted to try something different, I was shot down by management. This didn't sit well with me because I knew the computer industry was growing quickly in the 1970s, and the potential was there to place a lot of trained people. I approached a friend who also worked there and posed the idea of starting our own agency. He agreed and we set out to become millionaires (it didn't happen). We never had a written plan; we just went ahead in a seat-of-the-pants fashion.

We rented an office in a Chicago suburb, ordered the phone service, bought some used furniture, and were ready to go, we thought. We left the other company and officially opened our first new business the next day. With a lot of ambition, hopes, and a dream, we were ready to make some money. It really felt good that first day being in an office that was ours, win or lose, and we didn't have to answer to anyone.

Since we didn't have a noncompete agency contract, we were able to ask some of our former clients to follow us. We just gave them our new phone number and told them when our first day was. The only mini-plan we had was in our minds, and I'm sure a lot was missing. We learned quickly that we had to know how to operate from a business perspective, not just do the business. Neither of us had any experience operating a real business.

Luckily we made it through, but it probably took longer to be successful than if we had planned better in advance. We were able to hire a receptionist in a couple of months and then added several people to work for us on salary plus commission. For two guys in their twenties, we were making a decent living and had some other perks that come along with owning your own business like a car allowance, client lunch and dinner expenses, and free time off whenever we wanted it.

Even with no one to answer to, I ended up spending more time at work than I did before. I think we were able to have some success because the computer industry was growing so quickly at that time. We got in and took our risk when everything was on the upswing and the demand for this type of service was big. We didn't know it at the time, but it was one of those right places at the right time situations.

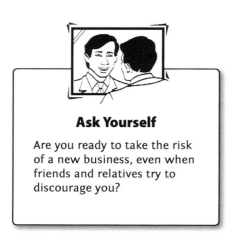

Ask Yourself

Are you ready to take the risk of a new business, even when friends and relatives try to discourage you?

Everyone can't be as fortunate as we were, and we probably wouldn't be able to do it again today. We beat the odds by being in a no-brainer, fast-growing service business. If you can find one like that in today's marketplace, you'll really have an advantage and a great chance for quick success. I think everyone in life gets an equal number of opportunities; it's what you do with them that sets us all apart. In the case of our new agency, I don't think we even knew about the opportunity, it just came when we needed it. Well, maybe we knew the industry was growing and sort of took a back-door approach. Blind luck still counts; don't knock it. When you're opening a new business, you use all the tools available, even if you don't realize you're using them.

Know Your Industry

You already know everything you need to know to start your business, you think. You are an expert auto mechanic on GM cars, and all your friends with GMs bring their cars to you for repairs. You even worked part-time at a quick oil-change place after high school. But what are you going to do if someone needs work done on a Ford or a Chrysler? Are they that much different? Can you stumble through a repair and learn as you go along? What about any needed parts—is your parts supplier set up? You can't buy retail any more—how do you know if you're getting the best possible wholesale prices? Why would anyone even give you wholesale prices—did you guarantee a certain level of volume to get it? What if you don't reach that volume—will there be a surcharge at the end of the year, or will your prices be raised next year? Did you check other suppliers and compare?

Okay, take a deep breath and relax for a second.

But you're not done yet, there's more. Will your suppliers offer you free delivery like they offer car dealers, or will you have to stop what you're doing and pick up parts? Will that delay finishing a job on time and if so, will the customer be unhappy about the delay and not come back or send referrals? You can hire people to run these errands, but you have to pay them. Will this extra expense be passed on to the customer and will that make you less competitive, or will you just take the cost from your profits until you build up enough volume to get free delivery?

Business Knowledge

Working in one aspect of an industry may make you familiar with many of the behind-the-scene activities, but without further knowledge in the field you won't be able to innovate and use your new ideas to make your business unique. Never stop learning.

These are questions that are more easily answered by doing. But if you're just opening your business, you don't have any experience to refer to. The answers won't be found in an auto mechanic's reference guide, either. You will have to discover the answers yourself. If you have the answers before you start your business, you will have fewer setbacks and headaches later.

These types of situations and questions will need to be resolved in any business or industry you go into. How do you get this valuable information that can make or break your first few months in business? You get it from your soon-to-be competitors, of course.

Work in the Industry

You may have already worked in the industry, and that's what got you inspired and motivated to open your own business in the first place. You saw what others were doing in your industry of interest and felt you had a better, faster, cheaper, or more service-oriented way. This is where a lot of ideas for new businesses come from, not necessarily from some textbook in high school or college.

You should consider working in your prospective industry, if you haven't already done so. You can probably get a part-time position and keep your regular job so you won't sacrifice your current income level. Don't even give a thought to a low hourly rate or salary. Who cares; you are there to learn, not make money. How else can you get a hands-on education in your area of interest and even get paid for learning? If you are just coming out of high school or college and haven't been working in your future industry, you definitely need on-the-job experience in advance of opening a new business. Even if you are considering a franchise, get some background on the company by working at one location before you make your investment.

While you are working for a future competitor, don't just learn the job you're being paid for—be nosy. Ask supervisors, managers, and the owner how their business works. Find out if there are slow periods and what they do if it gets too busy. Watch how they treat their customers and observe how the customer reacts. See if you can find areas and procedures that you would improve in your own business, even if they are small steps. After all, if you can't do it better, why bother starting a new business at all?

Being just like everyone else makes you a follower, not a leader. You want to have a new business that fills the wants, needs, and little customer service gaps that are being left open currently. And keep in mind that some of the customers you are servicing in your temporary job may become your patrons in the future.

Watch How the Business Works

Working in your industry of choice gives you the opportunity to observe the inner workings of the business. Be observant of where supplies and other accoutrements come from. Look on cases and boxes to find their origin and make a mental record of it. When you leave for the day or go on a break, write this information down for future reference. Check out the business hours and decide if they really suit the customers or if they need to be adjusted. When you have your own business, make your open hours convenient for customers, not just for your schedule. Everything you learn or observe is a lesson you can't even put a price on. Its value could pay off handsomely in your business. So be as curious as you can and ask, ask, ask.

You may also have a chance to see what the business is charging its customers and determine if the value is there for that price. Try to keep track of these prices, but don't write them down while you're working. Are they too high, too low, or just right for the product or services that are offered?

It's also helpful to watch other employees and see if they are dedicated to the business. Are these the kind of employees that you would want working for you? Are they really working to the best of their abilities or just slacking off? Is there any supervision or does everyone just report to the owner? And how well does the owner pay attention to what his or her employees do, and are there too many employees or too few? How would you handle employees differently, or do you even know? Watch them over a period of time and you'll see a trend in their abilities and behavior.

Maybe you learned all about the industry you want to enter from being interested in it as a hobby or pastime. You could almost be an expert in some part of it already, but that may not be enough to start and run a successful business. You will need to know everything you can about all aspects of the business. And you need to know how to operate a real business. You may have even made some extra pocket money from your pastime, but there's a big difference between that and a *for profit* business. A business is a much bigger operation, especially if you have employees.

Are you entering a field that you have absolutely no knowledge of or experience in at all but have always wanted to learn about? If this is the case, you will definitely need some on-the-job experience or a partner. If you have a partner, you must bring something of value to the table, even if it's only start-up capital.

Learn How a Business Works

If you have never owned and operated a business before, you're not alone. As I said earlier, over a million new businesses open every year, and I'll bet that two-thirds of these business owners don't know all the basics of how a business works.

When I opened my first business, I was one of those two-thirds—I didn't even know what some of the accounting terms meant. I knew we had to have financial reports and file tax forms, so I thought we would just hire an accountant or accounting service. When we did select a service, a business accountant was assigned to our account. But he had so many clients to handle that we didn't get too much of his time other than during quarterly and yearly reports. Plus, our monthly fee was higher than we had anticipated, maybe because we were getting too many reports we didn't want or need. And many were even blank because we had no data to put on them.

If you only need the basics at first, don't hire an accounting service with all the bells and whistles—it's a waste of money. Get the service or plan that will provide only what you need; you can always upgrade later.

This is just one example of the headaches that can be avoided by a better understanding of how a business works.

Continuing Education

If you never had any business college courses, it's not too late to go and take a few now. There's no age limit for going to college, and you'll probably see people there from eighteen to eighty years old. There are many community and junior colleges everywhere that have courses or special classes for what you need. Most will have very flexible class times, some early and some late. This way, you can continue working until you complete the courses and make the break to start your business. There are also many online colleges and schools where you can take courses or just learn about the subjects you desire. But as with

Business Alerts

Study the successful companies that made it big after starting small. Most of them took risks and changed direction many times. It takes more than book smarts to achieve lasting success. Learn from success stories and successful people.

everything else on the web, check them out before you send money or use your credit card. Some newer courses I've heard about actually specialize in small business operation and that's exactly what you need. Learn what you need to know in the time you have available.

If you don't have the time or desire to take a full course with homework and projects, consider a seminar or workshop on the subject(s) you need to learn more about. Many will last all day; some minicourses last up to four days at one location. You can find some of them by searching the Internet using the word *seminar* followed by the main word you're interested in. For example, *seminar accounting, seminar financing*, or just *seminar small business*. Send an e-mail to any of interest and ask for a list of dates and locations as well as a syllabus. There will definitely be a fee involved for attending, so ask about fees in advance. If a fee isn't listed or if the seminar is advertised as being *free*, be prepared for some arm twisting to get you to buy some bigger items (books or tapes) while you're there. We all know nothing is *free* (if you're that naive, maybe you shouldn't be going into your own business).

Read and Listen

I'm also a big advocate of learning from books, recorded tapes, and CDs. I have bookcases full of all types of business books and audio books. They're in my office at work and at home. I just feel a good business book (paper or audio) can give you ideas, suggestions, and solutions to problems that you can't find anywhere else.

When I listen to an audio book in the car, I know I will listen to it again in a couple of months. You can't remember everything the first time you hear it, and some of the information may not be relevant until the next time you hear it.

I sometimes mark pages in hard copy books with paper clips when they contain some unusual or important information so I can quickly refer to it when needed.

I don't think you can have too many books, even if many are on the same business subject. The new e-books are convenient to carry anywhere, so storage is no longer an excuse. Every time I see a new book from a famous businessperson come out, I have to get it. If they are so successful, I want to know what they know. Sometimes there are ideas in books that are ten to twenty years old that will still work just as well today. If I can get even one or two new ideas to try, I know that I've got my money's worth.

Several books on the same business subject gives you each author's unique perspective. Then you can decide for yourself what will work best in your situation, or you can apply parts of some or all of the ideas to your new business. Never throw a business book out; you may need information from it in the future. Most bookshelves are deep enough to store books two deep; I put the taller ones in the back. Books are like your kid's baby pictures, ten, twenty, or forty years from now, you'll still want to refer to them.

Business Knowledge

The more advice you can get regardless of the source will help you make decisions. Ask and listen to everyone, then use the information to make your own informed decisions.

If you are just starting your business book library, get some sturdy bookshelves and try to put them in your personal office within view of your desk. I like to look over and see my books so I know that help is always close by. You can begin by purchasing books at a discount at *Amazon.com* or *Barnesandnoble.com*, or you can search *business books* on the Internet. You might be able to find some good business reference books at used book stores or even at garage sales.

It doesn't matter that a book may look old and tattered as long as you can read the words. In fact, if it looks that used, it must have great information that someone referred to a lot. And since you probably get a few gifts every year (birthday, December holidays, Mother's/Father's Day), ask people to give you the latest business books coming out. It's a reasonably priced gift and you know that you will use it. Most e-books can be purchased at an even lower cost.

Get Business Assistance

As the saying goes, no man is an island—you can always use help in your business decisions, even if it's only to second guess your ideas and give you another perspective. Going blindly into something that you have never done before can lead to unexpected situations or even dead ends. It's always to your advantage to get some *street-smart* advice and direction from someone who has traveled the road before. Even Dorothy picked up some associates on her way to Oz, and so should you. Don't be afraid to ask for help or assistance; most people are happy to give it.

Finding a mentor to take a personal interest in your success would be great for you. Anyone who is currently in business or has a successful business would be a perfect candidate. You may be able to meet a mentor at a Chamber of Commerce or business organization meeting. There are a lot of people out there with loads of experience who would love to share their knowledge with you as long as you aren't going to be a competitor of theirs. Most will help you for no fee or return obligation other than a thank-you or a nice lunch. They get personal satisfaction from seeing you become a success using some of their advice. They may be able to introduce you to other important people such as bankers, accountants, and lawyers. You might be able to work with some of these people who wouldn't even talk to you without this sort of introduction.

SCORE

A good business resource that has been around for quite a while is SCORE. You have probably heard of SCORE but maybe never went any further because you didn't know what it was all about. Well, it's probably the best deal for business advice that you'll ever find. Actually, the cost for a lot of their services is *zero, free, nil*. These are experienced entrepreneurs, many retired, who love small business so much they can't get enough of it. They want to help you be successful using all the knowledge they acquired on their small-business journey.

The people at SCORE offer valuable information on start-up operations, expansion, and even overseas sales. You can receive two monthly e-mail newsletters that are well worth the time to read. I wish I had known about these back when I was starting some of my businesses. When you're not sure of your next step and don't know where to turn, SCORE may be a great resource.

SCORE has over 10,000 volunteer counselors who have on-the-job experience in many fields of expertise ready to assist you. You can select a counselor by business category (printing, construction, restaurants) or by business function (advertising, bank loans, pricing) or both. A counselor in your area of need will work with you for a couple of sessions or as long as a few years. In some cases, a counselor may even be able to visit your place of business and see your new operation firsthand.

SCORE also offers many convenient and low-cost local area seminars and workshops on specific business subjects. This is great for new start-ups that have a limited budget but still need the information. It also offers help with writing a formal business plan.

If you visit its website at *www.score.org*, you can ask some of your questions online via e-mail. SCORE has over 1,200 online counselors ready to assist you 24/7. You will get a response from someone within forty-eight hours and, again, the cost is free. How can you not take advantage of this when the need arises? Everything you ask is always kept

Business Knowledge

One of my favorite pages on the SCORE website is the *Success Story Archives*. There are at least one hundred short stories about how all different types of people started or grew their business and got around those roadblocks we all come to. You can select your *success story* by type of business, such as retail, food, industrial, or high tech.

confidential by your counselor who abides by a code of ethics.

You can find the location of a SCORE office near you that you can contact by phone or visit personally. If you are just starting out, have a basic business plan or outline and other information ready when you make your first contact. Then select or ask for a counselor who has expertise in the industry or type of business you need assistance with. You may even end up with two or more counselors, each of whom has expert knowledge in different but related areas.

When the need for business advice comes up, get on the phone or Internet and talk to someone at SCORE.

Ask Yourself

It does take a bit more than desire and drive to open and operate a successful business. Many of you who have been employed by a big corporation for most of your working life won't be *street smart* when it comes to small business. Sure, you may have shopped at a lot of smaller stores and offices, but there's a lot more going on behind the scenes that keeps those doors open every day.

There are a lot of questions you should ask yourself before you sign that lease and start buying furniture and equipment. Without the answers to these questions, your chances of a smooth path to opening your small business is doubtful. You can't just turn on your open sign or build a website and expect a line of customers to form. Your wait could be longer than you think—a lot longer. And why would anyone do business with you, the unproven new kid on the block with little or no experience? Come on!

Let's see how many of these questions you have quick answers for and how many you need to dig a little to resolve. These questions and possible answers are for you, not me, to see if you're really ready to open a business. Opening a business could be the most difficult thing you've ever done, but when it works, the rewards are the greatest!

➤ Do you really want to open a business? Why, because you're tired of working for someone else, or do you have a vision of filling the wants and needs of customers? (Pssst, the second one is the correct answer.)

➤ Will your product or service fill a need that is not being completely filled now, or is it just a copy of something already on the market?

➤ Do you have the finances to start this business? If not, do you know where you can get funding? Is your credit good enough so you can borrow money, and do you have assets to put up?

➤ Will there be enough demand for your product or service? Is the target market big enough to support your new business plus any competitors that may come in later?

➤ Do you possess the ability and skills needed to perform the tasks in your business? Are you able and willing to train others to do an excellent job?

➤ Is your product or service going to have a high value, or are you just going to compete on price? What if competitors' prices are lower than your cost? Can you survive?

➤ Do you have the knowledge to run the business end of your new enterprise? Are you willing to spend the time learning what you don't know, or will you take on a partner or two who can handle that aspect?

➤ How will you market your company? Can you afford expensive advertising and commercials? Will you use direct mail or telemarketing, and how long will it take to build a profitable customer base?

➤ Can you afford to hire good employees? How will you find them, and do you have the time for all the interviews? Who will train them? How will they be supervised to ensure acceptable performance?

➤ Will you devote the time necessary to make your new business a success? Are you prepared to give up weekends and vacations because your business needs you there in the beginning? Will you be 100 percent dedicated to its success?

➤ Do you have the support of your family, and are they willing to help you when necessary? Are your friends giving you encouragement or just warning you about possible failure?

➤ Have you been planning this move for a while? Is your plan written down and workable, or did you just decide to do this over the weekend?

➤ Have you done any research on your business idea? Can you make a list of pros and cons for your idea? Are there more pros and are you sure?

➤ Have you determined a time period when you feel the business will become profitable? Do you think it will be the first week or month?

➤ Do you have any type of backup fund for unexpected problems, expenses, or disasters? Is it enough to keep your business open while you recover?

➤ What if your idea doesn't take off like you've planned? Do you have a second and third idea? Have you thought about any government regulations or patent infringements? Are you sure your idea is original?

➤ Do you have enough savings to live on for up to six months? Is your spouse and/or family willing to be conservative until your business gets going?

Business Alerts

No one can decide when it's the right time to open a new business except you. Waiting too long or jumping in too soon may reduce your chances of success. You will know the correct time—then just do it!

> ➤ Are you involved in any lawsuits or a divorce that could adversely affect your new business? Are all your personal income taxes settled and up to date?

> ➤ Have you really made the full mental commitment to go ahead with this new business? Can you give it all your attention during its incubation and infancy?

> ➤ Are you willing to do everything necessary to make your new business a success, even those possibly unpleasant tasks that you can't predict? Will you give up if things get too difficult?

These are just some of the questions you need to answer before you spend any seed money. As you can see, just having a dream and an idea aren't enough; you need the whole package, or most of it. This is why many new businesses don't last for two, three, or four years. The new entrepreneurs don't really know all it takes to run a successful company.

All these questions are not intended to discourage you but make you anticipate all that's involved in opening and operating a business. Now that you have some answers, you may need a few more pages added to your plan before you start. And those new pages could be the most important of all, so don't overlook them.

Your Business Plan

Making and writing down a business plan gives your new enterprise a purpose for being and a road map, however incomplete, to where it's going. Don't make the mistake of just leaving your plan in your mind because parts of it will become lost or ignored.

It's OK to change your business plan whenever you anticipate going in a new direction or see a new opportunity on the horizon. We can't predict the future. We need to be flexible and adjust our plan along the way to take advantage of new ideas.

Your basic business plan should consist of the following:

> ➤ General description of your business: the products and services you plan to sell and why

> ➤ Goals and Objectives: the reasons you are starting this business and what you expect to accomplish

> ➤ Start-up capital: where is it coming from and how much do you need

> ➤ Growth capital: sources for additional funding as your business moves into its growth stage

> ➤ Target market: who you will sell to and its size (the market must be big enough to sustain your business and that of your competitors)

> ➤ Competition: who will be your competitors and where they are located

➤ Business strategy: your plan for entering your target market and what you have to offer buyers

➤ Your keys to success: Tools you plan to use to succeed and their availability

➤ Executive summary: why you feel this business will be a success and what you're willing to do to make it a winner

These are the basic concepts that you should know going into any new business. By writing them out in a business plan, you'll be backing up what you've been thinking about for a while. A written business plan will also make your new business idea seem more realistic because you can see it right there on paper. Remember, it doesn't have to be formal and can be changed at any time. Just get it done the first time, and the rest will be easy.

Your Mission Statement

Every business should have some type of mission statement that the owner-entrepreneur, employees, suppliers, and customers can use to define the purpose of the company. It's your opportunity to tell the world why you are in business, what your business stands for, your beliefs, your ideas, and your goals. Most mission statements are one to three sentences long and get directly to the point. It should not take more than twenty seconds to recite it by memory. Many businesses post their mission statement on their office and factory walls for everyone to read. Be proud of your mission statement and never hide it.

Some mission statement examples of well-known companies include:

➤ *Starbucks*: "Our Mission: to inspire and nurture the human spirit—one person, one cup and one neighborhood at a time."

➤ *Microsoft*: "At Microsoft, we work to help people and businesses throughout the world realize their full potential. This is our mission. Everything we do reflects this mission and the values that make it possible."

➤ *Nike*: "To bring inspiration and innovation to every athlete in the world."

➤ *Arby's*: "To provide an exceptional dining experience that satisfies our guests' grown-up tastes by being a 'cut above' in everything we do."

➤ *Omnicare*: "Our business is pharmaceutical care. Our mission is positive outcomes."

➤ *Hershey*: "Undisputed marketplace leadership."

CHAPTER 2

Your Business Structure

In This Chapter

➤ The five different business structures

➤ Advantages and disadvantages of each

➤ How to name your business

➤ Ways to protect your name

In this chapter you will learn to select the type of business legal entity that will work best for you. You will also learn why your new business name is important and how to protect it.

You will have many important decisions to make when starting your business, and choosing your business structure or entity is one of the first ones you'll need to tackle. The business structure determines how your financial reports are written and how taxes are paid. It also determines who makes financial, marketing, and other decisions after you are in an ongoing business. And the business structure determines who makes important decisions and who is responsible for government reports.

Business Facts

It doesn't matter if it's part-time, full-time, or out of your car, if you are providing goods or services for payment, you're a business. The U.S. Census Bureau estimates that over 12 million people are self-employed with more starting their own businesses every day.

There is no right or wrong entity; each owner or group of owners must choose what is best for them. Examine all of the five business structures thoroughly before making a final decision, and check with your Secretary of State office to find out what forms must be filed for each type. Many of the forms necessary to start a business can be found at the Secretary of State website.

Sole Proprietorship

Sole proprietorship, one person operating a business for profit, is the simplest, least expensive, and most basic form of business ownership. It probably goes back as far as records have been kept. The person is the business and the business is the person and absorbs all profits and losses. The owner-sole proprietor has complete control of everything that goes on in the business. A sole proprietor can be compared to a king or queen in a monarchy: everything he or she says goes (I think they stopped the beheading, though).

This type of business structure has many advantages and disadvantages that can be assessed before it's established by the current needs of the owner. It may also be changed to one of the other business structures later as the owner's needs change. The owner can operate the business under a different name but may be required to file a dba, or doing business as, form with the Secretary of State office. The owner can also operate under more than one business name and file a dba for each one.

Pros and Cons of a Sole Proprietorship

As with most things in life, each business structure has its advantages and disadvantages. Let's take a look at the pros and cons of running a sole proprietorship.

The advantages of a sole proprietorship:

> ➤ Easy and quick to start: in many cases, a business can be in existence in one day

> ➤ Low startup costs: most of the minimal paperwork such as the dba and tax filing can be done by the owner

> ➤ Low shutdown costs: when and if the decision comes to close the business, there is only a minimal amount of work needed to do it

> ➤ No business taxes: all profits and losses are filed by the owner as part of his or her personal tax return

> ➤ Complete control: the owner answers to no one when decisions are made

> ➤ Easy to sell: less complicated to sell or transfer assets

> ➤ All profits go to the owner: the owner does not have to share with anyone

The disadvantages of a sole proprietorship:

➤ Owner is responsible: all liabilities fall on the shoulders of a single owner

➤ Financial defaults: creditors can go after the owner personally if the business closes or fails

➤ Personally liable: owner is responsible for all debts of the business and may have to pledge personal assets

➤ Raising capital: may be more difficult to get loans and new capital to grow based only on the owner's assets and credit background

➤ The business is at greater risk: if the owner becomes disabled, retires, or dies and a succession plan is not in place, the business is terminated

➤ Customers' distrust: customers may hesitate to make large purchases guaranteed by only one person

➤ Slower growth potential: may be less desirable to investors and key employees

General Partnership

In a general partnership, two or more partners share in the ownership of a single business. Each partner is equally responsible and has the authority to operate the business. In general, any one partner can run the day-to-day operations of the business and make management decisions. The decisions of one partner can bind the other members of the general partnership.

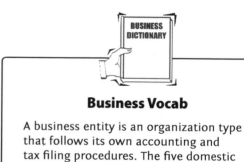

Business Vocab

A business entity is an organization type that follows its own accounting and tax filing procedures. The five domestic entities each have advantages and disadvantages for its owners.

If one or more partners die or ignore their duties or obligations, the other partner(s) are responsible. This is why a partnership agreement, which is a legal document, should always be drawn up when starting a general partnership, and then it should be reviewed periodically. Without the formal agreement, one partner could walk or refuse to honor his or her obligations. Many longtime friendships have been destroyed during a partnership business for lack of a partnership agreement. The agreement should include a provision to dissolve the partnership if one or more parties want out.

Pros and Cons of a General Partnership

As you read through the advantages and disadvantages of running a general partnership, keep in mind how they would affect the type of business you're thinking of starting to determine if a general partnership is right for you.

The advantages of a general partnership:

➤ Easy to establish

➤ Financial commitments are shared by the partners

➤ Two or more owners contributing start-up capital means more initial funds

➤ Lenders may be more inclined to give loans to a business with two or more partners signing

➤ Key employees may be attracted because of the chance of becoming a partner in the future

➤ Partners may have different skills and expertise that will benefit the business

➤ Two heads are better than one, and three are better than two when brainstorming for creative ideas

➤ Each partner has a vested interest in the business

The disadvantages of a general partnership are as follows:

➤ Partners may not agree on all issues, and arguments can arise

➤ Partners are jointly and individually responsible for all the debts and liabilities of the business

➤ Profits must be shared, and all partners may not put in the same time and effort

➤ Profits must be reported on the partners' individual income tax returns

➤ The business partnership may cease to exist if a partner dies or withdraws

➤ Partners must consult each other before major decisions are made, which can cause delays

➤ Outside investors may be hesitant to get involved in a partnership with several decision makers

➤ All partners have unlimited liability for all debts of the business

C Corporation

A general, or C, corporation is a legal business structure that is governed by the laws of incorporation in each state. A C corporation consists of a person or group of persons who are stockholders. Each stockholder can own a different number of shares or percentage of the entire corporation. Shares can be bought, sold, or traded according to the bylaws of the corporation. Shareholders do not have to be employed by or involved in the day-to-day operation of the business, but in new or small corporations many of them are a part of the business.

Ask Yourself

Many new enterprises now start at home to keep expenses down and to test their profitability. If the owner of a home-based business wants it to grow, he or she would need to find a new location and hire employees. It can be a tough decision and must be made in time by the owner.

Starting a C corporation requires more paperwork and fees than starting a sole proprietorship or general partnership, so it's wise to consult an attorney (see Chapter 4) to make sure it's done correctly. Many new corporations decide to become a close corporation, which limits stockholders to thirty to fifty people, and any new shares authorized must be offered to existing shareholders before selling to new shareholders. A corporation must have officers and directors and periodic meetings. This can be done even if there is only one person as a shareholder.

When setting up a C corporation, an Articles of Incorporation document must be submitted. This needs to be included when filing with the Secretary of State as a new corporation. The items that need to be covered are:

➤ Name of the corporation

➤ Nature or purpose of the business

➤ Maximum number of capital stock shares that are authorized to be outstanding

➤ Address of the registered office of the corporation

➤ Any special provisions or IRS code requirements

➤ The term of existence—usually perpetual

➤ Limitation of liability of directors, officers, and shareholders

➤ Any other information pertinent to the corporation

A small business attorney should be able to set up a basic C corporation and file the required papers for $400 to $800.

Pros and Cons of a C Corporation

Check the advantages and disadvantages below to decide if forming a C corporation will benefit your business.

The advantages of a C corporation:

> ➤ Personal assets of shareholders and owners are protected

> ➤ Owners can be considered employees and eligible to be reimbursed for expenses, travel, and insurance

> ➤ The existence of the corporation goes on after the owners die or leave the business

> ➤ The corporation can merge with another corporation or business with the approval of the board of directors

> ➤ Shares of the corporation can be freely transferred as provided in the bylaws

> ➤ Shares can be used to entice key employees to join the business

> ➤ If a corporation must declare bankruptcy, it usually won't affect the credit of the shareholders

> ➤ A C corporation is more attractive to investors because its existence does not rely on one person

> ➤ When the value of the owners' shares increase, the owners all benefit based on the percentage owned

The disadvantages of a C corporation:

> ➤ More expensive to form a C corporation with several fees necessary to incorporate, including Secretary of State filing fee, franchise tax fee and other government filing fees, and attorney fees for doing the paperwork. There are websites available where you can incorporate at a reduced cost.

> ➤ More formal than other structures and record keeping is more time-consuming

> ➤ Names and addresses of the owners and shareholders must be on file with the Secretary of State

> ➤ If payroll or sales tax payments are behind or not paid, the officers and possibly the shareholders can be held responsible

> ➤ In the event of dissolution of the corporation, the officers and directors are responsible for compiling the assets, paying outstanding creditors, and distributing the balance to the shareholders

> ➤ C corporations are taxed on any profits earned, and they're taxed a second time when dividends are paid to the shareholders

Most states require that corporations renew every year by filing a report form and paying a filing fee (of course). If the report and fee is not sent in a timely manner, the corporation can be dissolved without the directors and officers knowing about it. Don't ignore the yearly letter when it comes. Many corporations have it sent directly the their attorney.

Business Knowledge

Even if you think you know what legal entity you want to be, you should still compare all five to be sure you have chosen correctly.

S Corporation

The Tax Reform Act of 1986 created a desirable tax entity for paying corporate tax. The maximum number of shareholders, as of this writing, is one hundred by federal law, and they must be citizens or permanent residents of the United States. S corporations can issue only one class of stock and no more than 25 percent of the gross income can be from passive sources such as rent or royalties.

An S corporation is set up the same way as a C corporation, but the officers and directors must file IRS form 2553. Once this form is filed and accepted, the S corporation profits will be taxed only once instead of twice, as is the case with a C corporation. Profits are taxed only on the personal income tax returns of the shareholders, not at the corporate level. The personal liabilities of the company's debts are shielded from the shareholders just as with a C corporation. Several types of companies or businesses are excluded from becoming an S corporation.

> ➤ Some banking financial institutions

> ➤ Insurance companies taxed under subchapter L

> ➤ A USA corporation with international sales

> ➤ Certain groups of corporations

Pros and Cons of an S Corporation

S and C corporations are similar in many ways. Consider all the advantages and disadvantages of each before deciding on one or the other.

The advantages of an S corporation:

➤ Most of the same advantages enjoyed by a C corporation

➤ Single taxation of profits at the personal level

➤ No personal income tax is due when a dividend is distributed

The disadvantages of an S corporation:

➤ Many of the same disadvantages of a C corporation

➤ May have to file more accounting reports with its tax return

➤ Restricts some areas of international sales

➤ Requires a single owner to be classed as an employer and put on the payroll

➤ Additional expense and reports are needed to get started

Limited Liability Company (LLC)

An LLC business structure has some features of a corporation and some of a partnership but in fact is neither of them. Some people call this type of business a limited liability corporation but in fact the correct terminology is limited liability *company*.

All states and Washington, D.C., have LLC rules and legislation for in-state and out-of-state LLC companies. These companies can have an unlimited number of owners and members and they can be individuals, corporations, or other LLCs. There are a few states that require a notice in the local newspaper announcing the formation of a new LLC, so check your home state online to learn what is necessary to form a new LLC.

Many young professionals and entrepreneurs like this type of business structure because it's less complicated and quicker to form than a C corporation, plus it still protects their personal assets. It's wise to draft an operating agreement that defines ownership changes, and any profit sharing, 401(k)s, and ownership responsibilities.

Pros and Cons of an LLC

Consider the advantages and disadvantages of forming an LLC and decide if this is the right business structure for your new business.

The advantages of an LLC:

➤ A separate entity in which owners and members can't be held responsible for company debts or creditors

➤ More flexible than a partnership when distributing profits

➤ No requirement to hold regular directors meetings and keep record of the minutes

➤ No formal resolutions are required to operate the business

➤ No company tax on profits, which instead flow directly to the owners' and members' personal tax returns

➤ No ownership restrictions or number of members

➤ Owners and members can be other companies and corporations as well as individuals

The disadvantages of an LLC:

➤ Limited company life, not to exceed thirty years in many states

➤ Can be dissolved when a member dies or files personal bankruptcy

➤ Some states require at least two members or owners to start an LLC

➤ Articles of organization must be made and filed with the Secretary of State similar to the articles of incorporation needed for a corporation

➤ Not the best structure for a business hoping to go public someday; a C corporation is better

➤ More paperwork and filings than a sole proprietorship or partnership

➤ Can't offer stock options to entice key employees or investors

➤ Can't buy or sell shares in the company as it grows and becomes more valuable

Consider these five business structures thoroughly and do more research and due diligence before deciding which one suits your needs best. Seasoned entrepreneurs may have past experience and already know which one works best for them and their new venture. First-time business owners may find it useful and wise to consult an attorney, licensed financial advisor, or a banker in the business section of a local bank.

Even though you can change your business structure after it's started, it can be very costly and time-consuming. This is an important step in starting a business, so spend the time and effort to do it right the first time.

Naming Your Business

Your business structure and the name you select for your new business are the two most important decisions you will make before you actually start operating.

When choosing a business name, take your time and decide on a name that will work now and ten or twenty years from now. Changing a business name later can be expensive, and you may lose some of the target market recognition that has been built up over the years. Large corporations will pay a marketing firm millions of dollars to dream up a new product, division, or corporate name. But that's not necessary for a new small business. You can do it yourself or use a local company to offer several name choices for a few hundred dollars.

Make the Name Unique

Finding a business name that no one else is using and that will give your company easy recognition is a challenge, to say the least. But it's certainly possible and is done every day somewhere.

One idea is to take a common word and change the spelling to make it look different. With names, grammar doesn't matter and pronunciation is up to the business owner. Examples are making *autos* into *autoz* or *heat* into *heatx*. But this device is not wise if your business is in the health care or financial industry. People are looking for something more stable there, and not cute or clever.

Many people in a professional-type business use their own name and add *associates* or *company* after it. This doesn't explain what type of business it is unless you put a descriptive word after your name. One example might be *John Williams Accounting*.

Business Alerts

You can go to the United States Patent and Trademark website (www.uspto.gov) and file an application in about ninety minutes. Search the name right there on the site before you start the application process to make sure it's not taken or similar to any other businesses in your industry.

Another way to create business names is to select words that describe the business or its industry. Write down eight to ten words that people would know and look them up in a dictionary or thesaurus and collect synonyms for each one. You will then have forty to sixty words that you can combine to come up with name choices. Remember, you can also modify these new words to make more unconventional words.

Write each word on a small piece of paper and move them around to form different names. You'll end up with many choices to select from. The most successful business names are usually three words or less. Your name can be followed by a descriptive slogan to better explain your company.

Naming Dos and Don'ts

Here are some dos and don'ts that you can consider when selecting a name for your business.

Dos:

> ➤ Do keep the name general so you can expand into new and related products and services later
>
> ➤ Do think of how the name can be shortened into a nickname; eliminate any name that could be vulgar or embarrassing
>
> ➤ Do check out what the acronym of the words in the name spell out
>
> ➤ Do select a name that most people will be able to pronounce and spell easily
>
> ➤ Do choose a name that distinguishes your company from its competition
>
> ➤ Do research what your new business name might mean in other languages in case you ever go global
>
> ➤ Do ask friends, relatives, and strangers what they think of the name and if they have any suggestions
>
> ➤ Do see what the name looks like in different fonts
>
> ➤ Do experiment with what the name looks like on signs of one color and signs of multiple colors
>
> ➤ Do have three to five potential names ready in case your first choice is registered with the Secretary of State but not in use
>
> ➤ Do keep the name short and easy to say
>
> ➤ Do consider the length of the name and how it will fit on business cards, delivery vehicles, and packaging

➤ Don'ts:Don't choose a name that's too long or too difficult to pronounce

➤ Don't just use your name and add a product behind it, it will mean nothing to customers

➤ Don't lose your company name on a play on words; it will wear out quickly and may not relate in ten years

➤ Don't select a name that's similar to one from another business; you may hear from its legal department, complaining that it's confusing customers

➤ Don't use names of other people, living or dead, or a geographic location (you may move in three years)

➤ Don't pigeonhole your business with your name, like *Williams Pool Repairs*. You may want to sell it to *Johnson* someday.

➤ Don't include confusing slang or profanity in your business name

➤ Don't make your name look like you're affiliated with the local, state, or federal government

➤ Don't choose a name with just initials in it; many people won't have any idea what it means

Protect Your Business Name

It's always a good idea to register your business name if you're setting up a sole proprietorship or a partnership. This can usually be done at your state or county clerk's office. There will be a nominal fee, and you will also find out if anyone else is using the same name.

Registering the business name is part of the process when starting a corporation. Corporations can also register a dba (doing business as) name for other businesses they will operate.

Registering your business name gives you the right to use the name(s) in the state where you file your corporate papers.

You can also use a trademark (TM) or service mark (SM) symbol with your business name, product names, or services. Use TM or SM symbol after your business name to show you are claiming ownership. After several years of using the mark, there is a good chance that your ownership of the name will hold up in a lawsuit.

You don't have to officially register the names you are using the trademark or service mark with. If your product or service starts to really take off nationally and/or internationally, you should consult an attorney to see what further levels of protection can be used.

Since you have a serious investment in your business and its name, don't neglect some protection for it as soon as you determine the one(s) you will use. But the more unique the name, the less risk there will be. Most people will respect your business name and not try to use anything similar.

CHAPTER 3

Start-Up Capital

In This Chapter

➤ Sources for starting capital

➤ Working with bonds

➤ Using your home equity

➤ other places to find capital

In this chapter you will learn how to find the many sources of financing for a new business. You will consider each one and apply the information to your personal situation before making a final decision. You will see why a home equity loan can be your best choice.

The First Hurdle

Financing a business can be the first hurdle or roadblock that many entrepreneurs and new small business owners face. Without the adequate amount of start-up capital, a business can struggle right from the beginning. If all that the owners, members, or shareholders can think about is raising more money to cover expenses or for growth, a lot of time will be taken away from other important duties like marketing.

The resources needed for start-up should be found before a business starts, not after it's operating. Obviously, the first thing that needs to

Business Vocab

Start-up capital is the money used to pay for everything that is necessary to begin a business. There should be enough to finance the entire cost of a new business venture.

be determined is how much you will need. Most start-up owners estimate low to alleviate the pressure to raise funds from outside sources. But going back to the well for more money later on is even more difficult. A good rule of thumb is to figure what you honestly think you will need, and then add about 25 percent to that amount.

You must realize that when presenting your business idea to possible sources of start-up capital, you can't show any sales or profits yet. Why would anyone want to loan you money or invest in an unproven company? For those giving loans, the answer is in your collateral and your personal investment in the business. For investors, the answer is in your business plan and what you're willing and able to invest yourself.

Most entrepreneurs don't enjoy this part of starting a business, but without it there would be no new business. Once you have been successful raising capital for a new business, you become street smart and it will be easier and less stressful if you have to do it again. Let's look at some of the sources for start-up capital.

Friends, Relatives, and Angels

Once you have decided what your personal investment in the new business will be plus whether there will be any partners, members, or shareholders, it's time to investigate other sources for start-up capital. Your first stop: friends and relatives.

Friends

When looking for investors in their new business, a lot of entrepreneurs start by approaching friends, especially the ones who they think are doing well or have other investments. Friends usually have trust in the entrepreneur, which might outweigh the potential of the idea. You must decide if you want a loan from friends or an investment with equity tied to it.

Business Alerts

Be wary of borrowing start-up money from friends and relatives because you will see them again if the business goes bad. Small investments are fine, but big losses will strain relationships.

Don't involve friends who can't afford to lose what they give you because it can destroy a long-term relationship. The flip side of the coin is that if your new business really takes off and makes investors big returns, your friends may be upset that you didn't offer them a chance to invest. Whether a friend invests or just gives you a loan, always have everything on paper signed by both sides. All investors, including your friends, should listen to your business goals and have a copy of your business plan.

Relatives

Now here's a wonderful group of people that you have to live with during good times and bad. You can avoid or ignore your friends, but not your relatives. They will be there long after you're a success or failure, and you can't stop them from talking about the help they gave you.

First determine who, if anyone, in your family is financially able to help you with your start-up. Then decide what would happen if the business failed and they lost all their money. Would you have to leave town for holidays and birthdays, or would all be forgiven and life would go on?

Accepting capital from family members is a touchy situation. Every time you see them, you're likely to be asked how the business is doing. If your business starts going downhill, you may feel frustration, guilt, desperation, and gloom when the thought of your helpful relatives comes to mind.. Even if they say you are forgiven, you know it will never be forgotten, and you'll see that look in their eyes whenever you meet.

If you decide to take a chance with family members, always give them a copy of your business plan and get all the terms of the loan or investment in writing.

Angels

Angels are people you may or may not know, who on occasion invest in a new or growing business, hoping for a positive return on the next great idea. There are high- and low-level angels who invest different amounts. Low-level angels are usually very wealthy and can easily afford to take a chance with $5,000 to $30,000 without worrying about it. Even if they hit it big with your company and get a great return, they won't strike it rich because they already are.

High-level angels are usually looking for profits and capital gains. They may invest $25,000 to $300,000 in the hopes of striking it big with your enterprise. Normally after making their investment, these angels sit on the sidelines and let you grow your business. They are not interested in participating in the operation of any of their investments; that's why we call them angels.

Surveys have shown that there are about 250,000 angels currently functioning and investing in the double-digit billions. We don't hear about it on the news or in business publications because the investment is made privately. Without these angels, many new enterprises wouldn't have a chance of getting started, let alone surviving.

So the next question is, where do you find these angels? Most don't advertise or really make their availability known because they don't want to be bombarded with requests. But, of course, where there's a will, there's a way and you need to look in the right places. Here are a few suggestions:

- ➤ Your accountant
- ➤ Your attorney
- ➤ Corporation annual meetings
- ➤ Private country clubs and health clubs
- ➤ Other companies that angels have invested in
- ➤ Online pledge funds
- ➤ Successful professional people: doctors, scientists, CEOs
- ➤ Angel headhunters: firms online that charge a fee to bring together angels and entrepreneurs
- ➤ A referral from an angel who decided not to invest
- ➤ An entrepreneur who hit it big and cashed out
- ➤ Chamber of Commerce, the BBB, and business incubators

When you find an angel willing to listen to your presentation, make sure you are prepared. Have an ironclad business plan and a rehearsed dissertation that will show them why they should invest and how they can win with your enterprise. Keep the conversation businesslike at all times. You will probably only get one chance to meet the angel before he or she makes a decision, so make it count. The angel is meeting with you in the first place because he or she was intrigued by your initial idea. It's your job at the meeting to close the sale and lock up the deal.

Bank and Credit Union Loans

Bank and credit unions seem like the traditional source for start-up money, but they are more conservative than other sources. If you are going to approach a bank or credit union, you need to be well prepared. When the economy is struggling, banks are less willing to give loans, but it's certainly not impossible to get a loan from a bank under these circumstances. Keep an optimistic approach and be ready to answer any questions.

Questions Your Banker Will Ask

Before approving a loan, bankers will need answers to a variety of questions. Some of these questions will have no answer if the business is just starting.

➤ Can you repay the business loan?

➤ Can you repay the loan if the business fails?

➤ Does the business collect its invoices on time?

➤ Does the business pay its bills on time?

➤ Do you have a business plan?

➤ What inventory controls are in place?

➤ Are owners/officers committed to the business?

➤ Are sales and gross profits growing?

➤ Does the business have a profitable history?

➤ Do officers control the business expenses?

➤ Is there enough cash flow to pay employees and expenses?

➤ What is the outlook for the industry?

➤ Who are your competitors?

➤ How will you use the loan proceeds?

Reasons for Rejection

Many entrepreneurs leave banks empty-handed for a variety of reasons. Following are some reasons business loans are rejected:

➤ Incomplete loan proposal

➤ Unrealistic expense forecasts

➤ Lack of adequate collateral

➤ Underestimated capital requirements

➤ Applying with too many lenders at the same time

➤ Little or no business experience

➤ Overstated revenue and sales projections

➤ Cash flow projections that don't support repayment

➤ Borrower is argumentative with the lender representative

➤ Poor dress or presentation

➤ Poor communication skills

➤ Can't support documentation figures

➤ Trying to enter a dying industry

➤ Unable to explain use of capital

Business Knowledge

The Small Business Administration (SBA) can offer help with securing financial institution loans that you qualify for. Go to www.sba.gov and click on Loans & Grants. Follow the steps listed on how to apply.

Banks and credit union loans are not for everyone, as many will find out when they attempt to get them. Being rejected is not a sign of failure, but just one road that came to a dead end. There are other avenues to pursue, and some may be even better than a bank in the long run.

Credit Cards and Lines of Credit

When all else fails, many entrepreneurs turn to credit cards for available cash and purchasing power. Established cards can accommodate a financial need on a moment's notice with no questions asked. For this convenience, the user usually pays a higher interest rate if a balance is being carried. People starting a small business use their personal credit cards because they are not yet qualified for a business card. In many cases, the interest on a business credit card is a little higher than on a personal card because the issuer feels that there is more risk.

Ask Yourself

Are you ready to put your personal credit on the line if you use credit cards to finance your business? If your business fails and you can't pay off your credit cards, your credit score will also suffer.

Some entrepreneurs use credit cards as a first resource because it's easy and they don't want to bother with loan applications. They also shun the idea of asking friends or relatives for money, or searching for an angel.

The smart person will use credit cards as a last resort or for purchases that they can pay in full within the grace period of twenty-five days. Being deep in credit card debt when business slows down can spell disaster because missed payments can raise interest rates and add late fees.

Lines of Credit are Best

A line of credit from a bank or other financial institution tied to business or personal assets is just as difficult to set up as a regular bank loan. Credit lines can be more desirable because you only pay for the money you use and you can borrow more quickly when needed. As long as payments are made when they're due, this type of revolving account provides funds when unexpected needs arise. One of the best ways to set up a credit line is to use the equity in your home as collateral. The interest rate can be lower, and some tax advantages come with it.

Home Equity Financing

If you've been paying a home mortgage for several years, you may have built up some equity, which is the monetary difference between the current appraised home value and what you owe on your mortgage. This can be borrowed as a home equity loan, also known as a second mortgage. Most lenders will loan up to 90 percent of the equity and some even higher. I recommend borrowing no more than 90 percent of the equity, which leaves a cushion should home values in the area fluctuate. No one wants to have a house with negative equity, and in today's housing market, there is some uncertainty.

An equity loan is secured by real estate. A current appraisal of your home is usually necessary to assure the lender of its exact value at the time of the loan. A reasonable credit score and regular, verifiable income is about all you need in most cases.

If your credit score is lower than the lender's target number, you may be offered a loan at a lower percentage of the equity, like 80 percent or 75 percent. If you can't show a current salary, some lenders will accept stated income or monthly funds deposited in your checking account. They just want to be sure you have the money to repay the loan on time. The process usually takes about two to three weeks for you to receive your money. There's usually a three-day waiting period after closing before you can spend the money.

It May Be Tax Deductible

The best thing about a home equity loan is that in many cases you can deduct the interest on your personal income tax filing every year. Check with your bookkeeper or accountant to be sure. You can't do that with a bank loan or credit card interest. This means you will actually get some of the interest back in reduced income taxes. What else could you ask for—only in America!

Another type of home equity loan is a credit line instead of a lump sum check for the proceeds. Not every lender will offer this, but if you can find one who does, it has its advantages. For one, you don't have to pay interest on the entire amount until you need it, if ever. You can use the money on short notice and repay it in payments or all at once. Then it's there if you need it again, and it's yours without any further approval. As long as you make the monthly minimum payment, you can borrow at will. Only a computer will follow your trail, and you won't be bothered if you make your payment on time.

There are probably other types of home equity loans and lenders that are always trying to be creative with new ideas. It's certainly a lot less hassle than going to a bank or applying for an SBA loan. If you're really afraid to put your house on the line for your business, maybe you're in the wrong business or maybe starting a small business is a bigger risk than you want to take; it's not for everyone.

Business Knowledge

When considering home equity financing, ask the bank or financial institution up front if it offers HELOC (home equity line of credit) and what the maximum loan to value it can offer. This allows you to borrow, pay back, and borrow again at will.

Other Sources of Start-Up Capital

If these sources of start-up capital aren't right for you, don't despair. You have more options to consider.

Business Incubators

Many colleges and universities have set up programs to help new entrepreneurs start a business. There are support people with connections to start-up capital sources. This option takes longer to set up than the ones previously discussed, and it's usually not for an established business to grow larger. But for entrepreneurs with an idea and nothing else, business incubators may be worth exploring.

Venture Capital Firms

Venture capital firms are not for the average small business owner without a great and innovative concept. VC firms are usually looking for a high return potential. They may not invest in a start-up, but wait until the business is first established. They may also want to take part in some of the management of the business. VC firms have millions to invest, but they are very selective.

Bootstrapping

Bootstrapping is the art of launching a business with much less capital than is sensibly needed, or as we say in Chicago: launching a business on a shoestring. In many cases, the start-up funds are $1,000 or even less. There is no room for mistakes or early setbacks because the business will probably not survive.

The bootstrapping entrepreneur is hoping that cash flow and customer deposits will finance the early business and some marketing. If the cash flow is not there, then the business might not be either. But having said all that, these are some big success stories, including Apple Computer, Domino's Pizza, Nike, and UPS. It's not impossible, but it's not for the faint of heart either. If this is your only choice, it just may work for you.

Business Alerts

Opening a business with no regard for capital needs is sometimes called *winging it* by experienced bootstrappers. It's not advised for first-time entrepreneurs, who don't have prior knowledge of running a business.

Grants

One of the best kept secrets in financing is the Small Business Investment Company (SBIC) programs. In the last fifty-plus years, close to 100,000 small businesses have received billions of dollars in financing through SBIC. SBIC partners with government and private investors and are licensed by the SBA. You can find SBIC through its professional association National Association of Small Business Investment Companies (NASBIC). Some household names that have benefited from SBIC financing are FedEx, Staples, AOL, and Callaway Golf.

CHAPTER 4

 # Accountants, Lawyers, and Bankers

In This Chapter

➤ Why you need these professionals

➤ How to find and select an accountant

➤ What lawyer is best for your business

➤ How to use your banker effectively

In this chapter you will learn how to select three of the most important people you will use as advisors for your business. Although they are not on your staff, they will influence how you make many important decisions. Don't overlook the seriousness of your business accountant, lawyer, and banker; select them with care.

Why Do I Need Them?

There's a story in the Bible about three wise men who brought gifts and followed a star. Well, in today's small business world, you will also need your three wise men, and the gifts they bring can make you a success. That is, if you select the best wise men that you can realistically afford. Find a little extra room in your budget for an accountant, lawyer, and banker, and don't jump at the lowest price you are offered. You don't want to end up with the cheapest advisors; they could turn out to be the three stooges instead.

Chances are that you don't have an accounting, finance, or law degree yourself, so you need to acquire help in those areas. Even if you had all those degrees, when would you find the time to use them? Even the President has advisors, each with a different area of expertise, and so should you. It's vital to your long-term growth and success; the proper advice and guidance can keep your business out of hot water.

When you surround yourself with good professional people, you have a much better chance of success. Most small businesses can't really keep these three wise men on staff—there wouldn't be enough full-time work anyway. So you need to buy the time you need and pay only for that time.

The real challenge is to select the correct accountant, lawyer, and banker right from the beginning. You want to have complete confidence in all three of them because they will have all your records and past performance, and to transfer that to others is very difficult. These advisors should have the ability to handle large companies as well, so you can keep them as your enterprise gets bigger. Real pros want to be associated with a solid growth company and help keep progress on an upward trend.

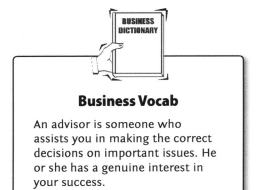

Business Vocab

An advisor is someone who assists you in making the correct decisions on important issues. He or she has a genuine interest in your success.

These three advisors should be selected as early in the business plan process as possible. They can assist or guide you in the right direction as questions come up from the beginning. And there will be a lot of questions and decisions to be made in the start-up process. They may also be able to introduce you to other professionals you may only need for a short time. With a recommendation from one of your three wise men, you can be reasonably confident that you are using the right person. Once you have your three wise men in place, use them as often as you can for anything you aren't sure of. They should be there when you need them and want to see you succeed as much as you do.

Your Accountant

It's always wise to check references before you hire an accountant. Ask for contact information of a couple of clients about your size or who have recently started up a business and contact them for a reference. You will want to know just how much help they received, especially in the beginning. Ask how quickly the accountant returns calls and if he or she prepares all the reports on time.

Your accountant should be willing to help to get your federal tax and state tax ID numbers when you are starting out, as well as set up your sales tax account and make sure you're not filing your reports late. Some states also have a use tax and who knows when or if an Internet tax is coming.

The Relationship

I think that your accountant, or CPA, is the most important of your outside advisors. He or she sees many other companies and can bring ideas from all of them to the table for you to use. You will most likely spend more time with your accountant than with your lawyer and even your banker. So you need a certain comfort level in your business relationship with your accountant.

Accountants should want you to feel very comfortable with their services. After all, most of them are really a small business also, and they don't have a lot of time to go looking for new clients to replace any unsatisfied ones. And a satisfied client is a good source of referrals and recommendations to grow their own business.

You will likely want to have a semi-personal relationship with your accountant so you can talk to him or her about any business issue that comes to mind. But keep in mind that your business is only a small part of the accountant's entire clientele, and it may not be cost-effective for him or her to spend a lot of extra time with you. So when you need this extra time for advice, try to set up a meeting very early in the morning, late in the day, or offer to buy lunch. Or you can meet when it's convenient for the accountant and adjust your own schedule.

Business Alerts

Accountants or firms that specialize in small business understand the challenges of smaller companies and can offer useful advice and direction when needed. It also helps if the accountant or firm has experience in your type of business. The more an accountant is familiar with your type of enterprise, the more help he or she can give.

Be wary of those who don't return calls promptly.

Who Works on Your Business?

A lot of small- and medium-sized accounting firms will assign two or more people to your account. One person with limited bookkeeping knowledge will do most of the data entry, routine reports, and tax reports. This person will probably process your monthly or quarterly data and run most of your reports. He or she should also figure your tax deposits and payments and get them to you well in advance of when they are due.

Business Knowledge

It's nice to get your tax reports a week in advance so you'll know if there is any payment due. That way if you haven't already put the money aside, you will have a little time to come up with it. There's nothing much worse than needing $2,000 for a federal tax deposit and having only $300 in your bank account. Of course, you are supposed to put this money aside when you do your payroll, but sometimes...

You want to meet personally with your accountant at least quarterly and review all of your statements and reports. This is the time to ask those questions you've been saving up for the last three months. You can also ask your accountant to look over your reports and comment on anything that he or she thinks is unusual. Most accountants will think many of your expenses are too high because they tend to be more conservative than entrepreneurs.

What to Expect from Your Accountant

An accountant who's worthy of your business should do more listening than talking. Let's remember that your accountant works for you, even if it doesn't seem like it sometimes. So he or she should take a visible interest in what you're asking, not just give you generic answers. I hate it when accountants take cell phone calls when I am meeting with them. I'm paying for their time and I want all of their attention while I'm with them. There are few situations that can't wait until your meeting is over. So if your accountant is taking calls in the middle of your meeting, ask him or her to please wait until your meeting is over.

Your accountant should be able to represent you and help you deal with the IRS and other government tax agencies. Some accountants may call themselves enrolled agents, which means they have been certified by the IRS in some way that gives them the right to directly handle your tax problems.

Your accountant should also know how to write letters on your behalf requesting extensions, reductions, or elimination of any taxes due, penalties, or interest. An experienced accountant has done this before and should know the limits and goals that can be used to protect you or give you more time. Dealing with the IRS is a little less scary when you have an expert on your team. So when considering a new accountant, be sure to ask if he or she will do this for you if it becomes necessary.

Business Knowledge

All your accounting records for the last several years should be kept in a computer file, backup disc, and paper file. At least one of these files should be kept off-site in the event of an unexpected disaster. Your accountant should also have a record of all your files.

If you travel a lot and don't really have anyone you can trust or is knowledgeable on your staff, your accountant may be able to step in. You can give him or her power of attorney, which allows your accountant to sign checks and handle other transactions in your absence. This is something you want to monitor, though, and go over when you get back.

Your accountant can be a business saver if something serious should ever happen to you. With someone you can trust stepping in and keeping your business running while you recover, you'll have something to come back to. He or she can be an advisor to your children or heirs, as well, in the event of your untimely demise. Make sure you have these things in writing where someone can find them so your wishes will be followed.

If It Doesn't Work Out

If after a couple of quarters with a new accountant you don't feel that things are working out as you had planned, you may need to make a decision to move on. You can first talk to your accountant and describe your concerns—sometimes there is a misunderstanding that can be easily cleared up. If your accountant doesn't want to discuss it or can't adjust to your needs, you may want to consider a change. But changing accountants is not something you do on the spur of the moment—you need to plan ahead.

Ask Yourself

If you don't feel comfortable with your new accountant, don't wait to make a change. It is your business and your accountant should make you feel important.

The best time to make a change is at the end of your fiscal year when all tax reports are received. Give your final yearly reports or copies to your next accountant, and he or she should be able to pick up from there. If the end of the fiscal year is too long to wait, the end of a quarter is the next best time. I wouldn't give any advance notice of your intentions until it gets close to the separation time. You want your last reports to be timely and accurate.

As I said earlier, your accountant can be your best business friend or just another aggravation. Set the groundwork for a strong, helpful, and prosperous relationship right from the beginning. When things don't go the way you had hoped, don't wait—bring it up right away. And if you don't know how to read or understand any of your financial reports, have your accountant explain it to you. It's always a good feeling to see the numbers of a growing successful business on paper. So read your reports as soon as you get them and file them for safekeeping. It will be fun to look back in a few years when you're double or triple your current size.

Your Lawyer

There probably won't be any lawyer jokes in this section, but sometimes I almost can't resist. Business owners may joke about or dislike lawyers because they feel lawyers are a necessary evil. You might even compare lawyers to taxes: you don't really enjoy living with them, but it's hard to be comfortable without them.

I've always had a difficult time finding a lawyer that I can feel close to. They all seem so distant and always "on the record." I even think that if I ask about a lawyer's golf game, he or she will charge me for the time. A lot of lawyers seem to have little or no sense of humor. Maybe that's how they are trained, not to let their guard down. Or maybe the serious demeanor somehow justifies their high hourly fees. My advice: keep your conversation about business and keep it moving; you're on the clock most of the time.

Well, regardless of how you feel about lawyers, there are times when you need their professional help and advice. And good legal advice is just as important as good accounting advice, even if you need it less often. When you hire a lawyer, you are paying for his or her knowledge, schooling, experience, and expertise. Maybe when you think of it that way, the $175 or more per hour doesn't seem so bad. You just don't want to be calling a lawyer about every little thing and run your bill into the thousands.

Plan your call or visit and write a list in advance of everything you want to cover. That way, you won't forget to discuss something and have to call back or set up another expensive appointment. And all that big money you are paying per hour doesn't go right into the lawyer's pocket. Besides the lawyer's education, you are buying the entire staff, office, and library with your hourly fee; it's a package deal.

Business Knowledge

Ask your lawyers for a list of set fees for things such as reading a lease, sales contracts, and registering a trademark. Many will have reduced fees if a paralegal can do some of the work. You will never know unless you ask in advance.

Finding a Good Lawyer

So where do you find these wonderful professional people who can make your business life easier and protect your interests? Friends and neighbors are a good place to start for a referral for a good business lawyer.

Business people in your area are a good source to tap into. Most of us know people who have their own store or office and who can offer their lawyer's name as a possible lead. If you have the time, it's always advisable to talk to a couple of different lawyers before you make your final choice. Even if you have to pay a reasonable first visit fee, it's worth it to give you that feeling of comfort.

Consider joining or at least attending a Chamber of Commerce or business organization meeting in your area. There will either be lawyers there as members or the executive officers can refer you to several. Discussing your needs with them at a meeting or luncheon could save you that initial visit fee.

When all referral attempts fail, you can turn to a local bar association for some advice. If there isn't one in your home city, look to the nearest medium or large city for one. Most will have a free referral service and will ask you what your needs are. When you tell them that you are starting a new small business and need a lawyer that specializes in that area, they have probably heard this request hundreds of times and should be ready and eager to help you. Their members, who are almost all the lawyers in the area, are subject to a code of ethics and are monitored for any infractions. You can feel reasonably comfortable with a bar association referral.

Besides finding a lawyer who is well qualified, make sure you can get along with and are not intimidated by him or her. That's why it's a good idea to talk to a few before making a final decision. Just like your choice of accountants, you don't want to keep changing lawyers.

Ask, But You Will Pay

Your lawyer can help you with all the legal paperwork for your business entity. You will need to select how your company will be set up— as a proprietorship, partnership, LLC, or C or S corporation (see Chapter 2)—and your lawyer can explain in depth the pros and cons of each. You should also consult your new accountant before you decide on your setup to find out how taxes will apply to each type. Don't rush into a decision too quickly, because it takes a lot of paperwork and cost to change the setup of your business entity.

Many small business lawyers have a set fee to legally establish a business entity. From my past experience, this fee ranges from about $500 for a proprietorship to $1,000 or so for a corporation.

Another key factor to consider when selecting a new lawyer is his or her availability. Most lawyers have regular Monday through Friday office hours, but what if you have an emergency during the off-hours? Will your lawyer give you an after-hours number for use in urgent situations? And what if you are ever sued for business or need to sue someone else? Can your lawyer handle these affairs or work with an associate who can?

Don't think that just because you're starting a bakery, computer firm, or dog washing service that these problems won't come up. They do occur and usually when you least expect them, so you have to be prepared to handle them. Good lawyers are available when they are needed, especially on short notice for consultation.

There are several prepaid legal services out there for either personal or business membership. They usually have a monthly fee that they charge to your credit card whether you use their service or not. My experience with them is that it's difficult to get a one-on-one relationship with them. They handle only certain situations as part of your monthly membership dues, and I never got the same lawyer twice. If your matter doesn't fall into the covered areas, you will be charged an additional hourly fee, but usually at a discount. I no longer use this service because the matters I need taken care of were never on the covered list.

There is also a company out there (and others I'm sure) called *We The People* that can do some one-time legal work for a lower set fee than a lawyer charges. I've never used it, but you may want to investigate for short-term projects at lower fees. If in doubt, you can always check with your local Better Business Bureau to see if there are any complaints.

Lawyers, like accountants, can really make a big difference in a small business. They can take the worry and decisions of many situations off your mind, allowing you to sleep better at night. But choose the wrong one and the effect can be the opposite. So it's always wise to spend the necessary time in advance to get that comfort level with the right ones. Just like dating and marriage, it's always easier to get into a relationship than to get out of one. If you don't want unpleasant confrontations later, do your homework in advance and select a lawyer that you are comfortable working with.

Your Banker

Oh no, do you really need a banker? Sometimes bankers seem like devils dressed in business suits. You know they try to nickel-and-dime you with fees, interest, penalties, and overdraft charges. They always advertise "free checking" with the asterisk after it, which means you're going to pay something. Their hours are usually short and never seem to meet your needs so you have to use the robot (ATM) machine. If you have questions during off-hours, you might as well ask your cat. Bankers always smile and offer to help, but the bank's interest (pardon the pun) is always the first priority.

With all kidding aside, you do need a relationship with an officer or junior officer at a bank of your choice. And believe it or not, banks need you almost as much as you need them, but I think they are trained not to show it. Without people and businesses using bank services and paying interest on loans, bankers are out of a job.

Since using a good bank is necessary for any business, you should start to build a relationship early. Even before you make the final decision to actually start a business, you can get some time with a banker. There is no first visit fee like a lawyer charges, so you might as well take advantage of it. You can even pick up the paperwork to open a business account and be ready if your plans are to go ahead. And remember to get the business card of the person who will be your main contact in the future. He or she can be a valuable asset that can help open doors for you.

If you plan to borrow money for your new business, get to know a loan officer who's been there at least six months. Explain what you are planning to do and ask what is required to apply for a business loan or line of credit. Don't be too surprised when he or she asks you to personally guarantee any loan; it's pretty standard for a small business owner. The loan officer wants to see that you will have as much at risk, or more, as the bank does.

Select a Bank You Can Visit

You should select one bank for most of your business accounts and services so you can be known and seen there often. Even if you're not borrowing money, regular exposure can get you a few perks like waived fees on money orders and cashiers checks. And when you're in the bank, be sure to stop and say hello to the bank representative that you know and may need in the future. If he or she is busy with another client, at least make eye contact or wave as you walk by. For these reasons, I like to physically go into the bank most of the time rather than use the drive-up or an ATM.

Try to get on a first-name basis with your banker so that you can stop and discuss business without an appointment. Even a bank that's tough to get loans from becomes a little easier when a key person is on your side. So develop a business relationship with your banker, and even invite him or her to your place of business.

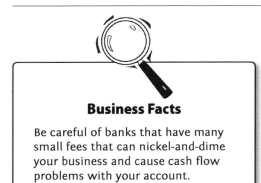

Business Facts

Be careful of banks that have many small fees that can nickel-and-dime your business and cause cash flow problems with your account.

Once you get to know a banker, ask for advice about any banking questions you have. Your banker may be able to check out and provide valuable information about a new large client you are about to acquire or get a Dun & Bradstreet report for you if you're not a D&B member. The banker wants to see your business prosper as much as you do and should be more than willing to help in any way he or she can. A good banker can be an asset, so treat yours professionally.

When it's Time to Change

The obvious time to consider a new accountant or lawyer is when you don't feel that you are getting the time and attention that you are paying for, and they don't return your calls or respond to your requests in a timely manner. When you're ready to sever your ties, don't get into an argument—just state your concerns and let them know you will be leaving soon. They are professionals and should continue to provide their service until the end.

Ask Yourself

Are you really satisfied with the help and response you are receiving from your three advisors? You are the client and they should treat you with respect.

It's probably wise not to dismiss your accountant or lawyer until you have another choice in mind and have already talked to them. Ask your current accountant or lawyer how you can make the transition smoothly so you can leave on good terms.

Both your accountant and your lawyer have files on your business that you will need to pass on to your new professional. In many cases, they will keep a copy in the event that a situation comes up in the future that took place when you were their client. This is OK as long as you remind them that the information is confidential and you should be consulted before it's used again.

Your accountant or lawyer will want to be paid in full before you leave and they turn over any files. If you have paid a retainer that's not used up, ask for a refund for the unused portion. Only an unprofessional accountant or lawyer will ask for a transition fee to turn over your records. If this happens, you were right in getting out of their clientele. Just like a marriage, some relationships don't work and each party will go their separate way. But to make the change the least stressful as possible, always be and act honestly and professionally.

CHAPTER 5

Location—Does It Matter?

In This Chapter

➤ Home-based business basics
➤ Distribution and Industrial space
➤ Finding retail space
➤ Reviewing leases

In this chapter you will learn why location is important for some businesses and not for others. You'll get advice on what to ask for when signing a lease and hints on what the landlord may concede to. Deciding where to start a new business can affect how customers value your new company.

The location for your new business does matter, especially if you select the incorrect one. Many new entrepreneurs have dreams of a big business and get way too much space in the beginning. A space too large for a start-up will put stress on its budget if it doesn't grow into it quickly.

Budget-minded new owners get a space that's too small and quickly outgrow it. When space becomes too tight or confining, employees may become disgruntled and use it as an excuse to do less than 100 percent of their expected duties.

Business Alerts

It's not worth going way over your budget for a prime location. Any start-up business can and must use draws other than location to get those first customers. A strategically placed sign or billboard can attract as many customers as an expensive location could. So don't overspend on rent for a new business.

Take the time to anticipate your real needs, and then lease space accordingly. The easy decision when just starting out is to establish a home-based business.

Home-Based Business Setup

Keeping your home-based start-up separate from the rest of the house can be a big challenge, to say the least, especially iI there are children in the family creating demands for more time and space. But starting a business at home can save hundreds of dollars a month in expenses for the average entrepreneur. If you don't need a storefront or warehouse, starting a home-based new business is a smart choice, even if it's only for the first few months or a year.

Once you've decided that starting at home is the best choice, you must also be prepared for some of the problems or inconveniences that it might cause. If your house is small, you can consider building a room in the basement or garage, or you could build an addition to the house either upstairs or in the back. But keep in mind that a new room will add extra start-up expenses that you may not be able to afford, especially if you hope to get a separate location within a year or two.

But if this room is used only for business, as it should be, you may be able to take a tax deduction as part of your mortgage. Check with your accountant to find out how to establish your working space so it meets IRS standards and won't be questioned later. Saving the rent and even getting the deduction can give a financial boost to a start-up company.

Business Facts

Many home-based businesses never make it past the first year and have to close. Some of the main reasons are lack of focus and passion for the business and lack of dedication to working hours. Some businesses start as a part-time hobby and never get beyond that concept. A home-based business is a real business and needs to be operated as one.

When you have decided on what space you're going to use, you must keep it off-limits to most of the family, especially during business hours.

Here are some other things that you might want to do for the best chance of success:

➤ Lock your business room door when you're away and during nonbusiness hours

➤ Use a separate landline phone system with at least two lines; don't operate with just a cell phone

➤ Forward calls to your cell phone if you feel that you can answer them professionally when you're out of the office

➤ Have dedicated lines for your fax machine so it's not busy when the phone lines are busy

➤ Use the top of bookcases and file cabinets to put your printer, copier, and other tabletop equipment

➤ Have a working smoke alarm, CO detector, and fire extinguisher in the room

➤ Consider a small refrigerator or water cooler in your office room so you don't have to keep leaving the area

➤ Have a large waste basket that doesn't have to be emptied every day

➤ Use a comfortable cushioned chair that rolls and swivels

➤ A large mirror on one wall will make the room look bigger

➤ Install a closed-circuit television to monitor any children

➤ Don't let callers hear children or baby noises in the background

➤ Lock all file cabinets and the desk when not in use

➤ Paint walls a neutral color and hang motivational posters on them

➤ An air purifier will keep the air fresh in a closed-in room

➤ Put tall bookcases in any unoccupied space

Business Facts

According to the research firm International Data Corporation (IDC), there are about 35 million home-based businesses in the United States. The U.S. Census Bureau and the U.S. Bureau of Labor Statistics estimate there are approximately 20 million home-based businesses. The SBA says that the number of U.S. households with a business exceeds 12 percent, big numbers and growing.

Check Local and County Laws

Most areas have local zoning laws that apply to home businesses. Most state websites describe these laws and list any restrictions for certain businesses operating in residential areas. These sites include rules and codes that specify what you can or can't do even with acceptable home-based businesses.

Deliveries

Your home-based business will also need a place for mail to be delivered and packages accepted. Since you can get only mail with a P.O. box, a better choice is a mailbox at a UPS store or a Postal Annex. These stores can accept all carrier-delivered packages as well as mail, and they give you a street address you can use for your business. They are about the same price as the post office but have many more advantages, including shorter lines. It also makes your business seem larger and keeps deliveries away from your home. It's a very popular option for home-based start-ups.

If you have a delivery vehicle or company car with your company name and contact information on it, always keep it clean. In the evening, try to find a nearby high-traffic area and park it there for free advertising. Make the phone number and web address big enough that it can be seen easily by passing cars. It's your business billboard, and it may attract new customers.

Number your van or truck with a high number like 6 or 12 to give the impression that you are bigger than you are and have a fleet of vehicles. This can make prospective customers a little more comfortable when giving you a first order or sale.

Distribution or Industrial Space

If you are opening a manufacturing or distribution business, your space requirements will differ from other companies. You will probably need a larger area than retail or office start-ups, but you also need to keep costs within your budget.

If you are going to use an agent to show you buildings and warehouse space, be sure he or she specializes in industrial and commercial space. If your agent takes longer than twenty-four hours to get back to you, consider getting a different agent.

Agents get paid by the landlord or leasing company, so it's a free service to you. If an agent asks you for payment, it's time to drive away and change your cell phone number.

There are many combination office-warehouse units available that may work well for you. In these units, most of the area is warehouse or industrial space with 10-20 percent office. If you expect your business to grow substantially during the lease term, consider a little larger space. But you will have to pay for unused space until you need it.

Another option is to get a clause in your lease that says you can cancel the current lease and move to a larger space that the same owner has with sixty days' notice. Be sure the space is at least 30 to 50 percent larger, or moving expenses and the hassle will eat up any extra profits you intend to make. It's great to grow your business physically, but there are always added expenses involved.

Considerations

There are some other considerations to take into account with this type of space. Make a list or just copy this one and take it with you.

➤ Adequate electric power and amps

➤ 220 voltage or other electrical requirements you may need

➤ Enough space outside for waste and scrap

➤ Dock(s) for truck deliveries and pickups

➤ Enough parking for employees and visitors

➤ Adequate office space for your needs

➤ Enough water pressure, if water is used in your process

➤ Enough storage space for finished product

➤ Adequate ventilation for machine exhaust

➤ Heating and AC as needed

➤ Floor material that is acceptable

➤ Enough lighting in any manufacturing areas

➤ Any zoning restrictions for your raw materials

➤ Any zoning restrictions for hazardous materials

➤ Any noise restrictions for the neighborhood

➤ Is the space available for use 24/7?

➤ Are there major roads or interstates nearby?

➤ Is there available room for signage as needed?

Retail Space

There has always been a debate on where to locate your brick-and-mortar store, and there is probably no easy answer for everyone. I think that you need to make a decision based on your type of business. Does it need to attract an impulse buyer or will your business be a destination? Each type of business pursues customers in a different way. The businesses that rely on impulse buyers appeal to potential customers by sight and need to be in a good location. Buyers who are looking for specific items are likely to look up businesses online or in a phone book and drive directly to the business, so location is not as important.

Following are some examples of businesses that need a great location:

➤ Sit-down and fast-food restaurants

➤ Grocery stores

➤ Ice cream shops

➤ Convenience stores

➤ Banks

➤ Cleaners

Business Facts

Restaurant sales in the United States are over $500 billion a year. Location of a restaurant will attract a first-time patron and impulse customer to stop in. But it's the food, service, and value that keeps customers coming back. People will go out of their way to patronize a restaurant that they enjoy and can afford. Restaurant sales in the United States are over $500 billion a year. Location of a restaurant will attract a first-time patron and impulse customer to stop in. But it's the food, service, and value that keeps customers coming back. People will go out of their way to patronize a restaurant that they enjoy and can afford.

Following are some examples of businesses that don't depend on a great location:

➤ Plumbing supply stores

➤ Vacuum cleaner repair stores

➤ Day care centers

➤ Music lessons studios

➤ Office furniture outlets

➤ Furnace and AC repair shops

Obviously a great location should have high vehicle and pedestrian traffic. It needs to have demographics that consist of many of your target customers. It should be convenient to get to, have plenty of parking, and be well lit for evening business. If you are in a strip mall, it's desirable to have a well-known and popular anchor store that will draw in more people than you can. Even a large national store within a block of your business will attract attention and benefit you. You want as much customer traffic as possible regardless of what store customers are going into. Your store and sign will be visible to them, and many will remember that you are there when they need your products or services.

Selecting Your Store and Location

Find at least two commercial real estate agents on the Internet or in the yellow pages. The best ones will have two or more years of experience in the area that you are considering. Never use residential agents who claim to do it all because they don't, at least not effectively. Not every agent will know or show you everything that's available, because they just don't have access to them. There are commercial spaces available that are not on the Internet listing service. Look at as many properties as you need to before making a decision.

Business Knowledge

If the exact size and type of space is not currently available in the area you want to open, don't accept a second choice. Ask your agent to check with building owners to see what leases are going to expire in the next ninety days and look at those spaces.

Have a series of questions ready and your agent for a demographics report. You want to know who lives in a two-, three-, and five-mile radius and what their income level is. Your agent should be able to get the demographics at no cost to you. A great location is only one if your target customers live nearby and can find your business easily. You may even want to check the demographics before you even visit the sites.

Before You Decide

When you think that you have found a possible retail site, it's time to do the rest of your due diligence. You want to be sure that you can have your business open 24/7 for any all-night sales or inventory counts. There may be a neighborhood restriction on lights and noise during some late hours—find out in advance.

Introduce yourself to the owners of the neighboring businesses to see how they feel about the property management. Ask them if they do any group sales or promotions during the year.

Visit the site in the early morning, midday, and later in the evening to monitor traffic and activity. You don't want to be surprised later if there's a teen gathering or motorcycle clubs that meet in your parking lot at night. These and other things may deter customers from coming at those times and may also leave a mess that needs to be cleaned up.

Business Alerts

A retail store needs to keep up with the times and appeal to regular and new customers' senses. About every six to eight years, you should remodel, paint, and reorganize merchandise. Use your brand name everywhere on signs, walls, and bags. The new look and feel can give a boost to customer visits and profits.

Ask the landlord if all maintenance is included in the rent. This means that if the AC or heat goes out, you make one call and it's taken care of quickly. Many sites have what is called triple net charges added to the monthly rent. These charges cover general area maintenance, property tax, and anything else the landlord or management company can add on. It's like the extras you get when you buy a car; the base price is not always what you pay.

Be sure you know the total amount required for rent each month with everything included. Don't assume that because something wasn't mentioned up front, you won't have to pay for it; ask.

Your Friendly Shopping Mall

If you have the type of retail business that attracts both destination and impulse shoppers, you may want to consider a store in your local mall. The rent for space will be 30 to 70 percent higher than the rent at a strip mall or free-standing store. You will have to abide by the mall management rules and regulations and be open during the mall's posted hours.

There will be some requirements for signage and design of your store front to appeal to all shoppers passing by. This is to keep the standard that all stores expect to keep the shoppers happy and comfortable. Usually, wild flashing signs and loud noises outside your store are not accepted.

The big advantage of being in a shopping mall is all the extra shopping traffic it attracts. Many of these people might not have even heard of your business and will now stop to check you out. But you need to assess if this extra traffic will produce the extra profits necessary to pay that additional rent. It's great to have a lot of shoppers, but you need them to buy something to make it worthwhile.

Ask the neighboring store owners about customer traffic and purchases. Sit on a bench nearby for an hour during the week and weekend and watch the people go by. Are these the type of people you expect will be your potential customers? Do they look like they will want or need what you will be selling? You may even want to ask a few of them if they would be interested in the kind of store you may open. This is not scientific research, but it will give you some answers to base your decision on.

Business Knowledge

When selecting a retail space in a shopping mall, consider one that's closest to a large anchor store. These big stores attract many shoppers who will see your store on the way in and out. It doesn't even matter what type of business the anchor store is in as long as it has a lot of shoppers who may also stop and browse in your store.

Some additional things to check are how many stores have moved out of the mall or closed in the past year and two years and what their reasons were for moving. Ask managers in the other stores if they are making the number of sales that they expected. How responsive is the mall staff when there's a problem or an emergency? Is the mall located within a mile of an interstate highway or a main road? Does the mall management hold events occasionally, and how is the mall decorated for the holidays? Does the mall advertise using different types of media (radio, TV, billboards, Internet) to drive traffic to the mall? Are the landscaping, common areas, and parking lots attractive? Is there a security force on site to solve problems and offer late-night escorts to cars? Add your own concerns and get the answers *before* you sign a lease.

Internet Business

If you're starting an Internet-only type of business, not much work is needed to find a location. You can work from your home or from a small office outside your home. There are also executive sites available that receive mail, ship packages, and have office help on call. They can be leased for a short as three months, but a year would probably reduce the monthly rent. You can always have a traveling business by just taking your laptop, notebook, iPod, or other such device with you to coffee shops, restaurants, beauty salons, or nearly anywhere else when you're starting out. You will need to have at least one phone number that customers or clients can call to increase the credibility of your business.

I recommend a physical office, even if it's small or at home, where you can install at least one landline. The quality of sound is better and anyone calling will feel more comfortable buying from you. You can also install an Internet connection so you don't have to rely on Wi-Fi all the time. Internet businesses are open 24/7, so check e-mails often in the early morning and late at night, and respond right away if you can. An office also gives you a place to store backup files away from your computer in case of a crash or loss of the entire unit. Internet businesses are new and exciting, but you should have a physical base to work from.

Leases and Options

As I said earlier, finding a location and space that you like is always a challenge, and once you decide on a space the process is not over. You must read and sign all the paperwork for the rental agreement. Start-up owners should have a lawyer look over the paperwork and point out any unusual or restrictive areas in the lease. Most are standard leases and can be from just one page to twenty pages long. If you are leasing from a corporation, the lease is likely to be longer but not necessarily anything to worry about. You do have the option to ask for any changes and you may get a few—maybe. Once you sign the lease, you are obligated to abide by it because it's a legal document.

Business Alerts

It's important to work with a real estate agent who is not associated with any specific property. He or she should have your needs, wants, and interests as the number one priority. Always make sure the agent is independent and willing to show you as many commercial spaces necessary to find the best one for you.

When signing a lease for the first time at a new location, it never hurts to ask for some free rent up front. If you're signing a year lease, ask for one month free rent, but if you're signing a three-year lease, ask for two months free rent. You will need to pay a security deposit of one month's rent as well as the first month's rent, which starts after the free period. The free month or two will help you get started.

Most landlords will allow the free rent period so you can become stable and pay future rent on time. If the space is currently vacant, you might also be able to move in a week or so early and get everything set up and ready for business.

Always ask for a clause in your lease the gives you the right to renew at prevailing rates when your lease is up so you don't have to move because of a rent hike.

Lease Dos and Don'ts

Here are some dos and don'ts that you should consider before signing a lease for your business.

Dos:

> ➤ Do look at several sites before deciding
>
> ➤ Do check zoning and codes for the space
>
> ➤ Do have all extra agreements put in the lease
>
> ➤ Do use a lawyer to read your first lease
>
> ➤ Do read the lease
>
> ➤ Do check demographics for a retail store
>
> ➤ Do get a clause in the lease allowing you to trade up to a larger space
>
> ➤ Do check signage rules before you buy a sign
>
> ➤ Do ask for a month or more free rent
>
> ➤ Do negotiate for a little better rent rate

Don'ts:

> ➤ Don't jump at the first place you like
>
> ➤ Don't take the cheapest rent without other considerations
>
> ➤ Don't believe everything the leasing agent tells you
>
> ➤ Don't personally guarantee the lease

Business Alerts

Don't ever be pressured into signing a commercial lease too quickly and before you have a lawyer review it. A new start-up needs to be very comfortable with its location, which can add a lot to the initial success. If you are told to "sign now or lose it," then let it go and look for another space—there are many out there.

➤ Don't be rushed into a decision

➤ Don't make the deal with a handshake—if the owner sells the property during your lease, the lease won't be valid

➤ Don't ask for unreasonable things—the landlord must also make a profit

➤ Don't let the potential landlord bully you

➤ Don't be discouraged if the landlord asks for a lot of references because you're a start-up

➤ Don't forget to check on any licenses or permits you will need

➤ Don't take the lease commitment lightly; it's a legal contract

A commercial lease can seem a little scary for a new start-up business owner, but it doesn't need to be. If you just follow the procedures above and don't settle for less than you want or need, everything should work out fine.

Selecting a location for your new business is a big decision, but once you make it and sign a lease, stop worrying about the decision. You have already made the commitment, and now it's time to go on to your next step in the start-up process.

CHAPTER 6

Franchises

In This Chapter

➤ Are you ready to go it alone?

➤ Is a franchise for you?

➤ Where to find franchises

➤ Franchise dos and don'ts

In this chapter you'll find out if you are ready to start a business on your own from scratch or if you need the guidance of a franchise. You need to ask yourself questions that will determine if you're ready to risk your start-up capital on your own idea or innovation. Many new entrepreneurs prefer the comfort and possible safety of buying into a franchise. But owning a franchise is not always a sure thing free of problems, as you will find out in this chapter. You will have to make a personal decision about which is best for you, your family, and any investors.

Do You Have the Expertise?

Many people want to open a business of their own. It's sort of the living dream to be your own boss and test your ideas. It's just human nature to think you have a better way of managing or making a product.

We all have our own ideas and opinions about how to make a business better, but how many of us follow through with those ideas? How many people take that first step and put those ideas into action? How many people can handle the possibility of failure? And how many people actually have the knowledge and expertise to start a business on their own?

Business Vocab

Expertise is the skill and knowledge of an expert in an industry

Some people seem to be born entrepreneurs and can just jump in with both feet and succeed most of the time. Others have to work hard at it and study the methods of proven winners with business success. I don't think anyone has the answer to why some people are more confident going into a new business and others need guidance, but that's just the way it is. The confident entrepreneurs must have had so much interest in their own business that they listened and picked up a lot of information in their early years and filed it away in their mental filing cabinet. Those mental files kept building and updating until it became time to start a business on their own. They were ready and the world was waiting to see what they had to offer.

Business Facts

Every year, over 1 million people start their own business and almost as many decide to terminate a small business. The majority of these are home-based businesses that are not planned well or were started with little or no capital investment. Taking the time to study, read, and investigate a business opportunity in advance gives you a better chance of success.

If You're Not Sure

You may want to be a born entrepreneur, but you are not really sure if you are. You think that you have most of the knowledge necessary but have not tried it yet and feel a little apprehension or hesitation. If this is how you're thinking, you are probably not a born entrepreneur, but that's not all bad. That just means that you have the drive, passion, and focus to start a successful business but lack in some of the mechanical expertise. These abilities can be learned and most of them are in this book; they will be here if you need to refer back to them. Without a gung ho attitude, you have two choices and need to select the correct one.

One option is to start your business on your own anyway, and learn as you go along. You must be willing to take your chances with what you don't know and hope that you can learn quickly or hire a staff member who's in the know. Your odds of success are still good as long as you don't ignore the tasks that need to be part of your start-up and you make a sincere effort to learn them. Remember, it's the drive, passion, and focus that are most important; the rest will fall into place if you let it.

Starting a business can change your life for the good and sometimes even for the bad. Not everyone can be a business owner or entrepreneur; not everyone can handle the risk. But when you accept risk as just part of the process, your chances of success are much better.

Another option is to rent a franchise. A franchise is a business you rent from a franchisor and includes the established trademark and the franchisor's standardized approach to delivering a product or service. With a franchise, you're not alone; you have a place to get your ongoing questions answered. Let's take a closer look at what it means to own a franchise.

Business Vocab

A franchise is a license granted to an individual or group to market a company's goods or services within a certain location. A franchisor is the company granting the license and a franchisee is you, the business that's marketing the franchisor's goods in a specific location.

Is a Franchise Right for You?

There will be some rules that you will agree to by signing your franchise agreement. One of them will be the minimum number of hours your business will be open. Many franchises have a planned and possibly advertised number of hours or times that you will be expected to adhere to. You may be able to be open longer hours, but not shorter hours without permission from the franchise main office.

If the amount of time that you spend working is a concern of yours, ask about the hours early in your consideration of each franchise company. If you want to open any type of retail store, you can almost be assured that the hours will be long. You must agree to work the required hours or hire people to do so if you're not able.

Ask Yourself

Many businesses fail or produce low profits because the owners only work the hours that they want to. A successful growing business will be open when customers want to buy regardless of how many hours that is. Be sure you're willing to work the necessary hours required by your franchise.

If you are buying a franchise because it's a proven concept, then you must follow that proven concept and the rules that go with it. The franchise owners know from current and past experience the working hours necessary for the best chance of success.

If you refuse to work the specified hours after you are running, you'll risk losing the franchise because you'll be violating your agreement. If you think that this is just an easy way out, consider that your initial franchise fee, which could be substantial, will not be returned. One minute after you pay the franchise fee and sign the agreement, that money is gone forever. It doesn't matter whether you are a big success or failure, the fee is nonrefundable for the proprietary information you'll receive.

Where to Find a Franchise

When you have decided that you want a proven partner for your start-up and a franchise is the answer, you need to find the best one to meet your goals. Of course, you can find many franchises by driving up and down the main streets in your city or town, but that's far from the best choice. Statistics have shown that there are between 1,600 and 1,800 franchise companies operating in the United States, plus hundreds or perhaps thousands more worldwide. Even if you narrow the franchises to your industry of choice, you will probably still have over a hundred to choose from. It's in your best interest to look at and investigate all of them.

Finding All the Choices

So where do you start to look for all of the franchises that could possibly work for you as a start-up? You can start by looking at your local or online bookstore for books and magazines that list available franchises. There are many publications available, but none will come even close to listing all of the franchises. So if you want to check all franchises in a specific industry, you will need to combine several sources.

The following are just a few of the websites with franchise information. You can also use your search engine and type in the industry name followed by the word *franchise*. For example, you can search *automotive franchise* or *pet franchise*.

➤ www.franchise.com

➤ www.everyfranchise.com

➤ www.franchisesolutions.com

➤ www.franchiseopportunities.com

➤ www.franchiseleader.com (resales)

➤ www.franchiseresales.com (resales)

Business Facts

It's estimated that there are 2,000 or more different franchise companies in the United States, and that number is growing. The number of actual franchisees who own these businesses is approaching 1 million and is also growing. The entire franchise industry employs approximately 18 to 20 million people and accounts for over $1.8 trillion of the U.S. economy.

You can also drive around your city and write down the names of places that interest you. Then go back to your computer and search the name to see if it's a franchise or if it's corporate owned. It's also a good idea to walk into the place of business to see if the owner is available to answer some questions. No one will know better about a business than the person who is operating it.

If the franchise fee and start-up capital are more than your budget can handle, just search for other franchises in the same industry. Long-time and well-proven franchise names always charge more to

Business Knowledge

You must know how to read and understand a franchise agreement before you sign it. There are many things that can be changed to your advantage if you just ask. Good franchise coaches can be well worth their fees.

start. But an intermediate or newer franchise company may be just as good and require less money to start. You just don't want to be the first or second one to open a particular franchise. It's better to let someone else get all the bugs out first.

When you find several franchises that are in an industry you feel comfortable with, request start-up literature from them. Laws prevent anyone from even trying to sell you a franchise until you have the literature in hand for at least three days. There is no shame in asking for literature from ten or twenty or more franchises before you make a decision. It's sort of like getting married: most of us don't marry the first person we meet even if we go back to him or her later. We want to see what's out there before we make that final decision. And a franchise, like a marriage, is easy to get into and difficult to get out of.

Do Your Due Diligence

I can't stress enough how important it is to thoroughly check out the franchises you're interested in and to be sure the franchise you choose is the one you really want. Whether it takes you one week or six months, find out everything you can about your franchise final choices. You may not like the company colors, which you will have to look at every day, or you may feel that its product or service is not up to par with its competitors. Some may be too expensive to start, or the monthly royalty may be high for its industry.

The royalty is an important consideration when weighing the pros and cons of a franchise. A percentage of sales must be paid to the franchise company periodically to pay for advertising and other such support activities the franchise company performs on behalf of all its franchises. This royalty varies from one franchise company to another.

Use all of the information you gather to eliminate your choices until you get down to four or five of the best ones for you and your goals. Then you will need to contact each franchise and ask some serious questions so you can make your final choice and write your deposit check.

Business Facts

Studies show that approximately 40 to 45 percent of all retail sales in the United States come from the franchise industry, and most franchise companies have fewer than one hundred units. The average length of a franchise contract is ten years and the average royalty is between 3 and 6 percent.

Following are some questions to help you determine if a franchise is right for you:

> ➤ Are the prices for the products or services high, medium, or low compared to those of the competitors?

> ➤ Are the products or services good, better, or best compared to those of the competitors?

> ➤ Is the franchisor a well-known name in the industry, or will you have to introduce it to customers?

> ➤ Does the franchisor have corporate-owned stores so it knows the day-to-day business firsthand?

> ➤ What are the normal business hours?

> ➤ Can you sell anything you want or only franchise-approved products?

> ➤ Is there a hot line that's available seven days a week and at least twelve hours a day to address problems?

> ➤ Will the franchisor help you find a location and order equipment?

> ➤ Can you get a list of at least twenty other franchisees, a few of which you can call for more information on the franchisor?

> ➤ Does the franchisor have store design plans, or do you have to hire and pay an architect to design your store?

> ➤ Does the franchisor offer any financing to assist with the start-up expenses?

> ➤ Is the franchisor listed with Dun & Bradstreet and local Better Business Bureaus?

> ➤ Do you personally like the products and services well enough to feel comfortable selling them to friends and relatives?

> ➤ Do you get a big enough protected territory to allow you to make a decent profit?

> ➤ Does the franchisor offer some type of on-site training for your first few days?

> ➤ Can you open more than one location if you're successful and what will that cost?

> ➤ Is the franchisor on the cutting edge of the industry or does it sell old products that have been successful for years?

Are You On Your Own?

When you're running a franchise, you are somewhat independent but also have a larger corporation to rely on. If you go into a franchise with the attitude that you're a businessperson who is buying into a proven idea, you will enjoy your business much more.

But if you feel like you're just an employee of the franchise company, then that's what you'll be.

The franchise will be your business, and you will be responsible for it and reap the rewards when it's successful. The corporate office will offer advertising and promotions, but you can go beyond that and do your own marketing. In fact, you should be active and known in your target market, whether local, national, or international. You will be your own boss but also have the franchise corporate office to assist you in any decisions or problems.

Business Facts

A new franchise business unit is opened or started every eight minutes of every day. A U.S. Department of Commerce study shows that less than 5 percent of all franchised businesses are closed each year. Non-franchised businesses had a much higher rate of failure. The average income of established franchise units is between $70,000 and $125,000, with some much higher.

Franchise Dos and Don'ts

Here are some things that you can consider if you feel that a franchise might be for you. Think about these dos and don'ts when starting to investigate different franchises. Better yet, make a copy of them and carry it with you or attach them to your computer so you won't forget them.

Dos:

> ➤ Do decide what industry you want to be in

> ➤ Do look at all the industry franchises first

> ➤ Do spend enough time to investigate each franchise

> ➤ Do talk to several existing franchisees

> ➤ Do meet your chosen franchisor in person

> ➤ Do ask all the questions in this chapter

> ➤ Do decide if you can and will work the hours required

➤ Do have a lawyer read the franchise agreement

➤ Do ask the franchisor if it offers financing

➤ Do be aware of the commitment you're making

➤ Do consult your family before making your final decision

Don'ts:

➤ Don't rush into a decision too quickly

➤ Don't expect instant success from any franchise

➤ Don't expect it all to be easy because it's a franchise

➤ Don't be the guinea pig for a new franchise

➤ Don't overextend your finances on a large franchise fee

➤ Don't ignore competition; a franchise is not a 100 percent sure thing

➤ Don't sign papers unless you know what they are

➤ Don't hesitate to walk away from a deal that seems shaky

➤ Don't neglect to investigate the franchisor

➤ Don't look back when you've made a final decision

Ask Yourself

Whether you start a franchise business or one on your own, you must be dedicated and take it seriously. Being a business owner is hard work and the market is changing constantly. The most successful entrepreneurs are aware of all changes before or as soon as they occur and are ready to act on them.

CHAPTER 7

Buying a Business

In This Chapter

➤ Should you buy a business?

➤ Where to find one

➤ What to check out

➤ What about the employees?

➤ Seller financing

➤ How it works

In this chapter you will learn how to investigate a resale business and what to look for on the balance sheet as well as in the target market. You'll find out that learning the reason a business owner wants or has to sell can be just as important as the financial numbers. You'll have the facts and basics to decide if you should buy an existing business or start a new one.

Why Buy an Existing Business?

In the last chapter we looked at buying into a franchise system where you are provided with a game plan that has worked in the past. We saw that you must follow the corporate plan and pay a royalty based on sales, pretty much forever. But there is another alternative to opening a franchise or starting from scratch, and that is to purchase an existing and operating independent business. There are millions of them around—yes, millions—but not all are for sale.

One reason to buy a business is the ready-to-go position it's in at the time of purchase. The time it takes to start a franchise or your own business doesn't come into play, so it may be profitable sooner, if not right away. You can concentrate more on operating the business than on how to get it going. Of course, there will be some things you will want to change, add, or eliminate, but the business will already be open and providing cash flow. This incoming money will pay ongoing expenses, suppliers, and personnel while you think about ways to grow and improve your new endeavor.

Business Facts

Here are some facts regarding purchasing an established independent business:

➤ Only about 20 percent of businesses that are listed for sale ever complete a sale

➤ A business broker is involved in less than 15 percent of all sales

➤ Of all the people who are looking for a business to buy, 90 percent never actually buy one

➤ Half of all negotiations between buyer and seller fall apart during the due diligence process

Another reason to purchase an independent company is that you don't have to pay a royalty or answer to a corporate office. When you make a decision, it's your decision and no one can stop you. It's your baby and you will live or die with your decisions. You can, of course, seek advice from staff or outside advisors, but you make the final call.

For some entrepreneurs with a strong will and success drive, purchasing an independent business is the only way to go. They want the independence and are willing to accept the risk to get it. Changes can be made whenever and wherever they want and on short notice. An existing business even with some problems can be very desirable to a strong-willed entrepreneur.

Where to Find an Existing Business

When you decide that you want to investigate several of the independent businesses for sale, how do you find them? There are a few ways to locate businesses that are for sale and available for your due diligence.

Advertisements

Ads in local papers, magazines, and the Internet are good sources for finding businesses that are up for sale. When answering these ads via voice mail or e-mail, just say that you may be interested in the specific business for sale and would like someone to contact you.

Leave a phone number or e-mail address and expect a response within forty-eight hours. If it takes longer than that for someone to get back to you, pass on that opportunity and keep looking. Don't send another e-mail or call again if you don't get a response, and never give out any personal information such as social security number, date of birth, or bank account numbers to anyone you don't know well. You are just in the beginning stage here.

Business Brokers

Business brokers have access to available businesses in the areas and the industry you are interested in joining. Commercial sale listings are different from residential real estate because there is no clearinghouse like the MLS network where all for-sale properties appear. So it may be wise to talk to several different brokers who may have different listings.

Business brokers are usually safe sources because they monitor and assist in every step in the process. They get paid by the selling party and handle all the forms and legal filings. They will, however, ask questions to qualify you before presenting you with a business for sale. Answering their inquiries should be safe, but if in doubt check the Better Business Bureau. But even with business brokers, don't give out too much personal information until you get to know them.

Referrals

Getting referrals, or word-of-mouth recommendations, is a way to find a business for sale that is not being advertised or listed with a broker. These referrals can come through the Chamber of Commerce, SCORE, banks, sales rep groups, Rotary, networking groups, or friends. Many owners who are not desperate to sell their business may just put the word out to see what happens. These owners may not want the general public or their customers to know that they are thinking about selling or to see a sign in their store window or website. Getting a referral from someone you know who is familiar with the business can create a little more comfort in the beginning.

Business Knowledge

Business brokers say that people who eventually buy a business select a different type than the one they were originally looking for. Some buyers will investigate too many businesses before attempting to make a decision. They feel that they never get the best deal but need to focus on one or two and make an offer.

What to Look For

You will need to do your due diligence for each business that you consider buying. Most people start with the financial reports, but they may only tell half of the real story. Financial reports are just numbers on paper and may not reflect what's really going on in the business. Here are some questions to consider:

> ➤ Do you like the business—the products and services?
>
> ➤ Do you like the location?
>
> ➤ How old is the business?
>
> ➤ Is it profitable (not always important)?
>
> ➤ Will any suppliers transfer account credit to you?
>
> ➤ Why is the seller interested in selling?
>
> ➤ Are there any employees?
>
> ➤ What are employees paid and what are their benefits?
>
> ➤ Will most of the employees stay?
>
> ➤ Is there inventory and what is its value?
>
> ➤ Is equipment working properly?
>
> ➤ Will the landlord (if any) transfer the lease?
>
> ➤ Who will train you to operate the business?
>
> ➤ How long will it take you to learn the business?
>
> ➤ Where can you turn for answers to problems?
>
> ➤ Is there a customer mailing list?
>
> ➤ Will the current owner sign a noncompete agreement?
>
> ➤ Is the target market large or small?
>
> ➤ If retail, can you get the demographics?
>
> ➤ Would you buy from this business?

When looking at the financial statements, do not be overly concerned about the profits, there may be reasons why they are low or nonexistent. For instance, many small business owners like to use profits to pay expenses and keep their taxes low, or the owner could have unusual expenses or loan payments that you won't have. What you should look at are the total sales, or revenues, and the cash flow. Have the sales been increasing over the last year or two, or are they stagnant and possibly decreasing? This will tell you more about what's been happening in the business. Cash flow will tell you if you have enough money coming in to pay your bills, and sales will tell you where that cash flow is coming from. In a small business, these are the two numbers that really tell the story.

Business Knowledge

Before a purchase contract is executed, take a close look at past financial performance, inventory, and other assets. Also talk to employees and sellers about how the business works, and who their customers and competitors are. This in-depth information should help determine if a new owner will make a difference and be successful.

If a business is showing profits that are higher than you expected, it could be from some creative accounting to make the business look more valuable. Even if sales are not growing, it may be worth a second look. Maybe you can come in with some new ideas, better customer service, product line and service changes, plus new marketing strategies that will turn sales around quickly. Some businesses that look marginal on paper can be purchased at a good price and become profitable in a short time. So look between the lines on the income statement to see the real picture and what can be done about it with a new owner.

Another area that you need to look at is the debt the business has and if the current owner will pay it off from the proceeds of the sale or if you inherit it. Loans that were signed by the current owner were probably personally guaranteed and should be finalized by the current owner. But payments due on equipment, supplies, and inventory can be negotiated. If you are using a business broker, he or she can work that out for you. If you are assuming payments to suppliers and others, will they transfer those payments to you as the new owner? Some of them may want to do credit checks before agreeing to that.

Business Vocab

Financial statements show in numbers how the business is doing now and in the past. You can see if it made a profit and what the expenses are, plus who the business owes money to and how it's paid.

Here are some other considerations:

> ➤ Financial statements: Read between the lines and ask questions. Decide if you really care how profitable the business is or if you are going to make new changes when you take over. Potential may be just as important as profit.

> ➤ Corporation or business: Which are you buying— just the business part or the entire company? Be sure this is all spelled out completely in the contract so there are no surprises later.

> ➤ Non-compete clause: Will the seller agree not to open another business that competes with the one you are buying? A certain area or time limit can be specified.

> ➤ Yellow pages: Are any phone directory ads tied to the phone bill that you will have to pay? And how much are they?

> ➤ Key employees: Will the current owner stay on after the sale? If so, how is he or she being compensated? If not, how will you replace him or her?

> ➤ Brand: Has the name or product already been established in the target marketplace? Does it have a good reputation?

> ➤ Security deposits: Do you have to replace the security deposits if the seller gets them back? How much will it be to replace them and did you figure for it in your budget?

> ➤ Office or store lease: Will you take over the existing lease or start a new one? Have you been preapproved and talked to the landlord?

> ➤ Face lift: Do you have any extra money for renovations or needed improvements?

> ➤ Long-term obligations: Are you going to be bound by any deals the seller has made with creditors, suppliers, customers, or banks? Can you negotiate a better deal with any of them?

> ➤ Supplier accounts: Is the business in good standing and does it have open accounts with its main suppliers? Can you change suppliers if you find better ones?

> ➤ Customer lists: Are these included and who else, if anyone, is using them? How were they compiled and can you enhance the process?

> ➤ Patents and copyrights: Are these included in the sale and will you own them exclusively?

> ➤ Licenses: Will you need any (i.e., liquor or gambling) and how long will it be before they would be approved or transferred? Will there be any interruption in the business?

> ➤ Employee relations: Talk to some of the employees and get their opinion of their job and the company. You may find out things here you won't hear elsewhere.

➤ Lawsuits: Are there any lawsuits still outstanding that will have to be settled after you take over?

➤ Business neighbors: Talk to the neighbors briefly to see if they have any comments and check for any noise or fumes coming through the walls.

➤ Customers: Try to meet some of the customers and see how your new ownership can continue or improve their loyalty. Ask what their likes and dislikes are.

What About Leases?

If the business location is leased, check to see if the landlord will just transfer the lease to you or your business entity before making a formal in-writing offer to purchase. It may be to your advantage and the landlord's if you sign a new lease adding a year or two from the current one. This lets the former owner off the hook if anything should happen when you take over. If the lease is just transferred to you and you sign to make the payments, the landlord still has the old owner as a guarantor in the event of any defaults. It will matter a lot more to the seller than you if a new lease is executed and they may not even know it.

If there are leases on equipment or vehicles, they must be negotiated before any sale is made. Consider these questions:

➤ Have all the payments been made on time and how many more are there to make?

➤ Do you want or need the vehicles and if not, will the seller take them?

➤ Is the equipment that's on lease state-of-the-art or becoming obsolete?

➤ Do any of these leases have a buyout option that will save any interest?

➤ Is the lease able to be cancelled if you need to upgrade the equipment?

➤ Is there anything else in the business that is on a payment plan?

Leases can be a big draw on cash flow, so be sure to ask all the questions.

The Employees and Training

The business you are considering buying will likely have some employees, or staff. These people already know how the business runs and you will need most of them to stay, at least during your break-in period. However, it could be a challenging situation if many of them are part of the seller's family. You will need some guarantee that most of the employees will stay until you understand the basics of the business and get new people trained.

When you purchase an existing business, you need to learn how the business works. It's best to leave everything the same for at least the first month. Meet with all of the employees as a group and explain that no big changes will be made right away and that there will be a transition period for both you and them. During that time, you will begin to see who the important and best employees are and what they can contribute to your overall plan. Some will be great customer contact people and some will be great backup people. And, of course, there will be some that will not fit in your plan at all and will need to move on.

Training the New Owner

If you decide to buy an ongoing business, you'll need some training in how the business works. The best person to show you the ropes is the current owner or one of the senior managers. When making your purchase deal, there should be some provision for the seller to provide two to three weeks of on-site training. After that time period is over, there needs to be another ninety days for the trainers to be on call for anything else that comes up.

When a new owner takes over a business, unexpected mistakes can happen, especially if there is not some quality control plan in effect. For instance, mistakes on orders can happen unless a key employee is given some authority right away.

Let's say you have purchased a non-franchise pizza company and a customer requests certain toppings or for the finished pizza to be cut in a specific way. People who are making the pizzas may forget or disregard customer requests. Customers who don't get what they ordered may call to complain or, worse yet, not call and never order again. A new owner needs to know as much as possible when taking over and who the key employees are that they can count on.

Retraining the Employees

When the time comes, in thirty to sixty days or so, to make a few changes, make them gradually. Those first few weeks will let you see how the business was run and what customers and employees think about it. You may already have a list of changes you want to make, but why not open your mind to everything that's possible. Here are three groups of people that you can brainstorm with for new ideas.

➤ Employees: the employees have either had customer contact or back room experience with the business much longer than you have. They have seen and heard things that they feel will make the business better, stronger, and more appealing to customers and potential customers. Listen carefully to their ideas and consider anything that may be possible.

➤ Customers: The regular and semi-regular customers of the business are accustomed to the previous service and procedure. They may want to see some changes or have ideas for changes. What better source for new ideas than the people who will buy from you.

If you have a retail store, roam around at different times of the day and talk to people. If you work by phone or through a call center, ask that a few calls be transferred to you after their business is finished. If you only work on the Internet, send e-mails or questionnaires to your valuable customers asking for their input and ideas. Listen to or read the responses and thank everyone for their suggestions.

➤ Suppliers and vendors: Normally these people won't offer suggestions for your business unless you ask them, so ask. They may tell you about new products or services and how to sell them. The key ingredient to brainstorming with suppliers is that they know your competitors. They probably won't reveal any secrets, but they may offer some general ideas that you can use. They may be aware of an expanded target market that you didn't test or think of yet. They want you to be a success as much as you do and are likely to help you as much as they can.

With all this brainstorming information, you can decide what new procedures you want to phase in and train your employees to offer. It's best to meet with them and explain why you are making changes and how it will benefit the company and them. Anything that improves the business also makes their job more secure, especially in a tough economy.

You want employees on your side as a team who wants to learn new things that will move the company in a positive direction. Occasionally you will find someone who will rebel against change, and you must decide if that person is worth keeping. When you make changes, do it slowly or have a target date when they will be implemented. Some people may catch on to change faster than others and that's okay. What you really want to see is a positive attitude; the rest will follow.

Seller Financing

When you decide on a business that you would like to buy, the next steps can be challenging. The purchase money may become an obstacle unless you have all the cash up front. Since most buyers are ambition-rich and cash-poor, a source of capital needs to be found. Of course, you will need a down payment, but the rest can be financed in one way or another. Most banks, especially in a tight economy, shy away from small business loans unless they are backed by the SBA. In fact, all of the ideas discussed in Chapter 3 can be used or investigated, but there may be a better way: seller financing.

When the seller agrees or offers to carry some of the purchase price, he or she opens the door to more potential buyers who now have a way to purchase the business. This can allow the seller to increase the price slightly, especially if the down payment is low. Seller financing can also give some assurance to the buyer that the seller will be involved for a while and have a serious interest in seeing that the business does well. All this ongoing help and interest by the seller can put the buyer in a better comfort zone and also be worth a little more in the purchase price.

How It Works

Whether you are using business brokers or finding businesses for sale through ads or referrals, you want to ask about seller financing. It may be available even if there is no advertising or discussion of it up front. The seller might be waiting to see what you bring to the table first.

It's all about negotiating and making the best deal for both sides of the transaction. Of course, the seller would prefer an all-cash deal but in most cases won't get it. You, the buyer, would like to offer the least cash possible and carry the balance over several years. Remember, you may need resources to keep the business running and to pay for your new marketing ideas. Go into any buy-sell negotiation slowly, and don't show your entire hand right away. As we say in poker, keep your opponent guessing.

A seller will almost always require some cash down, somewhere between 10 and 50 percent of the sale price. Most of the time the down payment will fall somewhere in the middle, around 25 to 33 percent of the sale price. This is a good range for both you as a buyer and for the seller.

The next step, if you're interested in seller financing, is to ask the seller to finance the rest. As with any loan, you would be making regular payments. If the payments are too high and the business profits low, you won't be able to keep up. The seller usually knows how much the buyer can pay and how often. The payments may even vary for peak and slow times of the year. There is no rule that says the payment must be the same for every month or quarter.

Business Knowledge

A letter of intent to purchase a business is a nonbinding agreement. It tells the seller that you would like to buy his or her business for a certain amount, so be sure you have thought out the finances thoroughly. It usually has several contingency clauses allowing the buyer to look at the business more closely. The seller will probably ask for proof of funds for the down payment or approval for a bank loan. Without some evidence that funds are available, the seller may not open all the books to the prospective buyer.

Most small business sales will be in the range of $50,000 to $300,000, and this is usually more than a buyer has in cash. A business broker or small business accountant with no connection to either side can help structure the deal and payment process.

The seller will likely ask for a promissory note signed by the buyer and a spouse, if applicable. The spouse's signature protects the buyer from transferring assets if something should go wrong along the way. The seller should also request the buyer to sign a personal guaranty for the financing, and sometimes this can be negotiated. The seller may also ask the buyer to provide a life insurance policy or key man insurance that covers the outstanding balance. This policy can be term insurance and is usually low in cost. These requests are not unusual, and it's the least that any bank would ask for.

Business Alerts

Part of your due diligence will be to find out if the business has any legal issues pending or in the past that could surface again. You also want to be sure all federal and state taxes have been paid to date. Check what the unemployment rate is for the company at the State Department of Labor. Are there any claims against the business that could turn into lawsuits? The more you know, the more comfortable you'll be after the sale.

The buyer can also request a few other things such as an open line of communication for any problems as long as there is a balance due. The seller should be happy to oblige because he or she wants you to be successful as well. Most seller financing deals carry a low interest rate, lower than a bank, and sometimes no interest rate at all. One idea is to offer to pay the seller's legal bill for setting up the seller financing contract in exchange for zero interest on the debt. If the business has been for sale for a while, the seller may agree, just to get the deal done quickly.

Seller financing can be a great way to buy an existing business without using all of your available cash or going through the long, agonizing borrowing process with a bank. Most sellers are just ordinary people who years ago started a business, made it grow, and now want to get out for any number of reasons. You, on the other hand, are ready to jump in and take that business to another level. In most transactions, both the seller and buyer are dedicated to seeing that the business not only survives but thrives with the new ownership.

CHAPTER 8

 **Defining Your Target Market**

In This Chapter

➤ Who will buy from you?

➤ Why will they buy?

➤ Know your competition

➤ Where to find customers

➤ Jump start your business

In this chapter you find ways to determine who and what your target market is and why they should buy from your new business. You'll also determine who your competition is and how strong they are. Tips on where to look for customers and reasons you may need to expand your target market are also included.

Target Markets

Knowing the who, what, where, and why of the market you are in is one of the most important parts of any business start-up. When you determine the buyers that are most likely to be your customers—your target market—you can budget most of your marketing dollars to reach them. Knowing everything about your target market is essential before making any investments or serious progress in your start-up.

Your target market is where you will make your sales, get your cash flow, and grow your business. So understanding as much as you can about it is imperative to making your start-up a success.

It's even a good idea to study the history of your target market—the products that have become obsolete and how long they were popular. Search the Internet, library, and talk to people who have been selling to this market for a long time. There is no such thing as too much information about the market you'll be selling to.

Business Alerts

There's old advice that says what worked yesterday may not work tomorrow. Always be on the lookout for what's new in your industry because many customers want the latest products and innovations. Don't be selling VCR tapes in a DVD world.

Who Will Be Your Customers?

To determine your target market, you need to find the people who will be your buyers. This is important whether you are selling to consumers or to other businesses.

What You Need to Know

Following are some of the details and questions you need to ask about your consumer buyers:

- ➤ Are they predominately male or female (or even)?
- ➤ What is the average age range (young, adult, mature)?
- ➤ What is their education level (if it matters)?
- ➤ What is their income range (low, medium, high)?
- ➤ How large is their family (kids, pets, relatives)?
- ➤ How old is their neighborhood (need repairs, landscaping)?
- ➤ Are they mostly professional or blue collar?
- ➤ Do they buy somewhere else now (your competitors)?
- ➤ Does their ethnic background matter for your products or services?

Following are some of the details and questions you need to ask about your business customers:

➤ How solid is their industry (growing or stagnant)?

➤ Are your products essential to their business?

➤ Are your products and services a commodity?

➤ Are there custom products in your line that need extra selling?

➤ How often do they order your type of products and services?

➤ How many competitors are in your target market?

➤ Will great service make a difference in repeat business?

➤ What will it take to create loyal customers?

➤ Are your target customers always looking for new, innovative products?

➤ How long has your target market been in existence?

➤ Can you take customers from competitors and what will it take to get them?

➤ What is your advantage over the competitors that are already in this market?

Once you answer these questions, you will need to plan your marketing to reach your target market. Coming into a market too slowly can show weakness and be a deterrent to new customers. You need to make your presence known quickly and with force. As they say in poker, act strong even when your hand is weak and you will stand out among competitors.

Before you even open your business, while you're still in the planning stage, watch how your future competitors are doing their marketing. See if they are targeting one segment of the market more than the others. For example, McDonald's and Chuck E. Cheese's direct their ads to children because they will convince their parents to take them there. And toy manufacturers get kids interested in new products so they can beg their parents and grandparents to buy them. You can be sure that they wouldn't be directing their marketing to children if it hadn't worked for them in the past.

Learn from past marketing who to direct your promotions to, even if it's not the person who will eventually make the purchase. I call this indirect marketing and if it's the way to produce sales, use it.

Why Will Anyone Buy from You?

When you have determined who your customer is supposed to be, you need to find reasons why they should buy from you. Just blasting the market with ads and direct mail, saying

"Hey, I'm here" will not produce great results. There must be something to justify buying your product over your competitors'.

There are people who will buy something from you once because you are new and they want to see what you're all about. Although many may not plan to return unless you wow them, you do have that one chance. There will also be people, consumer and business, who are unhappy with the company they are currently buying from and are looking for a way out. This is also a great opportunity to pick up those valuable first customers.

Business Knowledge

People spend their money where they feel confident that they are getting the highest value and expertise, and the best service. When people and businesses begin to trust and rely on your company for exactly what they need or want, your sales will build quickly. Start early, establishing your position at the peak of your industry.

What You Need to Offer

Try to find what is lacking in your industry or what concern is not being addressed, and use that to attract customers. Here are a few things that you can consider using to create interest in your new business:

➤ Bigger selection than competitors

➤ Outstanding customer service

➤ Easy special orders

➤ Add value to services

➤ Your unique selling proposition (USP) is superior to others

➤ Faster delivery or availability

➤ Loyalty rewards for regular customers

➤ Customer education and training

➤ State-of-the-art signage

➤ Longer business hours

➤ Several ways to order or purchase

➤ Experts on the front line

➤ Easy returns and exchanges

Price is not the factor that will attract the loyal customers a new business needs to grow and prosper. Low prices, other than a special sale, will only bring in fickle customers who may never come back unless your prices are still the lowest when they need to purchase again. And reducing prices too low will bring competitors into play and may start a price war where no one wins. It can also bring in the large companies who are able to beat your price every time and still not harm their overall business. Pricing low is not a way to start or build a business and is not recommended for a start-up. Offering a better value for the price is a much better way to build a business.

Your Competitors

The first thing you need to know about the competitors in your target market is who they are.

If you're a retail business, you should be aware of every other retail business within a two- or three-mile radius of your store, whether they are a competitor or not. Every time you see a building going up or a building permit on a window, stop and see who's moving in. If you sell to other businesses, know your five biggest rivals in the market you serve: local, state, national, or international. Be sure to subscribe to all the trade magazines in your industry; many of them are free. You need to know everything competitors are doing or planning to do as early as possible. Then you can develop your strategy to stay one step ahead of them as you open your new business.

Ask Yourself

If you think that you have no competitors because your product or service is so unique, think again. You may not be aware of them, but there will always be competitors planning to take some of your business by coming up with a better idea, lower price, or faster service. Even if your start-up business has the best idea since sliced bread, competitors will come after your customers, so be ready for them.

By knowing the answers to the following questions, you just might keep a little ahead of the competition:

➤ Exactly who are your competitors? If you're in retail, you can simply check the phone book and drive around your main selling area. If you're in business-to-business sales, you can search your industry on the web or check out the library.

➤ Are they big, franchises, or small? If your competitors are big public companies, you can easily find financial information from any of the stock service companies. If they're franchises, you can check the website of the franchisor and find out about the business: how many units, how long in business, franchise fees, royalty fees, etc.

➤ What are their strong points? What do your competitors stress or emphasize in their advertisements or yellow page listings? What are people saying about them, and why would anyone buy their products or services? What are their best-selling products and why?

➤ Do they have niche products? What are your competitors offering to customers and prospects that is unique in your industry? How are they promoting these products or services—or are they? Are they always offering something new or relying on the same old line?

➤ Are the owners active in the business? In a retail business, you'll want to find out if the owners actually work regularly in the business or just visit occasionally. It will take absentee owners longer to find out about any changes you make.

➤ What is their pricing strategy? How do your competitors price their products or services—are they expensive, rock-bottom, or middle priced? Are they looking for the low-price customer, or are they giving the impression of selling a high-priced luxury? Are you using this information to determine your own price position?

➤ Are they opening new locations and offices? Is your competition expanding? How will this help or hurt them in the marketplace? Will you need to expand or add locations soon to keep up?

➤ How many employees do they have? You may be able to find this out by visiting the competitor's store or office, asking people who work there or their customers. Are they hiring, laying off, or downsizing by attrition?

➤ How do they pay their employees? Do your competitors pay higher, lower, or about average wages for your industry? Have you talked to any of their employees during the interviews and are they satisfied with their wages?

➤ How are customers treated? One way to find out is to be a customer or hire a friend to browse a competitor's store or call the business. Are the employees courteous, helpful, and informative? Are you left standing at the checkout or on hold for a long time?

➤ What are their weaknesses? Your competitors will have some weak areas you can attack by doing things better. Do they offer poor quality, rude service, a small selection, or late delivery? Are their popular or sale items always out of stock?

➤ Where are they? Are your competitors near or far from you, and if you run retail stores, are the stores easily accessible? Are your competitors near your target customer base?

➤ How do they market? Do your competitors use a lot of print advertising in newspapers and/or magazines? Are they on the radio or television regularly? Do they have large, attractive signs at their location and elsewhere? Do they do direct mail and are you on their mailing list? Do they offer coupons and frequent customer cards? Are they selling on the web and how is it promoted? How will you counter these methods?

➤ How will they react to you after you're open? When you make changes, have sales, offer new products, or have promotions, will your competitors counter with similar offers? Do they do nothing or seem to pay no attention to you? If they do respond, how quickly? Do they try to outdo you or just match what you have advertised? Do they let you do your promotion and then have one of their own at a later date?

➤ Are you afraid of them? Does thinking about your competitors keep you awake at night? Can they come out with products or services that will make yours obsolete and put you out of business? Do you run your business more on the defensive rather than the offensive? How can you turn the negatives into positives? Does staying ahead or even with them drain your finances?

➤ Have you researched and studied the answers to all of the above questions and know where and how to position your new business? Are you ready to compete head-on and develop a profitable customer base? Can you compete in this market?

➤ Have you visited or called your new competitors and introduced yourself? Were they cordial and did they welcome you to the industry?

These are questions you want to keep asking yourself every six months or so. Don't think that the situation today will be the same a year from now. Even if you're not making changes, you can be assured your competitors are. You will need to constantly come up with new ideas and changes to keep a step ahead. Once your new business is open for a couple of months, the changes that you need to make will become apparent. And, don't ever ignore your competitors, because they are not ignoring you.

Where Will You Find Customers?

Finding those first customers that will give your business its much-needed cash flow can be a challenge. Every business goes through this stage when it first starts, and it never gets any easier. Maybe even more important is how you will treat and service your customers so they will come back over and over and refer others. You have what you think is the best business ever with the best ideas and products, but without customers you have nothing. So don't spend all your start-up money creating a beautiful location—spend it on getting those first customers in the door, on the phone, or at your website. There's an old sentiment that the customer is king because the customer holds the cash.

Business Customers

The first business customers should come from people you know or have met in the past. If you were employed in the industry prior to opening your business, you should have many contacts. You will know what they were looking for and not getting from the people they have been doing business with. If you have available what customers want or if you can solve their problems, it should be your lead when you are contacting them. You can also ask for referrals from any who will talk to you because they usually know others who buy the same products. People you know should be your first contact.

You will also find business customers at chambers of commerce, the BBB, and networking meetings. If you have attended a great meeting, join the group or offer to speak at an event. The people you meet there may not be direct customer possibilities, buy they may know others who would be. Whenever possible, ask for referrals' names and contact information so you can call or e-mail them.

Retail Customers

Your potential retail customers are the ones walking or driving down the street or shopping at the mall. You need to entice them to visit your store, restaurant, salon, or whatever through signage, ads, direct mail, or publicity. We will go into these marketing methods more in Chapter 16, but do whatever attracts attention to your business with the least cost per response. Don't just stick with one marketing method; try everything and assess the results. A good marketing mix always outperforms one good marketing idea.

You can start by asking friends, relatives, bankers, accountants, and even your commercial real estate agent to tell people about your new business. All these people are interested in seeing you succeed and should help you any way they can. Check out the local flyer service, Valpak, or others and decide if you want to participate in the mailing at around the time of your opening. The main thing is to get people in your retail store and get that initial cash flow in motion.

Online Customers

If you run an online businesses that sell products on the Internet, you need to make people aware of you. Join all of the major social media sites and find others that may specialize in your industry. Start a blog for your business and post items and articles regularly. Don't just put ads on them; give some real usable information and include your contact numbers and website address at the end.

Also see if there are any online directories that you can be listed in so people can find you. Have printable coupons or coupon codes that can be used for Internet purchases. Give out a lot of free information and even secrets for your target market. Secrets won't make you lose business; people will contact you to learn more or hire you. Expose yourself online so people know you're alive and where to find you.

Business Knowledge

One of the basics of effective marketing is knowing who, why, and where your target market is. Your market can be divided into three sections:

➤ Your best prospects

➤ Your casual prospects

➤ Your maybe prospects

Of your marketing efforts, 50 percent should be spent on your best prospects, 35 percent should be spent on your casual prospects, and 15 percent should be spent on your maybe prospects.

Business Alerts

Your target market should know about you and your new business long before you open. Use all the ways available to make your coming presence known as early as you can. Many large companies do this, and they have a long line at their door on opening day.

Jump-Start Your New Business

Marketing and sales promotion should start before you are ready to officially open your business. Once you've made your decisions on store layout, office construction, or home business equipment, it's time to start getting those first customers that are so important to new businesses. Without them, you'll have bills to pay with no money coming in to pay them. Your start-up capital will be depleted very quickly without a regular cash flow in the beginning. Don't let this happen to you; go after those customers early and use several different methods to see what works best. Here are some ideas to consider and have in place before you actually open for business:

> ➤ Toll-free number: A toll-free number can be fed into voice mail or your home phone number so customers and prospects can begin to ask questions and request information. You can do this even before your physical phones are actually installed. Later you can have the calls go to your office or store phone where you can answer them during business hours.

> ➤ Direct mail: Send letters, flyers, menus, etc., to your biggest pool of prospects in advance. You can do this yourself on a small scale or turn it over to a mailing house that can select the correct lists of prospects and do the entire mailing for you. This first mailing will make future customers aware of you, make it easier to contact them later, and create some sales. Your initial image will be created, so make it look as good as you can.

> ➤ Offer free literature: Use response cards, e-mail, and a toll-free number for prospects to request free information. Your literature should explain what your company is all about and why everyone should buy from you. Describe any unique products and services that will be available and how they are different from competitors'. Give them a reason to buy.

> ➤ Set sales appointments: Make sales appointments in advance, so you're busy from *day one* visiting prospects. You can use your home or cell phone to set up meetings with the most receptive prospects. If you have friends with a business, offer to pay them for a desk and phone until your office is ready. If the appointment is more than a week in advance, you can mail a postcard a few days after your call to remind them. You can also invite larger prospects out to lunch and meet in a nice restaurant.

> ➤ Start telemarketing: You, your staff, or an outside firm should be calling your most likely prospects as soon as possible. Tell them about your new business, when it will be open, and why they should be your customers. You can also accept advance orders if you know what your prices will be. Don't promise delivery or store pickup unless you are absolutely sure you can do it. You don't want to break your first promise to a customer.

> ➤ Announce introductory offers: Entice people to try your new business with special

offers, but don't give the ranch away—it will cheapen your image. Make offers that you can afford and that the prospect will value. Always set a *time limit* or *end date,* or your introductory offer will become your regular offer. You want people to try your product or service, then return to buy at its regular price.

➤ Offer gifts: Offer something extra for the first 100 or 500 buyers to get the cash register ringing. Everyone likes to get a gift as long as it's usable and has some value to them. Try to find things that relate to your business either directly or indirectly. After you open, you can have a special prize for the 1,000th customer and make a big deal about it. Take photos and send them to the media.

➤ Have a contest: Hold a contest, no purchase necessary, to get people to try your product or listen to your sales pitch. Be sure to follow all state and federal rules. It's wise to offer one big prize to attract attention and several smaller prizes so there will be more winners. If you're having a drawing, announce the time and day far enough in advance so you can have as many people in attendance as possible—they may make a purchase while they're there. Make the contest duration short (four to six weeks is desirable), and enter any names on a mailing list when it's over.

➤ Offer a free trial: To get prospective customers to use your products, give away free samples. Nothing sells better than the actual product or service, especially when the user doesn't have to pay for it. If the product is as good as you say it is, it should sell itself. Don't provide a large sample that supplies all their needs for a long time; you want customers to purchase more as soon as possible. In a food business, hand out taste samples freely.

➤ Place advertising early: You'll want your print ads to be out when you're ready for business. Many publications have a one- to two-month lead time. A lot of times, the November issue will be released the second week of October. Always check with the publication to find out when the ad will actually hit the public. If you are running a retail store, provide directions. Also inquire about multiple run discounts.

➤ Send press releases: Find something newsworthy about your opening and send the press release to newspapers, magazines, trade journals, radio, and TV at least a month or more in advance. The media may be interested in a revolutionary new product or even a contest if the prize is unusual.

➤ Offer free consultation: Free consultations, including quotes, estimates, samples, and advice will give you that face-to-face contact and could close the sale. These can be done in your store, office, or at a neutral place for breakfast or lunch. Offer your expertise to local radio talk shows and take questions from callers. Promote your expertise in your industry to create confidence in these first customers. Everyone likes to work with an expert.

➤ Hold a seminar: Offer a *free* seminar. Make it convenient and include demonstrations and an informative agenda. A seminar of sixty to ninety minutes is enough to create interest in your new business. You may also learn what new products or services your attendees are interested in and find a way to offer them. Offer at least two different times to accommodate all your prospects' schedules.

➤ Stress your guarantee: Make a *big deal* about your guarantee so first-time buyers can feel comfortable—no one likes to be a guinea pig. Some customers may be apprehensive when it comes to a new business because of past experiences. You need to assure them of your commitment to the highest standards, and then back it up. Make sure it's in writing.

➤ Offer cash discounts: Gifts or discounts for paying in cash can increase your short-term cash flow and make your purchasers feel they received a good deal. If you can't ask for the total amount in advance, try requesting a 50 percent deposit on the first order and the balance on delivery or within ten days. Any money you receive early will help with expenses, paying suppliers, and advertising.

➤ Get your website up: Even if your physical location is not ready, your website can be. People can find information, send e-mails, learn about your products, and even order before the brick-and-mortar store is open. Get on all the relevant social media sites and direct people to your website.

➤ Start networking: Go to all the meetings you can; find them in your Sunday or Monday newspaper. Bring plenty of business cards and give them to as many people as you can. Explain how your new business is different and ask for referrals or permission to call for an appointment.

➤ Advance order specials: Offering extra quantities, discounts, freebies, and free delivery for advance orders can give your first day a big boost. You may make less profit on these orders but you will have a cash flow, which is extremely important in any new business. Offer whatever you can to get those orders without taking a loss. A small profit is better than no customers at all, and this could lead to repeat business.

➤ Teach a class: Colleges and business schools offer short-term classes and clinics in various subjects. Teach a class in your field of expertise, asking for little or no pay. People in your sessions will want to know your current business and may produce some new customers.

It's always an uphill battle with a new business, and the sooner you start moving, the sooner you'll reach your goals. Don't overlook or put aside the task of getting those first customers. They will help your new business survive and grow on your way to an early success.

Business Alerts

When it's time to open your doors, phone lines, or website, don't do it quietly. Let your target market and, yes, your competitors know you are there in a big way. Use multiple methods plus all the bells and whistles to make your new presence known. Direct all your efforts to the people who will most likely be your first customers.

CHAPTER 9

Setting Up Suppliers

In This Chapter

➤ Finding suppliers

➤ Getting lower costs

➤ Establishing credit

➤ Outsource

In this chapter you will learn how to find suppliers for the products you want to resell. Many suppliers can be found in manufacturers' directories at the library and exhibiting at trade shows. You will learn how to set up credit with new suppliers so there won't be a drain on your start-up capital. You will also be able to decide what to outsource and how to monitor the outsourcing entity for best results.

Who Will Make or Supply Your Products?

An essential part of any business is finding supply sources for what you want to sell or provide to your customers. Even if most of these products are also your services, there will be other things that can also be added for additional profits. A new business is usually lured to the suppliers that are most prominent in the industry, but don't overlook the smaller ones.

Every large company today started as a small business with a great idea and no budget to promote it effectively. Always give an up-and-comer (like yourself) the opportunity to share some of your supplier needs. And you must seek them out in the wake of all of your industry's big advertisers. Getting suppliers in place should be done well before your opening day.

If you have already worked in the industry of your new start-up, you may be familiar with describe your new business so you will be able to set up accounts with them. Ask for all their information. You may find products that you weren't aware of and can also offer in your business. It may be wise to visit the supplier's nearby offices or plants to see how the products are made and to bond with important personnel.

Business Alerts

Never get so comfortable with one supplier that you overlook or ignore others that you find or that find you. Different suppliers may offer new products, better pricing and delivery, or terms that are easier to work with. Keep an open mind in your market and don't be afraid to change if something better comes along. You should also have a backup supplier for your fastest moving products.

If the industry is new to you from a working standpoint, you will need to seek out suppliers and make some comparisons. You can always search online, but two of the most reliable sources may be in your local library reference section. They are the *Thomas Industrial Directory* and the *Million Dollar Directory*. There are also several other national and regional industrial and services directories. Most of these will not be available free online, so you will need to spend some time in the library. There may be directories that specialize in your area of interest, so take the time to check out all of them.

Get Samples or Testimonials

Once you have selected several potential suppliers, don't just assume they will be good for your new business. You need to do some research. Call, e-mail, or fax a letter to each of them asking for information and samples, if applicable.

Check any product samples carefully, and if you know of prospective customers already, ask them to evaluate the samples also. You want to be sure you are getting the best possible product for the wholesale price you are paying. You should also ask every prospective supplier if it ever sells directly to the market and if so, at what price. You may not want to use a supplier who competes with you in the marketplace.

If you can find noncompetitors outside your target market area, contact them to get additional suppliers or to check a reference for someone you are considering. If you're not a direct competitor, they may open up a little more and reveal some things that you might not have found out until you're well in business. They may even tell you about a new supplier that you wouldn't find yourself or at least not for a while.

People in business for several years know a lot about suppliers that would take you a long time to find out. Send something like a thank-you gift card to people who give you a lot of useful information and offer to help them in the future. They will probably be your friend forever.

Become Partners with Suppliers

In times of economic uncertainty, two companies that are going in the same direction and helping each other have a much better chance of prospering. So why go it alone when you can have a partner who has the same general goals as you do, but is not a competitor? Who is this wonderful company that really wants to see you succeed? It's your supplier, of course. The supplier's success depends on you and many others like you.

Your suppliers can offer a tremendous amount of product information to make your selling job a lot easier. If you haven't taken a plant tour of several of your top suppliers, put it at the top of your to-do list. If you're out of town and a big enough or fast-growing customer, you may get them to contribute to your airfare. You can probably get great training for you and your staff in how to present their products.

At a business forms company I owned several years ago, we had a different supplier come in once a month and make a presentation. We would always learn something about their company or products we hadn't known before. It was a must-attend event for all salespeople and those in customer service.

We would usually have the meeting early in the morning so the salespeople could use the ideas the same day. Usually the representative would bring doughnuts or sweet rolls and we'd be one happy family all going in the same direction, with increased sales as the goal. That's what you need to get and use the full effect of a supplier's knowledge.

Free Sales Literature

Many of your suppliers will have literature that is available to you at a nominal cost or for free. Never pass up the opportunity to use these product flyers. It's one more thing you can offer to customers to show you're informed in your industry.

Ask your suppliers if you can have your business name printed on some of the flyers the next time they do a print run. Or you might be able to convince them to share some of the cost of your flyers if you highlight some of their products. Either way, you're getting professional flyers to promote your business.

Supplier Loyalty

One way to make a supplier need you and your business is to be loyal to that supplier. Giving more orders to the same supplier results in volume sales that means growth after a while. After this lasts for a reasonable time, you may notice a few perks tossed your way: faster delivery, faster returned phone calls or e-mail, a little extra in your order, or maybe even better pricing. Like anything else, there will be an occasional problem, so don't make unreasonable demands and threaten the loss of your business.

After you've built a relationship over a longer period of time, you may be able to set up volume discounts based on a year's worth of orders rather than just one order. If you guarantee a certain volume over a year, can you get better pricing based on the overall quantity? It never hurts to ask, but make sure you're willing and able to fulfill the agreement. You can also request a prompt-payment discount if you're able to pay your invoices quickly. There's not much loyalty left in the business-to-business world, so when it's given, it's noticed.

Business Knowledge

Magazines and newsletters for your industry will have ads and listings for suppliers in that industry. Research many of them to find the best ones for your new company. Subscribe to the ones that relate to your industry and read them. A list of trade publications can be found in *Bacon's Magazine Directory* at your local library reference department.

Sure, you are your suppliers' customer, but if they provide the products, pricing, and delivery your business requires to grow, you also need them. Never take good suppliers for granted because they are motivated, like you, to increase sales and profits. If they don't see some loyalty from you, they'll look elsewhere for regular customers and may just become tight partners with your competitors. I guess you could say that a good supplier is like a good employee; treat them well and they'll do a great job for you. The longer the relationship, the closer you will bond, and that helps a lot in a slow economy.

Quantity Pricing and Shipping Costs

As your business grows, purchases from suppliers will also increase, and that creates another opportunity. Most business-type purchases have a discount for large-quantity orders going to one location. When increasing the size of your orders from suppliers, always ask what the next lower price level is, and if you're close, try to get there. The higher quantity adds to your supplier's sales and requires less paper or computer work to ship. Everyone benefits as long as you're able to pay your invoice within terms.

Ask Yourself

When searching for your first suppliers, the most important criterion is that they want to see you succeed. The ways they can help is by providing a quality product or service at a fair wholesale cost in a timely manner. And taking care of any problems with an order quickly is also a major plus. But one excuse after another why something went wrong is not the type of supplier that will help you grow your business. Do you want to keep going through this hassle?

Another option for volume pricing is to guarantee that you will buy more product or services within the year. With this written or e-mail guarantee, you can ask for a special volume discount for all orders during that year. This will keep your cost low during slower times and assure you of a continual supply during peak times. Because the supplier has agreed to a certain lower price, your orders should ship first if supply gets tight. Both you and the supplier will have what you need.

You may also be able to combine orders with some of your competitors and have them shipped to one location. By grouping orders together, you'll get the lower price for all of you. Then you will know that no competitor has a lower cost than you and everyone is starting on a level playing field, at least for these products.

Some suppliers may even let you and other businesses order together and ship to separate locations. They will probably charge a split-shipment fee, but it's usually minimal. If this is possible, you won't have to reship or send a truck for pickup to each location. Once you are working with a supplier for a while and paying on time, there are many advantages that you can work out together. Remember, the supplier needs your business.

Establish Credit with Suppliers

Once you have found your suppliers and worked out a plan of ordering for best prices, you need to establish a way of paying them. As a new business, you will be considered a high-risk account unless your supplier is your uncle. And even then, there is always that lack of proven track record for any new business. Everyone will want to sell to you as long as they know they will be paid. And if your business entity is a corporation or an LLC, the supplier knows that you can walk away without liability. Having painted this grim picture, don't lose faith—it's not that bad.

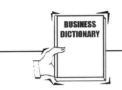

Business Vocab

Open credit means you will not have to pay for purchases up front or in advance when you order them. The seller will allow you to pay with terms of ten to thirty days after the purchase.

Establishing credit with suppliers is an ongoing process that gets better with time. Many of them will ask you to pay your first or first two orders in full and in advance. This can be expected, but you will want to phase out of that situation as soon as you can. The best way is to ask that your prepayment be changed to a deposit that keeps decreasing over time. Try to pay a 50 percent deposit with twenty- to thirty-day terms on the balance. After a few more orders paid on time or early, ask if your deposit can be reduced to 25 percent, then ask for it to be eliminated. Request a small credit limit at first that increases a little every three to six months. Remember that the suppliers want and need you to keep ordering and just want to feel comfortable about payment.

If the supplier won't budge on the full prepayment terms, you can ask for a discount of 2 to 5 percent for advance payment. You should get something for being your supplier's banker at no interest cost to them.

Another option to establish some open credit is to offer to personally guarantee payment of invoices for the first three to six months, but no longer than that. Have something on paper or e-mail that says your personal guarantee ends on a specific date. During that period, always pay on time or early to build confidence with the supplier.

When you have tried most of these ideas to get some open credit but nothing works, it's time to take your business elsewhere. The supplier is telling you that it doesn't care about your business, and that certainly won't help you grow your company. There is always someone out there who can provide what you need at acceptable terms. You need your suppliers to be partners, not dictators, to grow your business.

What Can You Outsource?

Outsourcing can save a business a great deal of expenses and personnel problems by taking routine duties out of your hectic daily schedule. The availability of outsource companies is growing by leaps and bounds. Maybe your new business is even going to be one. I think that if there were as many ways to outsource in the 80s and 90s, a lot of closed businesses would have been able to survive. That's how important using outsourcers to your advantage is to survival and growth. You should look at every task in your business and see if it can be outsourced successfully. It's no longer a luxury—it's a necessity.

The new trend is to have fewer employees in your company, not more. This reduces payroll costs, unemployment taxes, benefits, space requirements, supervision, hiring costs, and general babysitting in some cases. I'm sure there are even more advantages for outsourcing I didn't mention here. The more outsourcing you do, the more time and resources you will have to grow, promote, and improve your business. If you ever look at the *Inc.* magazine list of fastest growing companies, you'll notice that many have few employees but millions in sales. They have perfected the use of finding outsource companies to increase their growth.

Where Do You Find Outsourcers?

As a new or growing business, you don't have past businesses to turn to, so you must find them another way. The routine accounting, payroll service, cleaning service, and delivery services are easy to find. But areas close to your type of business may be less visible. You can search the Internet, industry directories at the library, and trade publications to locate some of them. A local business organization or association or your Chamber of Commerce may also lead you in the right direction. Another option is to ask someone you have already selected for your business such as a lawyer, accountant, or banker to recommend sources.

Other ways to find specific outsource companies is through online networks such as Facebook, Twitter, LinkedIn, and

Business Alerts

Following are a few tips for successfully setting up outsource companies:

➤ Clearly explain the project

➤ Check references

➤ Get everything in writing

➤ Start with a small test project

➤ Cover all costs in advance

➤ Specify delivery or finish times

➤ Promise future work if done well

➤ Don't hesitate to change outsourcers if problems arise

others. People from all over the world use these networks, so you're not just limited to the country you live in. There are also online directories that you can search by industry or location. If you want to outsource manufacturing, search the type of product followed by *manufacturer*. Always investigate thoroughly any company you are not familiar with and always ask for references—and then check them.

Keep Checking on Outsourcers

While outsourcing is great for growing a business and keeping expenses down, it can have a few drawbacks that you need to be aware of. There will be people doing the work for your business that you have little or no control over. You need to evaluate the quality of the product or service being performed on regular intervals, especially if you are outsourcing to a call center for inbound or outbound calls, or both. The call center is the first contact with your customers and you want to be sure it's done correctly. Listen to the calls that are monitored and let the management know what needs to be corrected immediately.

Have a written list of what you expect from your outsource company and review it with the outsource representative often. Watch for changes in the management of your account and meet with anyone who is new to you to review your objectives.

But when you explain what you expect and it's clearly understood, you will need to step back and let the outsourcers take control of the task. Don't try to nitpick every little item or change you feel needs to be done; have a preset time when you will meet with the representative to go over performance. After you have used an outsource company for a while, things should run smoothly by themselves.

CHAPTER 10

Accepting Credit Cards and Giving Credit

> ## In This Chapter
>
> ➤ Selecting your merchant service
> ➤ Alternate services
> ➤ Getting set up
> ➤ Beware of scams
> ➤ Extending credit

In this chapter you will learn how to select and where to find the best merchant service for your new business needs. Accepting credit and debit cards will open doors to new customers, but you need to control the costs and watch for scams. You'll also learn why you will need to extend credit terms to business accounts and how to be sure you get paid.

Choosing Your Merchant Service Provider

Part of opening a new business is setting up your system to accept credit cards. There are three steps to complete this process and get you up and working and accepting cards:

> ➤ Step 1: Applying to a merchant service provider
> ➤ Step 2: Acquiring a credit card machine
> ➤ Step 3: Acquiring processing software

The Application

Applying with a merchant service provider consists of providing basic company and owner's information, which must be approved by the merchant service provider's main office.

A good place to look for a service provider is the bank where you have your checking account. In some cases, the bank will give you a slightly lower processing fee, and it will be convenient to have your merchant service provider based where you have your account. You can also check rates and fees being charged by other providers, but be very cautious of many of the unsolicited calls you will get. Always compare the transaction fees, the start-up charges, and the early cancellation fees. These can vary widely and may be in the small print in the contract. If in doubt, just ask the representative to show you exactly where it is in print.

BUSINESS DICTIONARY

Business Vocab

A merchant service provider processes your credit card charges through the major card companies. The amount of the charge will be deposited in your bank account in twenty-four to forty-eight hours after a daily settlement. There will be a processing charge of 2 to 5 percent deducted from your account.

The process is simple once it's set up and ready to use in your retail, office, or online business. The credit card is swiped in the machine, entered manually for phone call orders, or entered through your shopping cart software online. The merchant service provider processes the card for the amount of the purchase and shows an approval code. You will complete the order or purchase knowing that the money has been paid.

Daily charges will usually settle or be transferred to your bank account at a preset time, in most cases around midnight, then a new tally is started. You can also settle early by processing the charge manually, which you may want to do for larger amounts so you can send it to your bank account

Ask Yourself

Do you really want to deal with the hassle of processing credit cards?

Most people like the convenience and safety of charging their purchase or using a debit card instead of carrying a lot of cash with them. About 30 to 35 percent of consumers pay off their balance immediately or within a few months. The card companies also entice users with perks, rewards, and higher credit limits for their most credit-worthy customers. Cards are here to stay, and you must accept them or suffer much lower sales.

quickly.

Before you select the merchant service you plan to use, do some checking and even ask for references. There may be a security deposit requested because you are a new business with no track record. This is because there may be a chargeback from a cardholder for any number of reasons, and the merchant service provider wants to be sure there is enough money in your account to cover it. If a deposit is required, be sure to ask that it's refunded to you in six months, or at the longest a year. But never sign a personal guarantee to cover any chargeback amounts; find another service to use. Once it's up and running, everything you agreed to in advance should not come into play again.

Getting a Credit Card Machine

The next step is to acquire a credit card machine to do the processing. The service you are signing up with will have a couple of different ones available and most new applicants just buy or lease them from their service. But there is a better and cheaper way.

For our last business, we found out which models we could use that would accept our service provider's software and went shopping online, comparing prices. We found www.merchantwarehouse.com and www.usamerchantsolutions.com, who both had what we needed at 40 percent less than what the merchant service provider was offering. This can be a big savings, especially if you need more than one machine.

Another option for credit card processing equipment is for it to already be in your point-of-service (POS) register. If you buy an intelligent cash register that is computer based, everything you need will probably be included. The POS terminal processes the credit card that is swiped, completes the sale, and prints a customer and merchant receipt, which needs to be signed. These all-in-one POS systems cost much more than a simple credit card machine, but are worth it if you can fit it in your start-up budget.

There may also be some used and refurbished POS register models that you can buy at a big discount over a new one. Once your business is growing and profitable, you can trade up to the latest models with all the available bells and whistles. The lower cost of the used older equipment will leave money in your budget for other needed expenses. Save now and upgrade later is the smart thing to do.

Processing Software

Getting your processing software should be the least painful of your chores because the service provider you have selected will download it over the phone lines. You will need a separate dedicated line that is not connected to your regular phone lines. We use the fax and credit card machine on the same dedicated line because seldom are they both needed at the same time.

Since your representative from the service provider either makes a commission or has a quota, let him or her do the software download for you. It usually takes fifteen to twenty minutes plus the steps to get it started. Tell the service provider before you sign the contract that you want someone to instruct you and your staff on how the system works. Not only will you save time, but you'll know that the money from the transactions are really going into your bank account. You should also get a verbal commitment from the representative that he or she will be available for at least the first thirty days to assist you with any problems or questions. Ask for cell phone numbers so you can contact him or her quickly. You don't want the rep to tell you to just call the customer service number.

Accepting credit and debit cards is now a necessary part of most consumer and business sales. You can decide if you want to accept only MasterCard and Visa or also add American Express, Discover, and others. However, your lowest processing rates and fastest deposits will be from MasterCard and Visa. If you are marketing higher priced or luxury items, you may need to consider the others. Just find out in advance how much each transaction will cost you and how quickly the money will be in your account. Credit card payments can be fast and easy for both sides of the transaction, but like anything else in business, you must do your homework first.

Business Facts

There are over 100 million PayPal users with open accounts. A person does not have to have an account to receive money from PayPal, and anyone can open a free account to deposit it. About 95 percent of eBay purchases process the payment through PayPal. As of March 2010, even Chinese consumers can use PayPal to shop online.

PayPal and Others

PayPal is known worldwide as the most popular middleman payment service for Internet purchasing and money transfers. Even though it seems like PayPal has been around for decades, it actually just started in March 2000. The company we know today was created as a result of a merger between Confinity (1998) and X.com (1999), two Palo Alto, California, businesses. Each had software that complemented each other and when merged made it the best, safest, and easiest service for cautious consumers. Over the years since its inception, many upgrades and security features have been added to

boost user confidence.

PayPal grew quickly as more transactions were processed. It was the first dot-com IPO after the 9/11 terrorist attacks. But it didn't remain alone for long and eBay acquired PayPal in October 2002 for $1.5 billion. As a wholly owned subsidiary of eBay, PayPal became too much competition for the other payment services, Billpoint and Pay Direct, which both closed in 2003 and 2004, respectively. There are other competitors in the online payment and money transfer business, but PayPal is by far the number one choice for most consumers and vendors. The fact that it's associated with the eBay name gives it credibility.

How It Works

PayPal is an Internet-based business that processes and allows payments and money transfers to most of the technology-smart world. It's gained the trust of both buyers and sellers because it shields the personal and confidential information of each. Strangers can safely send money to each other without seeing each other's credit card and bank information. PayPal acts as the transaction broker and follows the instructions of its users based on its policies and business integrity. It provides an electronic alternative to checks, drafts, and money orders, and does it at computer speed.

A PayPal account can be opened free at www.paypal.com and only requires a valid e-mail address and a valid bank account or credit card. The account can be funded with an electronic debit transfer from a bank account or with a credit card. Once it's set up, the movement of money is easy, safe, and fast. The recipient of a PayPal money transfer can have it deposited in his or her own PayPal account or bank account, or can request that a check be sent to him or her. The several options for funding an account and receiving payment has opened the doors to many users on both sides of transactions.

For all the ease, security, and speed of transactions that PayPal offers, it receives a processing fee. It's usually a percentage of the transaction and can also vary based on the amount of the transaction, payment method, and the country of the sender and receiver. There could also be additional fees to convert different currencies being sent. And just like credit card processors, the larger the account uses per month, the lower the fee might be. Big sellers on eBay may pay the lowest fee rates.

There are a few other payment and money transfer processors available such as Google Checkout, Moneybookers, Wirecard, and the new Instant Pay, but even the biggest of these is a distant number two to PayPal. These and others such services should be checked out thoroughly to see if they have the services and security you require. It's always good to know the country where the processor is based and what laws they are subject to follow. Check to see who is using the service and if any large companies are represented. Then check the fee rate and speed of deposits.

Scams and Excessive Fees

Like anything else in this world, there are good and bad companies to do business with.

This is certainly the case with merchant service credit card processing companies. There are plenty of them out there and they come and go regularly. Many will close under one name and reopen with a different name. They are in business for only one reason: to get as much money as possible from unsuspecting businesses as possible. But now you will know about them and not fall prey to their hard sell and false promises.

Business Alerts

You'll get many offers from merchant service companies to save a few tenths of a percent on fees. But unless you're having problems with your current service, it's best not to change for small savings. Stay with your current service provider and build a working relationship.

A lot of the so-called merchant services scams are guilty of charging excessive fees and upfront setup costs over and above the card processing fees. These are somewhere in the contract you sign but often not clearly stated or hidden behind some factious jargon. Few business people, especially start-ups, will have a lawyer review the merchant contract, so these pitfalls sneak by. Some may even require you to purchase a marked-up terminal machine, but as I discussed earlier, you can purchase it elsewhere for less.

Watch Out

Following are some of the hidden or excessive fees I have seen or heard about:

- ➤ Hidden setup charges
- ➤ Gateway fees
- ➤ Software fees
- ➤ Licensing fees
- ➤ Annual renewal fees
- ➤ Customer support charges
- ➤ Cancellation and termination charges

➤ Chargeback fees

➤ Daily settlement fees

➤ Bank account setup charges

➤ Minimum fees

➤ Retrieval fees

➤ Report charges

➤ Batch-out fees

➤ Statement fees

➤ Tech support fees

➤ Training charges

➤ Voice authorization fees

➤ Card decline fees

The list can go on and on and is only limited by the imagination. A reputable merchant service provider will have few if any of these fees and charges. The scam companies will try to prey on new and novice businesspeople, so you may want to have your lawyer or at least your accountant review your first contract. Don't be enticed by a low transaction charge without thoroughly investigating everything else.

Many of these card-processing scam companies try to lure you in with false or misleading ads that promise what they won't deliver. Some may even offer free process credit cards, which is impossible because they are going to make a profit somehow. Other too good to be true offers are the lowest processing fees, and a cash reward if you find lower fees, but they will get you on other hidden fees. Another scam is that they will start taking credit cards right away, which is not possible because you have to submit an application, which takes twenty-four to seventy-two hours to be checked out. Don't fall for these gimmicks and only partner with a reputable company.

Giving Customers Credit

Extending credit to customers is another challenging part of starting a business. Business customers expect it, but consumer customers do not. If you are selling to both groups, you may have to initiate two different policies. All of a sudden you're on the other side of the transaction that was discussed in the last chapter. The only difference is you will be extending credit for possibly only one order or maybe two. That customer may not have the urgency to pay because he or she won't need to order again for several months or longer.

If the customer is tight for cash and you didn't find out in advance, you may have to wait longer than you expected to be paid.

One way to reduce the risk of slow payments from customers that you extend credit to is to request a deposit on a new first order. Since I'm not a fan of checking references because it's time-consuming and sometimes not that accurate, I request a deposit from all new customers. It saves time and if something goes wrong, I at least have some of the total money owed. I usually ask for 40 to 50 percent of the total order as a deposit and offer twenty-day terms on the balance when the order is finished. We let the customer pay by check or credit card and are considering also using PayPal in the future for international customers. The more payment choices you offer, the easier the transaction will be for the customer.

Repeat customers and large corporations may balk at the deposit, and you will need to decide if it's necessary for them. Normally a bigger company will pay on time or close to it and you have a track record with the repeat customers. If you're still in doubt, you can search the Internet with the words *How does ABC company pay its bills?* If there are major problems or a possible bankruptcy, it should come up on the first or second page of results. Offering credit to customers is not that scary, but you do have to do some common-sense thinking about who you give credit to.

One consideration when you're first starting a business that may extend credit is that some of your start-up capital may be needed to bridge the credit gap. That means that you may have to prepay suppliers in the beginning and wait until a credit customer pays you or the balance he or she owes. This is not unusual for start-up companies, and that's why I always say your starting capital should be 50 percent more than you think you'll need. As time goes on, suppliers will loosen credit to you and you will be a better judge of who will be your best creditworthy customers.

If you're going to have customer service employees or sales people who directly handle orders and payments, there must be a set policy in place. Everyone should know your credit policy well and should be verbally tested occasionally to be sure it's understood. People who ignore or disregard your credit policy should be informed that they are personally responsible for any unpaid debts within your terms. Since you are responsible for bills due to your suppliers, your rules should be followed to the letter. Any employee who is guilty of two credit policy offenses should be terminated immediately.

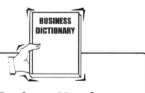

Business Vocab

Progress payments are partial payments made as the order is being finished and before it ships or the service is completed. It allows the seller to cover costs while the order is being processed.

With all the risks and chance of loss, why should you even bother to give anyone credit? As we said earlier, most business-to-business transactions are done with some credit offered, especially if they are going to be repeat customers. For very large orders or purchases, you may want to request a deposit or progress payments on orders that take a long time to deliver. When in doubt, always refuse credit or ask for the balance owed before delivery. Most honest and reputable customers will understand your policies and procedures and go along without too much disagreement.

If customers are looking for a long-term payment plan (over thirty days), you should not get involved and instead suggest they just use a credit card. As time goes on and if there are many more requests for this type of extended credit, talk to your bank and see if it offers this service or if it can refer you to someone who does. The buyer must qualify and will pay the third party directly, and you will get full payment within a few days of acceptance. The third party credit provider accepts all the risk (for a fee of course), and you receive payment up front. This can work well for large ticket purchases or *lease to buy* transactions.

Selling For Resale

If you are selling to distributors or dealers who will be ordering often and also need some credit to survive, there should be a watchdog on their account. Most of them will know that if they go past terms on old invoices their new orders may not ship. A two- to five-day grace period can be allowed, but much beyond that will start to harm your own business. Once you state your open credit policy and enforce it, most of these buyers will go along because they will need a continual source of supply. Watch the first few orders closely to see that they are following your credit requirements, but don't overly aggravate them unless payment goes beyond your terms.

A good way to start with people who will be buying from you for resale is to request prepayment on the first order. Most of them will have an adequate cash flow to handle this and may even expect it. Then you can ask for a 50 percent deposit on the next few orders and change to an open account (no deposit) only when you feel comfortable with that buyer. There is no set rule for when to change to an open account, and you, the owner or partner, should make that decision. If this customer repeatedly goes past your terms, you can go back at any time to the 50 percent deposit required. It's also a good idea to make a copy of their first check so you have their bank information if you ever need it.

Companies buying for resale can give you a lot of orders and business if you are able to work together effectively. Although you will want all this regular business, don't be tempted to change or relax your credit policy to get it. If your customer for resale starts to get behind on invoices, don't just cut them off abruptly, but meet with them in person or on the phone to resolve it. E-mail does not work as well as personally contacting the person responsible for

CHAPTER 11

 # Setting Up Your Website and Blog

---

In This Chapter

➤ Why you need a website

➤ Easy for visitors

➤ Using your site

➤ You also need a blog

This chapter will make it easy for you to get started designing and using your new business website. In today's world, a website for your business is no longer a luxury but a necessity. But the good news is that it's easier than ever before to set up a site and make changes regularly. You'll also find out why and how to use a blog, which will complement your website.

Business in the 2000s is done 24/7 and that means you must be available for your customers all the time. Since most of us sleep sometimes and need some family time, who will take care of your business? The obvious answer (if you haven't already figured it out) is your website.

The Internet is one employee who is not expensive and never sleeps. It loves to work all the time and never complains. You only have to pay a reasonable monthly salary (provider fee) and it doesn't need health insurance. If all our employees were like this, our job as owners and managers would be easy. So hopefully you can see that a website for your new business in not a choice, it's imperative.

Purpose of Your Site

For a new business, a website doesn't have to be that fancy, it just has to be there. It can be a basic site that gets updated as the business grows. A business, of any type, that does not have a website looks amateur and may not be taken seriously.

Make your site a place where prospects and customers can go to get information about your business anytime they want to, whether it's noon or midnight. Letting everyone know about your business and how to start working with you is the first step in setting up your site,

Make Changes Later

As time goes on, you can start adding some of the bells and whistles that will make your site more interesting and productive. Once you decide what the purpose of your site is, you can make changes as you need them. Don't feel pressured or rushed to have an extensive site; do each change with a purpose in mind to make it fun and easy for your visitors. The more prospective customers come back to your site, the more comfortable they will feel about

Business Knowledge

Potential customers and prospects usually visit a company's website before making any direct contact with it. The home page is the first thing they see, so it should load quickly and be easy to read and understand. The copy on the home page should be short, to the point, and not too small or blurry. If people don't like your home page, they may not go any further and just click out. A new business needs to put most of its website development time, effort, and resources into making that home page the best it can be.

your company and you as its leader. Keep them interested by giving them new information as often as you can.

There can be a variety of reasons to have a website, and the most important one is to tell people all about your business. You may want to explain how you started the business, why you started it, and its goals or core values. Some people will actually read this stuff because they want to know more about where they are spending their money.

Your website can address questions that people may not ask you directly. You may answer a lot of questions that people have asked in the past through a frequently asked questions (FAQ) link on your home page. This also gives visitors a place to go more than once if they forget the answer and need to inquire again. There should also be an e-mail link so they can ask a question that's not covered in the FAQs page.

The purpose of your website can just be to let people who visit become comfortable with your company and to give you some credibility as an established business. Later you can add features that let them browse products and services for sale and a way to purchase them. You can add a shopping cart software package for a few hundred dollars that provides safe and efficient transactions for both sides. But even with shopping cart software, some people may still want to discuss their purchase with a live person, so include a toll-free number. Your website can be anything that you want it to be, but it should always lead people in the direction of being a customer.

Business Facts

As of 2009 according to Royal.Pingdom.com, there were:

➤ 81.8 million dot-com domain names

➤ 12.3 million dot-net domain names

➤ 7.8 million dot-org domain names

➤ An 8 percent increase over 2008, and growing all the time

Make it Easy for Everyone

You may want to have a high-tech website with all the state-of-the-art stuff, but think of the people who will be visiting it. You need a site that's comfortable for them to use, not one that looks impressive but is hard to navigate.

First start out with a URL, or website address, that's easy to type and easy to remember. You can check the availability of your URL at www.godaddy.com or another such site. You may need to adjust the URL a few times until you find one that's not taken. Then you can register it for your company at a nominal fee. You may want to even register two URLs if you think that you will need more than one website in the future. Once you register a URL, no one can take it away or use it unless you sell it to someone yourself or if you let the registration lapse.

Once you have your site name and web address, you need to sign on with an Internet service provider to keep you connected and active on the Internet. There are many reputable providers available, and you can ask friends, business acquaintances, or even the Chamber of Commerce to recommend several. When you have selected a name and provider, it's time

Ask Yourself

You can't assume that every visitor to your website will be a high-tech person, so make your site easy and comfortable for everyone to use. Ask yourself if it would be easy to use if you were a first-time visitor. Following are some undesirable things you should avoid on your website:

➤ Choosing a difficult name to remember or type

➤ Using non-scannable text that visitors can't use elsewhere

➤ Using too many pop-up ads

➤ Asking visitors for too much personal information

➤ Using misdirected links that take visitors to unexpected pages

➤ Using excessive banners and advertising

➤ Using blinking or flashing signs, text, or both

➤ Trapping visitors on pages with no links back to the home page

➤ Using text that is too small to read easily for some people

➤ Making the contact us or e-mail link difficult to find

Always try to be user-friendly; not user-hostile.

to design the site and make it user-friendly.

You can either design the website yourself using one of the many software packages available from the store or online, or hire someone to do it for you. Either way, there are a few things to consider before jumping in and just adding graphics and text.

Define your ideal audience or visitor and determine whether they expect just the basics or require more high-tech info. Some people will want to visit your site and spend time looking at everything, but others will just want to conduct business and get out. Which one is your ideal prospect or customer?

After pinpointing your ideal audience, you may realize that there is a secondary group who may visit or use your site. These visitors may just be surfing a subject on the Internet and happen to find you. They may be possible customers either now or in the future. You will want to keep your site interesting for them, especially if they aren't as versed in your industry as your primary audience.

Design your site keeping in mind that 80 percent of the visitors will be in your ideal or primary group, and 20 percent will be other interested or curious parties. Secondary group members can become primary ones if the website so entices them.

Decide How Your Site Should Be Used

The people coming to your site will either be exploring or have a purpose for visiting. You will need to decide what they should do and guide them to it using links on your home page to other pages. Do you want them to just get information, leave messages and requests, or do you want them to actually purchase something during the visit? Visitors will probably make suggestions if you provide an e-mail address to do so. And you want these suggestions so you can serve your customers better.

Make Changes Regularly

Once you get people to visit your new website, how can you get them to come back again? Did they see and use everything they will ever see on that first visit?

To get some ideas for changing, updating, or enhancing your site as you go along, check out some of your competitors' websites.

Many websites are incorporating a short (one to two minutes) video on their home page or information page. A video is entertaining and easy to design into your site, but don't make it too big—one-quarter of the page is big enough. You can have it start running as soon as someone visits, but don't have it keep repeating. Have a repeat button for those who want to see it again.

Free E-mail Stuff

Ask visitors to sign up for a weekly or monthly e-mail newsletter, special offers, coupons, etc. Don't ask for too much information during sign-up or some will pass. The only required

Ask Yourself

Do you go to the movie theater over and over again to see the same movie? Most people don't because they are looking for something new and exciting. The same thing goes for your website if you want return visitors and referrals. Keep content current, and change or move images on your home page. Add new link pages, make new offers, and offer new ideas so people feel they have to return or be left behind.

info you really need is name and e-mail address. Make any other information optional. Always have an easy way to unsubscribe. Don't ask for a phone number—most people don't want to give that out. If you say you will send promotional e-mails weekly, do it weekly.

Have someone on your staff check your site at least twice a week to make sure it's still working and to alert you of what needs changing. You don't want to have a big Happy New Year! on your home page on Valentine's Day. Also be sure that the links to other pages in your site are working. I hate when someone calls my business and tells me that my website isn't working. This is not only bad news but lost revenue as well. Try to find problems before your visitors and customers do, and save a little face.

Other changes you can make are updating the background colors and content. Moving things around on your home page, even it's not changed, will offer some variety to repeat visitors. Adding a new page link or quote of the month will give people who come back a reason to do so. New graphics or photos can keep your site fresh and interesting. Even people who come back to reorder can be enticed to look at anything new that you have available. They may even buy an additional product right away or at the very least remember where they saw it for future reference.

Suggestion Box Link

I have always been in favor of anything that gets customers and prospects involved and to offer their input. Some of the best ideas come from those willing to pay you if you use them—you can't get better than that. So give them an easy way on your website to offer those ideas and suggestions.

Have a link on several of your website pages that that directs users to a suggestion box page. to the page can be an e-mail form that automatically has Suggestion Box printed in the subject line. Don't ask for personal information because some people may want to remain anonymous. Better to get an anonymous comment than none at all. Anyone who wants a reply should know to leave a name and e-mail address or phone number. By having the suggestion box on your website, people can use it 24/7 and not have to wait on hold, wait in your store, or leave a voice mail.

Soliciting anonymous feedback opens the door to a few unpleasant or nasty comments. But it's worth the trouble, especially in a newer business to get the other good suggestions. What a person may think is silly or useless could turn into something you could really use. You can include a statement by the suggestion box that you will reward the ideas you use if people decide to leave their name and contact information. Then when you do give a reward, make it something nice and of value so they will tell everyone and you'll get more suggestions— and possibly more business.

If you're not getting a lot of response with the suggestion box, try adding a question about your business regarding delivery, packaging, value, or variety and let people voice their opinions. Change the question two or three times a month and post the results of the previous questions. Also have an archive of older questions so that new visitors can look at those. If you make it interesting and even fun, people will come and participate.

Once people become more comfortable with you and your website, it will be easier for them to buy from you.

Get the Word Out

As soon as your home page and a few other pages are up, it's time to get people to visit the site. Just being listed in search engines is not going to bring those first visitors. You need to promote your site in other, nontechnical ways so people will find your site and be interested enough to visit it. Once they do visit, you hope that they bookmark it.

The initial visit is so important because there is no coming back, bookmarking, referrals, or online purchases if people don't visit the first time. Here are some places and ways to promote your site that you may not have thought of:

> - Always put your website address on your business card
> - List your website address on letterheads, invoices, and other office forms
> - Paint your website address on any delivery vehicles or put large magnets on the vehicles that advertise your URL
> - Be sure your website address is on all promotional literature and flyers
> - Buy a rubber stamp with your business name and website address
> - List your website address in your profile on all social networks that you join
> - Include your website address in your signature block when you send e-mails
> - Direct people to your site when you make posts on Twitter and Facebook
> - Print it on all promotional and giveaway products plus T-shirts and caps
> - Entice people to visit your site using word-of-mouth publicity every chance you get
> - Buy small ads in church bulletins and association newsletters
> - Start a blog and have your website address on every page
> - Exchange web links with other sites, but not competitors', that are looking for similar visitors
> - Include your URL in the byline of any articles you write that may be published

Business Knowledge

Spend the time to list your website in as many search engines and directories as you can. If there are ones specific to your industry, you may even consider paying for an ad or a higher position on page one. Including a video will always boost your position on the results page.

➤ Make sure your website address is big and bold in any advertising you use

These are just a few ideas for letting people know that your website is alive and well. You can keep thinking of other places to get the word out on your site. Don't be the person who spends a lot of money designing and developing a site but little on promoting it. It's like having an expensive dress or suit that no one sees because you keep it in the closet. Display it everywhere and anywhere you can to get the best results.

Affiliate Marketing

In simple terms, affiliate marketing is rewarding one website for sending visitors or web traffic to another website. The *affiliate*, or referring website, will receive some type of reward or payment for each incident. Normally, both websites will refer visitors to each other, and the excess will be paid according to their agreement.

Affiliates can be rewarded for the following:

➤ *Pay per click*: Every time a visitor or potential customer goes from the affiliate website by clicking on a link, an agreed amount of money is put in the affiliate's account.

➤ *Pay per sale*: Each time a sale is made as a result of an affiliate's referral or by ads or banners on an affiliate's site, a reward or money will be deposited in its account. This can be a set amount, a percentage of the sale, or a commission.

Affiliate marketing is being used more and more by online retailers and other businesses. If you can find other websites that appeal to the type of target customers you want, consider setting up an affiliate marketing agreement.

Blogs Create Interest

Along with a website, I feel that a blog or even two blogs are an important part of promoting your new business. In some cases, your blog may get even more visitors than your website because new material is added more often. If you make visiting your blog fun and informative, people will come and check it out regularly and tell friends about it.

As with your website address, put your blog address or link *everywhere* you can for maximum exposure. Your blog will grow in popularity quickly if you add posts three to four times a week and if they are easy and fun to read.

Business Vocab

A blog is a website or Internet destination where visitors can read posts by the blog owner. It may be casual information or business ideas, and each post is dated and saved in an archive.

Starting Your Blog

You can set up free blogs at Google, Yahoo!, and many other places. Just search *free blog* and you will get many choices to select from. Select one or two and just follow the setup instructions listed. It is usually very easy, and you should be done and ready to go in fifteen minutes or less (five minutes if you're a computer geek). If it's too difficult for you to get started, just exit and find another one.

If I can do it in ten minutes, because my computer skills are only average, anyone can set up a blog.

You will need to make a personal commitment to post on your blog at least three times a week, if not more. If people come back and find nothing new for a week or more, they will probably forget you and not return. You do want people to visit your blog several times a week and tell others about it. When you have started your blog and have several posts on it, send an e-mail to everyone in your address book with a link to the blog. The blog will usually have a counter so you'll know how many people have visited. Check the counter often to see if people are returning and sending others.

Business Facts

According to infoplease.com, the top seven most visited blogs were:

1. The Huffington Post;
2. Tech Crunch;
3. Mashable;
4. Engadget;
5. Gizmodo;
6. Boing Boing; and
7. The Official Google Blog.

Making Your Blog Interesting

Once people visit your blog for the first time, that part of your marketing is over. Then it's up to your content and the way you write. Keep your posts interesting, informative, and fun for the best results. Here are a few ideas to keep your blog hot:

- ➤ Ask your blog readers questions
- ➤ Answer questions readers left in the comments section
- ➤ Post new ideas
- ➤ Add humor and stories occasionally
- ➤ Give away some secrets in your industry
- ➤ Add a picture to some posts
- ➤ Post a tip readers can use *today*
- ➤ Announce an important event coming up
- ➤ Cross promote with another blog
- ➤ Refer readers to your website for more info
- ➤ State your opinion on a valuable subject
- ➤ Suggest new books and e-books
- ➤ Describe a recent industry event
- ➤ Include links to important sites
- ➤ Include links to important videos
- ➤ Post blog entries on Twitter and Facebook

These are only a few ways to keep your blog fresh, interesting, and fun for everyone. A blog that's always serious and technical will get boring and ignored. When and if you see the counter moving slowly, you know you'll need to make some changes on your blog to make it hot again.

Have more than one blog if you have more than one topic or area of interest. But keep posting to all of your blogs and keep each one fresh and interesting. This is a great way to promote you, your business, and your website; plus the only investment is your time.

CHAPTER 12

Your First Employees

In This Chapter

➤ Finding new employees

➤ Warning signs

➤ Train and retrain

➤ Supervise and mentor

➤ Superstars and trust

In this chapter you will learn if you need employees and where to find the ones that will help your business. You will also learn the correct way to select the best employees and why it's important to train them and retrain them.

Supervising and delegating will take a lot of routine tasks from your daily schedule and leave you with more time for important duties and management tasks. You'll learn how to recognize your best employees and trust them with more significant responsibility.

Adding Employees to Your Business

Having employees in your new business can be a great asset, but it can sometimes be a liability as well. You need to be ready to handle employees and properly supervise them for the best results. But every new business does not always need employees right in the beginning, and you must decide if your business can operate effectively without them at first.

Any growing business will usually require one or more employee to do some of the routine tasks and free the owner(s) to do more marketing and financial duties. If you are opening a restaurant, retail store, or delivery service, you will need good employees or associates to handle much of the day-to-day work.

The key to success in having employees at any time on your staff is selecting the correct ones from the many who will apply. Ads in your local paper and online, and posting on college bulletin boards will draw in many applicants to choose from. Most of these people will not be good for your company and only time spent interviewing will let you select the best. Rushing through interviews will only cause problems later and create a high turnover rate. A personal referral of an applicant is usually the best, but that's not always available. Interviewing is a serious business and it must be treated that way if you want the type of employees who will help you build your business.

Interview with Care

The interviewing process is the most important task for any new business owner because some of these people may become very important as the business grows. In a new company you may start with just hourly employees either full- or part-time and decide later who will become your permanent salaried staff.

When you put the word out that you are looking to hire, a lot of good and a lot of undesirable people will apply. So be prepared to weed through them effectively. This will take some time, but it's well worth the effort and the future of your business.

Hiring Hourly Employees

Once you have selected applicants to interview, it's a good idea to analyze their actions prior to and during the interview. Most of your employees will likely be part-time, and they may value the job less than full-time employees, so you need to qualify them in advance to foresee any problems. Look for these red flags that could spell difficulties later:

➤ Someone (friend or parent) comes to pick up an application for someone else

➤ The applicant showed up for the interview with a parent or friend who wants to sit in

➤ The applicant isn't carrying a pen or pencil

➤ The applicant forgot important information like Social Security number

➤ The applicant has had too many short-term jobs

➤ The applicant lists reasons for leaving a previous job as not liking management

➤ The applicant can't find your address and doesn't ask for directions in advance

➤ The applicant is poorly dressed for an interview or has a noticeable odor

➤ The applicant fills out the application with sloppy, hard-to-read handwriting, omits information, and crosses out a lot of words

➤ The applicant arrives late for the interview and doesn't call when on the way

➤ The applicant doesn't have a phone number or a way to be contacted quickly

➤ The applicant tells you during the interview that he or she needs a lot of days off for vacations, appointments, weddings, etc.

➤ The applicant is vague answering questions about a previous job

➤ The applicant is in a hurry to finish the interview because of another appointment

➤ The applicant has another job and wants to fill in more hours to pay unexpected expenses

➤ The applicant wants higher pay but will take your job anyway (won't stay long)

➤ The applicant can't decide to take your job until interviewing with other companies (not really interested)

➤ The applicant's parents want to decide when and what hours the applicant will work

➤ The applicant won't look you in the eye when talking

➤ The applicant brings a baby or a pet to the interview

Before interviewing, check your state regulations for rules regarding what you can and cannot do or say to prospective employees. Once you know the law, you can go to step two—hiring the best, or at least good, employees for your business. If you own a retail store, you're probably going to trust these employees to use your cash register. Make sure you feel comfortable with them and can give them that trust before you hire them.

Business Knowledge

To know how much income tax to withhold from employees' wages, you should have a Form W-4, Employee's Withholding Allowance Certificate on file for each employee. Ask all new employees to give you a signed Form W-4 when they start work. Make the form effective with the first wage payment. If employees claim exemption from income tax withholding, they must indicate this on their W-4. The amount of income tax withholding must be based on filing status and withholding allowances as indicated on the form. If a new employee does not give you a completed Form W-4, withhold tax as if he or she is single, with no withholding allowances. Additional withholding may be required on wages paid to nonresident aliens.

Hiring Telemarketing Employees

If your business will be done mostly on the phone, there are special considerations for those employees. Since your customers and prospects will probably never meet your telemarketers, looks and appearance won't matter much, but cleanliness and personal hygiene does. Telemarketers may have a different dress code than others in your company, especially if they are working in a separate area or have different hours, like late afternoon and evening, so they can contact consumers.

People who are successful at telemarketing are a different breed from other employees in several ways. They may not be as punctual and they may want to leave early. They need more breaks and shorter hours so they can be refreshed and ready for each series of calls. When your telemarketers are good, your business will see positive growth results. Put them in the right environment, with the right products and target list, and how can you not prosper? If telemarketing is right for your business, then the right telemarketer will help make you a winner.

So, how do you know if your telemarketers can perform the job necessary to increase sales? Not everyone is cut out for this job. Certain qualities are necessary and you should keep an eye out for them everywhere you go. When you find someone with the right skills, give that person your business card.

Here's a basic list to look for:

➤ Has a pleasant phone voice

➤ Speaks at a good pace, not too fast or slow

➤ Uses proper grammar and correct pronunciation of words

➤ Sounds positive and optimistic

➤ Has good listening skills

➤ Speaks loudly enough without offending

➤ Seems like someone you'd enjoy having a conversation with

➤ Can be persistent without being pushy

➤ Knows when to stop talking

➤ Has a sense of humor without being silly

➤ Keeps up with current events

➤ Has a friendly manner and likes meeting people

➤ Shows enthusiasm

➤ Sounds confident and reassuring

> ➤ Believes in your products or services

> ➤ Enjoys telemarketing

You may have other qualities you're looking for that pertain to your industry.

Don't settle for less than you're comfortable with or you'll just have to go through the hiring process all over again. Be sure to interview people in-person and over the phone to get a complete picture. Have every applicant do a trial run through your script or outline to get a sense of how comfortable they are and how successful they may be. Covering all potential issues in the beginning will ensure positive results later.

Business Alerts

Employment application forms are the most commonly used applicant document. A completed form is a dated record of a potential employee's interest in a position that is available. The application serves as a profile of the applicant for interview and later record keeping. If the applicant is hired, the information in the application becomes part of the personnel record and is filed in a confidential place. All applications should be signed and dated at the time of execution.

The Right In-Store Sales People

Sales people in a store should be able to speak the language and lingo of the group they are serving. They should also dress and act like the target customer base so that the customers can relate to them easily. It's not going to work in most cases if a flashy teenager is serving baby boomers considering luxury items. The same goes for senior citizens serving the twenties in crowd buying the latest fashions. Matching employees who will handle sales to your specific target market will result in more sales, especially if the products are technical or do-it-yourself items. Purchasers may also want some advice on how to use the products or how to accomplish a task.

Here are some qualities you should look for in candidates for your in-store sales job:

> ➤ Has knowledge of the products or the aptitude to learn about them quickly

> ➤ Likes to sell and takes pride in closing a sale

> ➤ Is dependable and can be relied on to show up for work every day

> Is intelligent and has the curiosity to expand his or her knowledge

> Has a pleasant and positive image, which mirrors that of the store and its core values

> Likes people and can easily relate to them

> Are helpful to customers as well as fellow employees and management

> Is a team player who believes in the company's goals

> Needs a job and is willing to work hard to keep it and grow

> Has ambition and hopes to someday have your job—or his or her own store

There are other factors to take into consideration. These include appearance, speech, charisma, past employment history, and references. In addition to former employers, ask the candidate to supply the names of former customers you can call for a reference.

Part-Time Outside Sales People

People without a full-time permanent position usually have extra time on their hands. They can turn that time into extra income by working for you selling products that don't need too much training to present. Let them set their own hours, but set a minimum number of hours they're required to work each week.

Business Knowledge

One way of controlling salaries and benefits is to use temps for those peak times of the year or when sales spike upward. Fast-growing sales make you wonder if the trend will last. Until you know the answer to that question, why add expenses that are difficult to get rid of if sales fall back to previous levels. Why put yourself in a position where you have to terminate someone you recently hired because you can't afford him or her? It's better to use temps for easy-to-learn positions with no set guarantee of how long the position will last. You don't have to pay taxes for them or even offer benefits. And if business stays strong, most agencies have a temp-to-perm program.

The other advantage is that you can see how temps perform their jobs before adding them to your permanent staff. Using temps is a good way to manage salary expenses when you're just not sure that business will remain at an elevated level. Find an agency and describe your needs and if they provide the right type of people, stick with them for future needs.

Pay a good commission on sales or profits, but don't pay an hourly rate or salary. Since you have no real risk, you should offer a better commission because you probably wouldn't have those sales without these workers. They will be on the honor system and should report their progress to you or the office regularly. You can offer a little lower commission on repeat orders.

If your products are highly competitive and you don't want competitors to see your literature and other specifications, ask your new reps to sign a confidentiality agreement. Under no circumstances should they be selling products for a competitor of yours at the same time they're working for you. Should they decide to leave your company, require that all materials and samples be returned before their final paycheck is issued.

This type of part-time arrangement also works for people who are employed in unrelated areas but have time available to work during selling hours. Real estate agents, car sales representatives, college students, and teachers during the summer are all good candidates. Pay them all as outside contractors and issue a 1099. Check with your CPA to be sure you're doing this correctly.

When and if one of these employees decides to leave, you don't lose very much, maybe the cost of training and some literature, but you do get to keep any customers who will likely reorder. Plus some of the contacts the employee has made may order later on, and then it's all yours. It's one of those win-win situations where each side has little at risk.

Some Good Interview Questions

After checking their past employment, frequency of changing jobs, and experience to perform the job needed, there are other questions that will tell you more about your job candidates. Many of these questions have no right or wrong answers but will give you a better feeling for the person you are considering. Here are some sample interview questions:

> ➤ What would you like us to know about yourself?
>
> ➤ How would people who know you describe you in three words?
>
> ➤ How did you feel when you lost in a competitive task or contest?
>
> ➤ Who was the best boss or supervisor you had?
>
> ➤ What duties did you like and dislike in past jobs?
>
> ➤ How did you prepare for this interview?
>
> ➤ Do you like to work alone or with others?
>
> ➤ Have you ever felt like giving up on a task?
>
> ➤ How do you get along with people you don't really like?

➤ What irritates you on a job?

➤ Describe one unpleasant work experience.

➤ What do you want to be doing five years from now?

➤ What do you feel are your strengths and weaknesses?

➤ How do you react to constructive criticism?

➤ What do you like to do in your spare time?

➤ Do you like making new friends?

➤ What type of people do you get along with best?

➤ Why should we consider hiring you?

Business Alerts

According to irs.gov, you are required to get each employee's name and Social Security number (SSN) and to have each employee fill out a Form W-2. (This requirement also applies to resident and nonresident alien employees.) You should ask your employee to show you his or her Social Security card. The employee may show the card if it is available. You may, but are not required to, photocopy the Social Security card if the employee provides it. Record each new employee's name and Social Security number from his or her Social Security card.

Train, Retrain, and Cross Train

Once you have selected the person or people who are going to make your business great and grow, it's time to train them to do the job that you expect them to do. Training can be classroom style, task demonstrations, actual on-the-job instruction, or a combination of all three to achieve maximum results. Whatever works best for your business, don't underestimate the importance of doing it right. Spend the time necessary for the person to know exactly what you want done and how to do it. You can't really reprimand people for doing something wrong if you didn't train them properly in the first place.

Some people learn faster than others, but that doesn't mean they will turn out good or bad as employees. Quick or slow learners can both be great employees as long as they do things the way you want them done. One of your best people may have difficulty with only one part of a task, so have patience and let that person grasp it in his or her own time. Don't treat any question as silly or a waste of time. If a question is being asked, it means the person is interested in learning and performing their job correctly.

From time to time it's necessary to review or retrain all of your employees to reinforce what is expected of them. Explain that you are not doing this because they are doing something wrong but just as a review of what's necessary to make the company successful. During this period, you or they may see something that would work better if changed or adjusted. So it's a learning session for both the employee and employer. This is the time to ask for suggestions from everyone, and implement the usable ideas right away. Schedule these retraining sessions every three to six months and take them seriously.

What Is Cross Training?

Cross training is training an employee to do someone else's job. It is something that will help you get through periods when a key employee leaves abruptly or is off for an extended length of time, especially if that person was doing a complicated job that takes a while to learn. Cross training employees to do a difficult job allows someone to step in when the person who holds that job leaves the company. Cross training can be done by the owner-manager or by the person who is currently doing that job. For an important job that affects the overall condition of the business, three or even four people can be cross trained to do it. The owner in some cases may not be able to step in because he or she may not have the experience or knowledge to do the task.

Another way of cross training is to develop a task manual that has a step-by-step list of each important task. This manual can be updated as changes are made and new procedures are added. The manual doesn't have to be too formal, just an outline of the steps involved. The person who is doing each task can write the page or pages for that task. Use a three-ring binder with hole-punched pages that can be replaced easily as changes are made. Once this manual is in place, you will see how valuable and useful it is.

Supervise, Mentor, and Delegate

Supervising employees for maximum results and satisfaction for both parties is not an easy assignment, to say the least. People who come to work every day and try to help your business prosper and grow are the backbone of any small organization. Some employees need more supervision and guidance than others and should be treated that way. A few employees will step up and be *superstars*, which we will talk about at the end of this chapter.

With all of the other duties that you have, you must find time to supervise your employees if you want them to follow the guidelines that you set up. People sometimes get off the yellow brick road and need to be helped back to the route they should follow. Only constructive supervision will do that effectively.

Employees Must Be an Asset

For your small business to succeed and grow, the people who work there must all be on the same page. That page is the one you set and the one they believe in. You and they need to be going in the same direction, both mentally and physically. If they're not, they are just a liability. It doesn't matter how long they have been with you or how much education they have, a liability is a liability. And as we all know, assets are valuable and liabilities are just a pain to deal with.

Maybe the correct asset to look for is attitude. A positive company attitude is a real asset you can build on. The more employees you have with a positive attitude, the faster your company will grow and prosper. People who believe in you and your ideas are the ones who should receive rewards and bonuses when you are doing well; don't forget them.

Ask Yourself

When reviewing an employee's performance, which you should do at least twice a year, determine if his or her presence is helping your business. Would your company be better off with another person doing the same job or is this person doing it well?

But what about those who are not on the same page and don't have that positive company attitude? You may try to detect attitude when you first hire someone, but many times you don't see it. I usually notice an employee's attitude within the first three months of employment. As soon as I see any signs of difficulty or rebellion, I sit down with the person and re-explain our goals. I reiterate what we need him or her to do to help us reach those goals. If the employee likes the job, he or she will usually come on board.

The ones that don't or won't be part of your team need to be replaced by people who will. You just can't afford to carry them as a liability that may infect others. As soon as you realize that there is no hope for an employee, it's time to act. Eliminating him or her from your staff may be the best thing for both of you.

Delegate and Oversee

Do you ever find yourself with little or no time to grow your business and implement new ideas? Are you always too busy *doing* your business instead of *managing* it and being the administrator? Many small business owners fall into this gap and feel there is no way out of it. They are so absorbed in the day-to-day operations that they can't step back and look at the bigger picture. And that bigger picture may show ways of acquiring new customers, adding new products or services, and maybe even expanding. It's like a horse running with blinders on: you see only what's in front of you, not what's all around. And the ideas to improve a business and grow it may not always be right in front of you.

You need to find quality time to be the owner and entrepreneur so your business can grow to its full potential. But you don't really want to give up all the tasks you do every day and let a subordinate handle them. Then don't give them *all* up, just some of them. There is no reason why an owner must do everything in a business, especially if you have full- and/or part-time employees. If you don't have enough people on your staff to delegate to, add part-time employees. The cost of adding them will be much less than the additional revenue you will make by growing the business.

To find out what you can delegate to free up some of your time, make a list. Start writing down everything you do in an average day at your place of business. I mean *everything*, starting with opening the door in the morning, making coffee, and turning on the computer. You should have at least twenty-five tasks and maybe a lot more. Carry the list around with you for a day or two and keep adding tasks that you had forgotten. You may be surprised at how long the list will get.

Once your list is close to complete, sit in your office or in a quiet room at home and go over it. Start crossing off things that you would never delegate like signing checks, ordering expensive equipment, or doing payroll taxes. This should eliminate no more than one-third of the list. The rest are possible tasks that could be delegated, even if only on a trial basis. You could easily have someone you trust open every day and get the office or store ready for the day's business. Interviewing and training can be done initially by one of your staff with you coming in at the end of it for the final decision. Making a schedule of employees' hours or what you need to

Business Alerts

It's a common trait among business owners that they hate to let go of many of their tasks and end up overloading themselves. But when they start to delegate some of the routine business chores and see how well it works, they usually have a change of mind. So delegate to people you trust, and then let them do the tasks to the best of their ability.

order can be submitted to you for final approval by an employee, saving you all the time of making them up from scratch.

As you look at your list, many tasks will probably jump out as obvious ones to delegate and should be entrusted to employees right away. You may want to delegate other tasks, but you may have to think about how to supervise your staff for a while until you are comfortable letting go. Some more important or difficult tasks can be phased in over a longer period of time.

Your staff will be ready and willing to learn new things and even feel more respected because of your trust in them. So maybe delegating tasks serve two purposes: freeing up some of your time *and* making employees feel they are a greater part of the company and its success.

Once you have extra time, use it wisely to investigate new ideas and roads to continued growth. And, yes, even take an occasional afternoon off and hit the golf course or shopping mall to regenerate. You will see the overall business much more clearly with fewer busy duties and be able to guide it in new directions. As your business grows, you will find it necessary to delegate even more tasks to employees who have proven themselves in the past. Start making that list today.

One area that should be delegated is the training of new employees. Your best people with *hands-on* experience should be used for this task. It's also easier for them to relate to new employees, especially if they're doing the same job. This can give you more time to handle higher-level tasks and maybe even take a little time off. But until someone has done a delegated task for a reasonable period of time, you need to be mentally aware of how well they're doing. This means giving constructive criticism when necessary, but not nitpicking. Once you've delegated, you need to step back and let your employees perform to the best of their abilities. You might be surprised by how well they do.

Open-Door Policy

As the owner of a small business, you have the *responsibility* to listen to all of your employees. This doesn't mean that if you have thirty people that they all can bring their problems to you every day. But it does mean that if difficult matters and unanswered questions can't be resolved by other supervisory personnel, you *need* to be available. You have to remember that what may seem trivial to you may be of great importance to an employee. People have different needs and they should be resolved on their level.

Unhappy, neglected, or ignored employees are not going to put the 100 percent effort into their job that you need to build your business. If people are doing the minimum, it will show in quality and service. Many times it only takes a few minutes of listening to a problem or situation to get an employee back on the right track.

If you're very busy or away from your store or office a lot, you still *need to find time to* listen to your employees. You can try to schedule an hour or so twice a week to be available. This will show your people you really care and want to help any way you can. Having a short meeting to handle any employee problems or inquiries is just as important as any other business meeting. Employees need to know they are not just a number on the payroll list.

You can set up a procedure for employees to follow when they have questions, problems, or grievances. But your door should be open to get involved with any situations that can't be resolved elsewhere. Your help and decisions need to be fair, honest, and in the best interest of the company *and* the employee. Needless to say, anything personal or confidential should be kept private or in locked personnel files. You want your employee to feel good when he or she leaves your office. You may have other business problems, but listening to your employees should be on your priority list.

It's your employees, more than you realize, that can help you get through tough times. So, you need to be there when they are uncertain as to where to turn. Sometimes just listening and acknowledging that a problem exists is enough to put them at ease. Be there when they need you and they will be there for you.

Frontline Authority

Every sales environment has frontline people who have direct contact with your customers. Hopefully you have selected your most cordial and knowledgeable employees for this important part of your business. In many cases, they will get to know your customers better than you, the owner, does. Good frontline people can supply customer satisfaction, and create repeat business and loyalty. It doesn't matter whether it's a retail or a business-to-business situation, frontline employees will get to know your customers—and your customers will get to know them.

Most sales of any product or service will go smoothly and your customers will be pleased with their purchase. But like life itself, occasionally something can and does go wrong. Isn't there a guy named *Murphy* who said this first? But it's not a question of whether something will go wrong, it's how well you handle it. And the most important factor in the resolution of a problem is how *quickly* you resolve it to the *customer's satisfaction*. Speed, not a rash decision, will be long remembered and can actually increase loyalty and repeat business.

> **BUSINESS DICTIONARY**
>
> ### Business Vocab
>
> *Murphy's Law* is a famous observation: anything that can go wrong will go wrong.

Look at it from your customers' perspective: they purchased something from you in good faith, paid for it, and it's not right. Why should they wait to have you make it right any longer than is absolutely necessary? You didn't wait to take their order and money. Please remember that fixing an existing problem is just as important, or even more so, than taking the next new order. As I've said before, think of the long-term value of a customer. And keep in mind that a disgruntled person whose problem wasn't solved quickly will spread negative word-of-mouth faster than you can sneeze.

One way to resolve some minor mishaps quickly is to give your frontline people some authority to do it. They will usually be the first to hear about any problem, and if they can solve it *on the spot,* your customers will be impressed—so impressed that they will probably give you positive word-of-mouth praise to everyone they know. You solved their problem much faster than their expectations and turned a negative into a positive. Giving your frontline people this authority, within a reasonable limit, is providing outstanding customer service that your competitors may not be doing. Your customers will forget the problem but will remember how it was solved.

You can set a limit of how far your frontline people can go before getting further approval. I've heard about one company that set up a monthly fund of $XXX that frontline employees can use to solve problems quickly with customers. Once the fund is used up, if it ever is, a supervisor must give them final approval. If they get to that point, a supervisor will always be readily available to make a quick decision. Rarely does it get to that point, but they are prepared if it does. Each month, the fund stats are at the full amount for the employees to use again. This way the owners can see what it's costing to solve problems and make any adjustments to eliminate recurring ones. This is money well spent because it helps your frontline employees save face and make the customer leave with a smile.

Ways to Make Employees Team Players

In sports, the coach and managers always stress that the team as a unit is *more important* than any individual player. If the team wins, all the players win *together.* Individual performance is recognized only after the team wins together. It's the same in busines: when the company wins, everybody wins. You need to make each person feel part of the team, and you need his or her best effort to succeed. Here are some ideas to generate the team spirit:

> ➤ Clearly define each person's duties and goals—a well-planned offensive succeeds more often.

> ➤ Train employees in secondary positions as backups when someone is off or if a position is vacant.

> ➤ Encourage employees' suggestions, discuss them at meetings, and reward the ones you use.

> ➤ Let employees solve minor problems with customers without prior approval, then have them explain their solution to everyone else.

➤ Have an open-door policy with managers and executives—employees should not feel apprehensive about discussing a problem at any time.

➤ Create a feeling of trust and respect—it goes both ways and makes employees feel important and needed.

➤ Follow through on promises and changes.

➤ Recognize outstanding performance in front of other team members.

➤ When good things happen, reward the team as a whole. It will bring them close together for the next challenge.

➤ Encourage team members to help each other, with the focus being on the overall goal.

➤ When awarding bonuses, treat all levels of employees equally.

➤ Start an after-work sports team so that employees can enjoy their team spirit away from the company.

➤ When a promotion becomes available, let team members suggest a candidate.

Employees who participate in a team effort are less likely to leave the company, which saves you the expense of hiring and training. When you have a good team, you feel less anxiety about leaving for a vacation or business trip. The team should be able to handle most problems and circumstances that arise if everyone works together.

Bully Employees

We've all heard of bully bosses, but how often have we seen the tables turned and had to face bully employees? Maybe more often than you'd think.

Bullying is bad for the growth and morale of your business and should be eliminated as soon as you're aware of it. Like a disease, it probably won't go away on its own, you have to treat it or it just gets worse. So if it exists, how are we dealing with it, or are we dealing with it at all? Do we just walk away, sweep it under the rug, or otherwise ignore this unpleasant situation? Larger companies may have staff psychologists or programs to deal with this problem, but in small business it's left to the owner or manager.

There are three types of employee bullying that need to be addressed. The victims of these are the customers, other employees, and the boss or employer.

➤ Bullying the customer: This is the reverse of good customer service and consists of making demands of customers or insisting they place their order sooner if they want a certain delivery date. Even if you have products that are not available elsewhere, you don't want your customers to feel like you're doing them a favor by selling to them. Don't allow your people to raise their voice or have an attitude when dealing with customers.

> ➤ Bullying other employees: This probably occurs more in larger companies but has no place in small business. This type of bullying will quickly destroy morale, and you may even lose a key employee or two. Many people won't complain about bullying to their boss, so be on the lookout for an employee making demands or demeaning another person, and stop it right then and there. If you let it go or ignore it, the situation could get out of control.

> ➤ Bullying the boss: How a person of authority lets this happen, I don't understand. But I've seen it several times over the years at various companies. People will make demands about work assignments, schedules, and even when they can take a break. They might insist on early pay increases or time off—extraordinary requests that other employees don't make.

Don't be bullied into submitting to these demands because there will only be more and more of them. As soon as other employees see this happening, they will all be at your door with complaints or their own demands. If you lose control and let employees bully you, the entire business will suffer. Even if after several meetings that don't resolve the problem a key person has to go, it's still the best solution.

Hey, nobody said owning a business was going to be easy, and it's not. You have to wear many hats and this is just one of them. But when these issues need to be addressed, there is no reason to wait. In fact, waiting only makes things worse and more difficult and time-consuming to deal with later.

Superstars and Trust

As you get to know your employees, you will see a few who stand out from the others. You can trust these employees and give them more responsibility. An employee can tell when you trust them and their actions, and will work even harder to keep that trust. If you can find even one of these assets in your new small business, you'll be lucky because employees like this don't come along very often.

Superstar Employees

We all want the best possible employees we can get for the money we're able to pay, but do we all take the time necessary to select them? You must remember that the people on your staff that have direct contact with your customers represent your total company. They are what can make you or break you, as the saying goes. If they don't please and *wow* your patrons, there's no impetus for repeat business. And without customers who remember your business, you're just another jelly bean in the jar. Great employees on the front line and behind the scenes are the foundation of a growing, prosperous, and successful business. Don't underestimate their power in your company.

Superstar employees care about more than just their paycheck and will want to become an important part of your winning team. They will want to develop into a key part of your business, so let them and lower the restrictive fences. Give them the opportunity to make small decisions without getting approval first. This will build their confidence.

No one likes a superior looking over their shoulder for every little thing, and superstar employees will appreciate the space you give them. Let them know you trust them and count on their support to make the company successful. The more comfortable they feel doing their job, the more creative they will become. Show them that you believe in their honesty and reliability.

Business Knowledge

Once you identify a superstar in your business, you will need to keep him or her challenged if you want to keep them. Superstars need some authority and to know that what they are doing is making a difference. They will look at difficult situations with a smile and dive right in.

So, how do you know if you have any superstar employees on your staff? You may suspect that you have some potential candidates when you hire them, but you never know for sure until you see them in action. Here are some of the traits that will tip you off to an employee's superstar status:

➤ The employee is a self-starter

➤ Customers make favorable comments about the employee

➤ You see it in the employee's smile

➤ The employee easily earns coworkers' respect

➤ The employee is eager to accept responsibility

➤ The employee is eager to assist customers or clients

➤ The employee is happy to work on problems

➤ The employee has no attendance or punctuality issues

➤ The employee shows confidence and self-assurance

➤ The employee never complains about duties or assignments

➤ The employee likes to stay busy all the time

➤ The employee is eager to help other employees

Superstars are easy to recognize because you won't see many of these traits in your average employee. As the saying goes, superstars "stick out like a sore thumb." They will make your job easier and your business shine in the face of competition. It's like a value-added service for your customers and clients.

Building Trust

Trust can go both ways in a business, especially in a new small business. You must feel that you trust employees to do their job to the best of their ability, handle any money transactions honestly, and to be truthful to you and everyone else. This trust will build over time and both sides will know it. The more trust an owner feels for an employee, the more responsibility the owner can give to that employee. Along with responsibility may be other perks or financial rewards. All is worth achieving for doing a good job.

The employee must also feel that his or her boss is fair and follows through on promises and rewards. When employees feel that their efforts are appreciated, they will work even harder. When both sides trust each other, the business benefits and the tasks are easier.

 # The Retail Jungle

---

In This Chapter

➤ Finding Employees

➤ Why Have a Grand Opening

➤ Hiring Tips

➤ The Customer Experience

➤ Having a Sale

Ask any seasoned retail owner and they will agree that it's a jungle out there. It's been said that selling to retail customers is like trying to catch a house fly. Once they land somewhere and you try to attach their loyalty, they are off flying somewhere else. You just can't seem to keep them coming back to one place for very long. But many owners really love the retail business and would never change. They enjoy the personal contact with customers and training employees how to service them. Retail is a difficult way to be in business but when it works, it can bring big profits for its owners. Learn all about retail and all that it demands before making the commitment which is easier to get into than out of.

Finding Retail Employees

If you are opening or growing a retail business it's likely that you will need at least some employees to assist with the customers and long hours necessary. Finding those employees at or near minimum wage can be a real challenge for any owner. The three most important characteristics to look for in potential retail employees is attitude, honesty and common sense. The rest of the skills and procedures you can teach but not those three things. So how do you find these fantastic people to help you operate your business? Here are some ideas:

➤ Current employee referrals - offer a small bonus for anyone hired and stays 90 days

➤ High Schools - Contact the administration office and ask them to post your job listings

➤ Craigslist - Free to post but if you list a phone number, it will never stop ringing. Ask for an email resume first.

➤ Free Internet Job Sites - There are many so be careful not to give them too much personal information

➤ Colleges - Mail, email or stop in and give your job specs to the Dean of Business, Finance, etc.

➤ Customer Referrals - Post a small help wanted sign near the check-out and verbally let customers and clients know

➤ Churches - They usually know people looking for work and may be able to verify the "3 important characteristics"

➤ Local Radio - TV Stations - Many have links on their website as a community service

➤ Local Unemployment Office - Be very specific with your needs and qualifications or you will have a long line of unqualified applicants outside your door

➤ Networking Groups - These local business people may know excellent people but not able to hire them now

Business Knowledge

The best retail employees should enjoy dealing with people, have a positive attitude, common sense and good communication skills. They are always trying to be helpful and smile a lot.

It's wise to have at least two people interview candidates and always check references. Explain what the job duties are and what you expect of them. No employee is perfect and no job is perfect for everyone but try to come as close as you can.

Training New Hires

Once you have made your selection of who will work for your business you must train them in both procedures and your policies. Don't just show them what to do and leave them on their own; supervise and guide them to do things the way you expect. Whenever possible, have a written description of each job that each new person can read and study. The more they know in advance will make them a better employee. Introduce them to other employees and let them watch their job in action before letting them get started. If they will be dealing with customers watching a little longer will give them more confidence.

Superstar Employees

We all want the best possible employees we can get for the money we're able to pay but do we always take the time necessary to select them? You must remember that the people on your staff that have direct contact with your customers represent your total company. They are what can make you or break you, as the saying goes. They are the first ones that customers meet and create that "first impression".

If they don't please and WOW your patrons, there's no reason to get repeat business and referrals. And without customers and clients who remember your business, you're just another jelly bean in the jar. Great superstar employees on the front line and behind the scenes are the foundation of a growing, prosperous and successful business. Never underestimate their power in your company and let them know it.

The Customer Experience

You will need to answer the question that every potential customer is asking themselves, "Why should I spend my money with this retailer?". Great products, great service and competitive prices is not enough anymore. People can get all that anywhere today. You must go beyond what everyone else is offering. It's just common sense that if you make customers and clients very satisfied and happy, they will return and send referrals. Make them say "WOW" and they will remember you and your business. Keep thinking of ways to add value to your products and services; the answers are there, you just need to find them.

Wear Your Customers' Shoes

Are you really treating customers how you would want to be treated? Yes, it's the old Golden Rule and it never goes out of style. Here are some ways to be sure that you're following the Golden Rule in your business:

> ➤ Shop at your competitor's business and see how they treat customers

> ➤ Review your refund, exchange and return policies

> ➤ Listen in on staff's handling of call-in and walk-in service

> ➤ Are your hours of operation adequate?

> ➤ Are your phones answered by real people?

> ➤ Do you accept all major credit cards?

> ➤ Do you ask customers what new things they want?

> ➤ Do you watch your customer's faces during customer contact?

> ➤ Do you treat complaints like an opportunity?

> ➤ Does everyone on your staff smile often?

> ➤ Do you offer samples or demonstrate freely?

> ➤ Do you periodically work the front lines?

> ➤ Can you say that you never cheat a customer?

Business Alerts

Customers will believe you and trust you until they find that you have not told them the truth about something important. Never, never lie to a customer and risk that trust..

Customers Want to Trust You

When someone decides to buy from your business or use your services they usually feel some trust that you will provide the best value you can for the money they are paying. That trust can increase or decrease based on what they receive and how satisfied they are after the transaction. If that trust decreases because of a shortfall on the value that they perceived, you will probably not hear from them again. Plus you will not get any referrals from them either. Don't let this happen.

Trust is always slow to get, especially in business, but it can be lost quickly as a result of a dumb act or situation. A new client or customer will be watching very closely to how you treat them and serve their needs. They are the most vulnerable when trust comes into the picture. Your job is to make it easy for them to trust your business by making every situation a positive one.

Trust from customers and clients may be the most important thing that can build your business.

Ask Yourself

The Golden Rule is no longer good enough. You must exceed it to make your customers say "WOW".

Create Loyalty

We all want our customer's loyalty but are we willing to do what's necessary to create it? You must make the effort and establish an environment that makes the customer experience better than competitors. Here are some ideas:

➤ Always say Thank You (every transaction)

➤ Have high value perception

➤ Ask their name and use it often

➤ Fast payment options

➤ Convenient business hours

➤ Rush service or orders without extra cost

➤ Stock specialty products and services

➤ Perks for regular customers

➤ Resolve problems quickly

➤ Smile a lot (even on bad days)

➤ Have knowledgeable people available

➤ Have an outstanding guarantee

➤ An open-door policy for questions

➤ Use customer suggestions

➤ Never ever lie to them, ever

Reasons Customers Will Pay More

Customers always want to pay the lowest price, right? But wait, them may be willing to pay more even if they can find it for less elsewhere. Here are some reasons why:

> ➤ Your products are easier and faster to purchase

> ➤ Your products arrive quicker when ordered

> ➤ It has an extra highly desirable feature

> ➤ There's a lower long term cost of ownership

> ➤ It gives the buyer a higher social status

> ➤ Your customer experience is unbeatable

> ➤ They know, like and trust you personally

> ➤ The price difference is not that much

> ➤ Your location and parking is more convenient

Ask Yourself

Don't assume that all your customers will want to purchase the lowest priced product. Have choices available for all levels of buyers.

Listen to Customers & Clients

> ➤ Everyone your business is part of customer satisfaction and here are a few things everyone should remember.

> ➤ Ask how you can assist and explain and then stop talking and listen to the answer

> ➤ Remember that the one customer you are talking to is the reason you have a business or job

> ➤ Again, stop talking when the customer is telling you how to satisfy them

> ➤ Really listen and make it show

➤ Pay attention to no-verbal clues, tone of voice and demeanor and you will learn more than is said

➤ Never judge a customer on manner of speaking or appearance

➤ Think before you respond and use all the information they give you to form an answer

➤ Realize that this person may be telling you how to make them a loyal customer

➤ Don't look around the room when listening, pay attention to them

➤ Don't answer phone calls when they are talking

The Unfriendly Customer

Some people just want to get their business done and that's it. You should be able to pick out these customers right away and fulfill their wants. You don't know or need to know what else is going on in their life, so complete the sale as quickly as you can and let them go. A pleasant hello, no questions and smile will be enough for this person.

Never force a customer to respond to "How are you today?". They may not want to answer and it makes them irritated by just asking. Avoid asking any general questions to this type of buyer and just finish the transaction. If you serve and treat this customer the way they want to be treated, you will probably long term loyalty. Your goal is to satisfy them not to ask questions they don't want to answer.

Customer and Client Rights

➤ Ask permission to stay in touch

➤ Listen to their wants and needs

➤ Keep your word and commitments

➤ Tell the truth about products and services

➤ Be sincere and honest

➤ Respect their decisions

➤ Never cheat them even if you can

➤ Treat them as intelligent buyers

➤ Respect their time

➤ Keep them informed

> ➤ Never promise impossible delivery dates

> ➤ Never assume they will always buy from you

Having A Retail Sale

Shopper always love sales where they can purchase something they want or need at a lower price than is normally offered. Don't reduce your level of service during the sale because you want everyone to return when the sale is over. Here are some ideas for planning successful retail sales.:

> ➤ Choose a name for the sale that will generate interest and curiosity

> ➤ Make sure you have enough stock of the sale items

> ➤ Have sale merchandise fit the name of the sale

> ➤ Price reduction should be a least 25% and higher if possible

> ➤ Popular best sellers work best for a sale and people will come to see what else is reduced

> ➤ Have a time limit for the sale, no more than 10 days is best

> ➤ Have big displays near the entrance of popular items on sale

> ➤ Have a lot of window and in-store displays

> ➤ Have a costumed character with a sign by the street

> ➤ Use newspaper advertising and a map to the store

> ➤ Post sale announcements on all social media

> ➤ Mail announcements to everyone on your mailing list

> ➤ Have related items grouped together and even bundle some of them

> ➤ Have signs at the checkout prior to the sale start date

> ➤ Let VIP customers into the sale early

> ➤ Decorate outside if possible to attract attention

> ➤ Extend OPEN hours a little and let people know

> ➤ Ask suppliers for extra product on consignment for the sale

> ➤ Do something outrageous and alert the media

> ➤ If you think you will run out of some items post "While Supply Lasts"

> ➤ Have fun, make money and smile a lot!

Business Alerts

Sales that last more than 10 days are no longer sales. The reduced prices you are offering then become your regular prices in your customers' minds. Why would anyone ever purchase at the regular price again? Have a deadline for all sales and stick to it.

Shopping At A Small Store

The consumer has many choices when it comes to spending their money. Why should they consider a small store over a large corporate chain or discount store? Here are some ideas that build loyalty in small stores:

➤ Better all-around customer service

➤ Well informed sales staff

➤ Owners on premises & available

➤ Every sale is very important

➤ People you can get to know

➤ They take the time to listen

➤ Faster check-out or payment

➤ Comfortable store layout

➤ Easy returns & exchanges

➤ Special orders are welcome

➤ They know your name

➤ They really care about your loyalty

➤ No corporate bureaucracy

➤ Consistent quality & prices

If your small store or business is missing any of these, get to work on improving your image today. You can and will survive any economic slowdown with loyal repeat customers who will also send referrals. But to get that loyalty, you must give them the feeling that their business is valued and appreciated. Never have a bad day or let problems show in front of a customer.

Business Facts

Have useful items within reach of your checkout counter or pay station and you'll benefit from impulse buyers. Low or reasonable priced items work better.

Small Retailer Holiday Ideas

As we approach the holiday season again, all the big box and corporate chains are trying to undersell their competition and have the earliest sales. They entice customers with low prices and limited availability. The profit margin is low so they have to sell more to come out ahead. They spend mega-dollars on advertising to lure shoppers into their stores and to their websites. It's the same old thing year after year and for some, it doesn't even pay off. They think ONLY the lowest price will get the sale.

But why should a small business retailer or online seller join the madness and try to compete for super low profits or any at all. The big stores aren't going to let you win anyway, they will just lower prices again, maybe below your cost. Why not fight back with something value-added that others are not offering instead of just low prices. Find something your customers want (ask them!) and offer it along with a fair price. There is an old saying that if everything else is equal, people just buy the lowest price. Add value so it won't be equal.

Don't let your business be "just equal", make it offer more with a smile and provide the added service that can't be found elsewhere. You won't need to spend big bucks on advertising because you will receive more valuable Word-of-Mouth publicity. Be involved in your target market community and the word will spread quickly. And remember these happy and satisfied customers will be repeat business after the holidays!

Retail Is Not For Everyone

If you hate long hours and possibly working 7 days a week, a retail business may not be for you. Sure you can stay open any hours you want but if competitors are open longer, you may lose business (and repeat business). You could always leave someone else in charge when you leave but will they do the job as well as you do and give outstanding service? Some of us love long hours and being involved in our business 24/7 and that's great. If you have a young family, it's tough to be away that long, so consider a partner or a different type of business.

Retail businesses have other situations to deal with in addition to long hours. You have to hire, train, retrain and supervise your staff and sometimes fire them. You also need to keep your store/location clean and in stocked condition. Handling returns, credits and exchanges also takes time and finesse so customers will come back. And of course that occasional nasty or unpleasant customer who can't wait to confront you. These are all part of owning a retail business and it's not for everyone. When it's doing well there is nothing better, if you can handle the stress.

Why You Might Lose a Customer

➤ A problem was not resolved

➤ They moved out of your selling area

➤ They are unhappy with your product/service

➤ They found lower prices & higher value elsewhere

➤ Your competitor has a better selection

➤ They don't feel their business is appreciated

➤ You stopped saying Thank You after every sale

➤ They had an argument with an employee

➤ They had an argument with the owner

➤ Technology left you behind

➤ Poor "customer experience"

➤ A competitor stole them away

➤ A new generation wants changes

➤ They now have a relative in the business

➤ Delivery took too long

➤ They no longer use your product/service

➤ Your products now outdated

➤ They can't afford to buy

➤ Your hours don't fit their schedule

Most of these can be fixed by making changes in how you do business. Responding to customers new wants and needs will enhance the customer experience for everyone. It's time to get out of your comfort zone and make positive changes.

CHAPTER 14

Planning Your Grand Opening

> ## In This Chapter
>
> ➤ Why have a grand opening
> ➤ Jump-start your business
> ➤ Using the media
> ➤ Giveaways and promo items
> ➤ Other celebrations

In this chapter you will learn how an effective grand opening celebration will get your new business off to a good start. You will learn ways to start getting your cash-flow quickly and how to attract the media for free publicity. Also, you'll learn how to use holidays and other celebrations to lure people to your business for fun and profit.

Planning for Opening Day

All the decisions, preparation, and work you put in to get your business started eventually leads to your opening day. Some new business owners wonder if they really want to have a grand opening celebration. It can be a fun and profitable endeavor that brings people to your door, phone, or website. A grand opening will make your new business stand out from the crowd for a short time, so if you're going to do it, you should plan it correctly or it could have negative effect.

Business Knowledge

Here are some ideas for you to use while you're planning your grand opening:

- ➤ Select the date as soon as you can
- ➤ Have a separate grand opening budget
- ➤ Have a ribbon-cutting ceremony
- ➤ Invite the mayor and congressmen
- ➤ Ask suppliers for signs and displays
- ➤ Have all of your staff and temps on hand
- ➤ Get a radio station to remote broadcast
- ➤ Hire an entertainer for the kids
- ➤ Ask the fire department to offer free blood pressure tests
- ➤ Alert the police of a possible big crowd
- ➤ Get enough sleep the night before

Business Facts

Many new businesses plan a grand opening without setting a budget for it. As a result, they overspend and use valuable marketing funds that don't show the results expected.

If this is your first business it's like a dream come true, and you are ready. It's a fabulous feeling to see all your ideas actually take form as a new business. This is just the beginning of a new era for you, and you want to do it right. A grand opening is like launching a new website, receiving an award, or adding someone new to your family; you'll remember it for a long time, maybe forever. It's your day, your ideas, your staff, and your success all wrapped up in a grand opening.

Some entrepreneurs may think that a grand opening celebration is just a waste of time and want to get down to business instead. But this is the business of promoting your business in a once-in-a-lifetime celebration. Use this opportunity to make your new business known in your marketplace, and take advantage of all the perks a grand opening has to offer. It lets people know right away who you are, where you are, and why they should become a customer. Oh, and by the way, it does create some immediate cash flow and much-needed sales.

Jump-Start Your New Business

Now that you've spent all your savings, all your investors' money, all your bank loans, what do you do? You need customers right away, and a lot of them! Marketing and sales promotion should start before you even open for business. You can use a toll-free number that feeds into voice mail to get customers and prospects calling early so you can begin to lay the groundwork for future sales. Here are some ideas to consider and have in place before you actually open for business.

➤ Start direct mail: Send letters, flyers, menus, etc., to your biggest pool of prospects. Test several lists for your target market.

➤ Offer free literature: Use response cards, e-mail, and a toll-free number where prospects can request free information. Describe your product, services, and availability.

➤ Set sales appointments: in advance so you're busy from day one visiting prospects. You don't need a store or office to make a sales call.

➤ Start telemarketing: You, your staff, or an outside firm should be calling your most likely prospects as soon as possible. Create excitement for your grand opening.

➤ Announce introductory offers: Entice people to try your new business with special offers, but don't give away the ranch; it will cheapen your image.

➤ Offer gifts: Something extra for the first one hundred or five hundred buyers to get the cash register ringing. You may even have a line at your door on opening day.

➤ Have a contest: No purchase necessary to get people to try your product or listen to your sales pitch.

➤ Offer a free trial: Get customers to use your product or give away free samples. You may even get a few testimonials from people who like it.

➤ Place advertising early: You'll want your print ads to be out when you're ready for business, and many publications have a one- to two-month lead time.

➤ Send press releases: Find something newsworthy about your opening and send press releases to newspapers, magazines, trade journals, radio, and TV at least a month in advance. Promote new products and contests.

➤ Offer free consultations: Free consultations can include quotes, estimates, samples, and advice. Get that face-to-face contact and close the sale before you open.

➤ Hold a seminar: Give a seminar that's free and convenient , and include demonstrations. Tell people something that they didn't know.

➤ Stress your guarantee: Make a big deal about your guarantee so first-time buyers can feel comfortable—no one likes to be a guinea pig. Print your guarantee on everything.

➤ Offer cash discounts: Gifts or discounts for paying by cash can increase your short-term cash flow. Sell gift cards and offer double value during your grand opening.

➤ Advance order specials: Extra quantity discounts, freebies, and free delivery can have a pile of orders waiting for your first day.

Promotions Help

Promotions can be expensive, inexpensive, or free. In slow times, you'll want to use one of the second two and spend as little as you can. Along with free publicity, you want as much exposure as you can that will generate sales. Promotions can be anything from coupons, contests, scratch offs, exhibits, games, or events.

One ongoing promotion I've heard about that's different concerns a local pizza restaurant. It offers a 25 percent discount to anyone who cuts out their biggest competitor's yellow pages ad and brings it in. It must be the original, not a copy. This works two ways: the customer gets an immediate discount and the competitor's ad is no longer in the phone book when the customer is ready to order again. This promotion costs nothing except a discount that customers could have received through a coupon anyway.

Scratch offs work because they are fun and give the customer or prospect a chance to win something or get a discount. There are stock cards available that are low in cost and available quickly. If scratch offs bring in more business when you need it most, it's worth the investment. And if it works well for you, try it again soon or on a regular interval. People will catch on and be waiting for the next time. Prizes or discounts don't have to be large; most people love to win anything.

If you're a business in a large mall or street mall, join in any mall-wide sales or special events. If it's a joint effort, the cost of promoting it will be shared with all the vendors, and your part of the cost will be reasonable. Don't pass up this opportunity to make quick sales and be part of the action.

Promotions of any type will bring attention to your business and remind past customers to visit you again. Most people love to participate in different events, rather than the same old sale. Be creative and find promotions you don't see every day. Be sure to advertise your promotion, post signs in your store, and send direct mail. You want to create an excitement so potential customers will put you on their to-do list.

Do It Now

You want to create a sense of urgency for your customers by making it clear that they may lose the offer if they don't act now. This sense of urgency will get customers in the store more quickly and will give you needed cash flow. It also starts the free word-of-mouth advertising working. Don't overlook or put aside the task of getting those first customers. They will be the foundation of your future success.

Business Knowledge

If you don't have a physical location or even if you do, celebrate on your website. Everyone in the world will be invited. You may even want to consider putting *Welcome* in several different languages on your home page. Offer great prices on your products for one day only. Give some great industry ideas or have a link to a blog with information customers can use at no cost. Promote the grand opening in e-mails, Twitter, Facebook, and anywhere you can.

Giveaways and Deals

Your grand opening and the first few months in business will tell the story of how well people remember your business. The more they remember, the less you will have to spend to show your presence in the market. One way to keep your name in their minds is to give them a small gift with your business name and contact information on it. Magnets are used by places that want their phone number or e-mail address readily available. Many pizza shops use magnets so people will have their number at hand for orders.

Many times magnets, pens, or note pads will serve as an idea to order or make a contact now. The person may not even be planning to call or e-mail, but the promotional item will create that desire. That's why gifts and giveaways should always be useful items that can be placed in a customer's home or office where he or she can see it.

Give Them Something

People like to be remembered and thanked for doing business with you. Giving them a small token to show that you care and to remind them where to buy again can pay off. There are thousands of promotional products available, but the most common are pens, magnets, letter openers, key chains, and water bottles. They are usually inexpensive and keep your name and image in front of customers when imprinted with your business information.

Check with your promotional products supplier to see if there are any new and unusual products that are unique to your business. The money you spend on these items can ensure some customer loyalty and return business. Don't overlook the power of promotional products. Check at www.americas-cards.com.

Surprise Customers

Did someone ever unexpectedly do something for you or give you a gift for no particular reason? How did it perk you up and brighten your day? I think most of us like positive and pleasant surprises once in a while, and we usually remember them long after they have occurred. When a business does something special for you or surprises you with a kind gesture, you remember it for a long time because it's so unusual.

Catching people off guard with a positive surprise can really build loyalty, at least for a short time. But six months to a year later, that feeling of gratitude may have worn off and needs to be refreshed. Find unique ways to surprise your customers and clients to help create that bond and loyalty.

Partner with Other Businesses

Many businesses work together to help each other create new business so that both or all can grow. That's how the local Chamber of Commerce and other organizations came into being. There are many monthly and weekly meetings that you can attend as a guest before you join and have to pay dues. Several that come to mind are Sales Pros, BNI, and various business women's groups. They usually have a speaker with usable and informative business tips and ideas. These groups charge dues and possibly for meals if the meeting is being held in a restaurant. It could be worth your while to join at least one such group and attend the meetings. You need only a few ideas and tips to boost your new business.

Business Knowledge

A soft opening for a couple of days before your grand opening will allow employees to get live experience and get the bugs out. Just open the door and turn on the Open sign and let anyone who happens by come in. You can invite family, friends, and business acquaintances for refreshments or a small party. When your publicized grand opening opens a few days later, you'll feel more comfortable with customers in larger numbers.

Cross Promotions

There are always other businesses that serve the same target market you do but have no interest in your type of business or what you sell. Why not work together and expand your horizons even more. You can put flyers with coupons advertising your business in the other business's store or on its website and even print Compliments of … on them for a nice personal touch. In return, you can give out information or have a small display where your customers can be referred to your partner's business.

You will need to investigate potential cross promotion partners to be sure they are offering quality products and services that your customers expect. Some businesses go together very nicely like:

➤ Hair salons and tanning parlors

➤ Day care centers and ice cream stores

➤ Printers and graphic designers

➤ Wedding photographers and tuxedo rentals

➤ Health food stores and exercise clubs

➤ Travel agents and car rentals

➤ Employment agencies and day care centers

➤ Casinos and jewelry stores

➤ Furniture stores and interior designers

➤ Auto parts and tire stores

➤ Book stores and coffee houses

➤ Pet supply stores and veterinarians

➤ Golf courses and sporting goods dealers

➤ Florists and funeral homes

➤ Chiropractors and massage therapists

➤ Auto repair shops and towing services

➤ Realtors and mortgage companies

➤ New car dealers and car washes

Once you find your best type of partner business and you set up a cross promotion, don't stop there. Search the web or look in the phone book for others in our partner's business and approach them with the same idea. It's better to have five or six working for you than just one. But get to know your partners and be sure they provide quality products and services. You're really giving an endorsement by referring customers to other businesses and you don't want it to backfire on you. Any time someone is referred to you through cross promotion, call the other business and thank them. It may inspire them to try to send many more customers your way.

Use the Media

For a new business, any free use of the media is a plus and can only help with business recognition. This publicity is not easy to get, though, because so many other business owners also want it. But it is possible and you should make every effort to get what you can as often as you can. Bringing your new business out of the shadows and into the limelight can do wonders for those first and cautious customers. And when you receive credit or publicity from the media, or anyone else for that matter, it's not you tooting your own horn; it's a third party saying it. Most people will believe third parties because they have no interest in the business and nothing to gain.

Business Alerts

A grand opening and other celebrations are great while they last and will bring a lot of attention to your new business. After about sixty days when their effects wear off, people will ask ,"What have you done for me lately?" Have a couple of new event plans and ideas in the works at all times and start publicizing them thirty days before they occur to generate interest.

The first way to approach the media is through e-mail or regular mail. It's always better to send announcements to a name rather than just a title, even if it's the wrong name. You can easily find names of contacts by searching the Internet for your state newspapers and magazines, then going to their websites for names and contact information.

There are several lists of radio stations on the web that can be found by searching: *(state name) radio stations*. You will find a lot of stations, but the search list should include their format : religious, country, talk, rock, etc. Find your best matches and contact them first.

If you're announcing your grand opening, be sure to note that something unusual or free will be given away, and make it clear that no purchase is necessary. Just a plain old grand opening is boring and probably wouldn't warrant being publicized by the media. You need an attention-grabbing headline that makes everyone stop, think, and take action.

Offer to be interviewed for more information and be available on short notice. Send your announcement to the media about eight to ten days before the event is going to happen so they have just enough time to use it.

Write Articles and Be an Expert

If you want to try for publicity outside your local area, write articles about your area of expertise and offer them to publications in that industry. Tell people something that they don't already know. The publications probably won't pay you for the article but you can put all your contact information in the byline. You can find many targeted publications listed in *Bacon's Magazine Directory* and *Bacon's Newspaper Directory*, which can be found at your local library's reference department.

The articles will not only give you exposure, but also tout you as an expert in your field. People like to buy from experts, so why not be one?

You can also offer to do fifteen- to twenty-minute talks at local coffee shops, community colleges, libraries, or anywhere else someone will have you. Pass out a brochure highlighting your business *at the end* of the presentations, and encourage people to call you with questions. All this exposure and interviews are going to keep you busy, but that's what it takes to get a new business going.

On-the-Air Publicity

Some of the biggest audiences you'll ever get will be on radio or television. We'd all like to be on Oprah's show to discuss and promote our company, but what are the chances? You may have a better chance of winning your state lottery. Only the best, the hottest, the most spectacular will get that chance in a lifetime. Don't walk away with your tail between your legs; there's still a chance at the local level—that's where to start.

Send a letter similar to a press release to the radio station manger or on-air personality stating you're an expert in your field and would be available to be a guest should the need arise. Offer to take calls from callers asking about your specialty and give free advice. Question-and-answer segments are very popular with most audiences. Send your letter to all the radio stations within an area you can easily get to on short notice.

Many stations will keep your letter on file and call your unexpectedly when a news story or public interest questions in your field come up. Radio is a great place to start because if you're nervous, no one can see it except your hosts and they're not going to tell. After you've done a few radio stints, if you know your subject well, you'll be relaxed and ready to try the *tube*.

BUSINESS DICTIONARY

Business Vocab

Publicity is any announcement or event that brings attention to your business or website. Unlike advertising, publicity is usually free, but you won't be able to control what is said or done.

Television is the *big time*, where people not only hear your voice but see you, your actions, and your body language. So start small and build confidence in yourself and your presentation. The key is to keep your audience motivated and interested. Any material you plan to use should be pretested with your staff, friends, and relatives. You don't want to sound boring, or your time will be cut short and you won't be asked back.

Find the best local stations to approach for your targeted audience. You can look in one of the media directories or check your local phone book. Many local stations have talk shows on Saturday and Sunday, early in the morning. Call or send mail to the show producer (*not* the station manager), offering your appearance and availability. Larger regional or national talk shows may monitor local shows to find new and interesting guests they haven't seen before or too frequently.

Once you've done one or more of these, it's infectious; you'll want to do more. Every three months send mail or e-mail to the producers of the shows you want to appear on most and offer a new *angle* each time. You may get a last-minute call to fill in for a famous person who cancelled at the last minute, so be ready. When starting out, don't expect to be paid or receive anything other than public recognition. After you become famous and receive many appearance offers, you can negotiate reasonable fees. But publicity itself is usually a big payoff.

Other Events and Celebrations

Once your grand opening is over, you're really in business and the day-to-day routine will occasionally need a boost. The low-price sellers will always have some type of sale going on to cut prices and draw in customers. A company that always offers a sale price doesn't really have a regular price. The sale price is its regular price and buyers are always waiting for it to go lower. Don't get caught up in this surefire way to reduce profits and deter loyal customers and clients. Instead, have an occasional event or celebration to draw in customers who will come for reasons other than low prices.

Try to plan at least five occasions when you will have some type of an event that will draw in your customer base. The event should somehow relate to your business or its core values. Let's say one of your core values is being *green* whenever possible. Everyone believes in helping the planet stay livable and will at least check out your idea. The event could be a weekend recycling drive, where you get a city or independently owned truck for people to deposit used plastic, paper, or aluminum. You may even get radio or TV coverage for an event like this.

Another event could be a clothing and shoe drive for the homeless. You could even ask for food for the local food pantry. Organize a drive that occurs at the same time as a national telethon and take donations at your business.

Ask Yourself

People love events where they can have fun and save money at the same time. Be creative and come up with event ideas that are new and exciting. Don't just copy some other business ideas that make you a follower, not a leader. Ask family and friends for event ideas; you may be surprised and get something great!

Events will bring people to your store or office, and some of the event attendees may make purchases while they are there. They will at least remember your business as the one that helped a cause they also believed in, so when they're ready to buy, yours will be the first business that comes to mind. Your not-so-well-known new business could be a household name sooner than you think.

When Is Your Birthday?

Everyone likes to be acknowledged on their birthday even if they don't show it. The world has made everyone's birthday a special day regardless of their age. Of course, kids love their birthdays and even older people have to smile when you wish them a happy birthday.

You can offer your customers a free gift or a discount on their birthday. If possible, put your business name and logo on any free items. To make a birthday special, the gift should be something of value. For instance, if you own a restaurant and someone is there celebrating a birthday, taking a photo of the party and giving the celebrants two prints before they leave will stay with them for a while.

This is one celebration that everyone can be a part of. Make this an ongoing event or have it last for at least one full year.

First Anniversary

An anniversary celebration can be held in a store, office, rented hall, at your website, or at several places simultaneously. Many new businesses never make it to the first year, so you should be proud when you do. All the credit for that first anniversary celebration can be given to the customers who supported you during the first twelve months. Without them, where would you be? If you have a mailing list of past customers, send a flyer thanking them and inviting them to participate in your celebration.

It's time for a little payback for those first-year customers, but don't go broke doing it. You can offer bigger than normal discount and maybe a drawing for a few nice prizes. You may even get your bank, accountant, or suppliers to sponsor a few prizes since they all made money from you and hope to in the future. If you have a retail store, invite your business neighbors to join in and make it an even bigger event. This is your one-time, first anniversary, so use it for all you can get out of it.

CHAPTER 15

Products, Services, Guarantees

In This Chapter

➤ Why offer a guarantee?

➤ Pricing ideas

➤ New products

➤ Sales follow-up

➤ Supplier special deals

In this chapter you will learn the power of a guarantee in new business sales and how it can put those first customers in a comfort zone. You will learn about pricing that appeals to customers but also lets you make a fair profit, new products and how to introduce them plus following up on sales, especially on large purchases, and you learn how to find ways to get deals from suppliers.

One-Stop Shop

By the time you have gotten to this part, you've already decided what your products or services will be. You may have a new great idea, an improved-upon product, or a better way of providing a service. These are all great, but you can build loyalty by providing the total sale.

If you are going to service a specific industry or need, don't just offer a product or basic service; have everything needed to complete the project—the total sale. You don't want your customers forced to go somewhere else for more accessories or services to get the job done. Be a one-stop shop for your customers' needs. If you're selling clocks, also sell the batteries that make them operate; if you're selling a grass edger or weed whacker, sell extension cords and replacement lines. How would you like to go into a hardware or home improvement store to buy paint and find out it doesn't sell brushes, rollers, or edging tape? You would have to go somewhere else for the supplies you need to get the job done. You won't get a lot of repeat business this way. Plus when your customers go somewhere else to purchase the accessories, it opens the door for the competitor to get all of their business.

Stand Behind All Sales

If you plan to stay in business for longer than a year, you must back up all products and services that you sell. This means standing behind all guarantees whether it's yours or a manufacturer's. Customers pay you for a product or service, and that's who they expect to back up its guarantee. Just telling them to contact your supplier or manufacturer is not going to build loyalty; it may destroy it, along with future sales. Some customers will count on your business to help them when a guarantee is needed, and you're obliged is to help them. Every customer will have a problem once in a while; it's how you take care of it that matters.

Business Vocab

According to Dictionary.com, a guarantee is a promise or assurance, especially one in writing, that something is of specified quality, content, benefit, etc., or that it will perform satisfactorily for a given length of time: a money-back guarantee.

A good policy is to stand behind every sale for which you've received payment. You should be your customers' one and only contact when something is not right. It's your responsibility to contact any other person or supplier to fix, replace, or refund the purchase. Customers should not have to pay anything for shipping or for anything else to have the situation resolved. And if you can loan them a replacement while the problems are being addressed, do so at no cost. Establish this policy when you first open your business and the word will spread quickly that there is no risk buying from your company.

A Little About Pricing

Pricing products so that you can make a decent profit and make buyers feel that they have received a high value has always been a juggling act for entrepreneurs. You have to consider your costs, including marketing costs, and still be in a price range that makes you competitive. Marketing experts have been scratching their heads for years trying to come up with the correct formula for pricing products and services.

Competitors, Price, and Value

Incorrect pricing, whether too low or too high, in a crowded market can send your customers flocking to your competitors' doors. People expect to get what they pay for, and if the price is too high or too low, they start wondering what's wrong.

You expect a fast-food hamburger to be under $5 and a designer suit to be over $100. If the suit is $39 and you are a trendy businessperson, would you really want it? When you go to the movies and see outrageous prices on popcorn, candy, and soda, you think twice or three times before buying anything. The concession stand line is not so long anymore. But in a movie theater or airport there are no competitors, so if you want it an item, you have to overpay for it.

Competitors won't always dictate your pricing guidelines if you provide reasons for higher value. Higher value can justify higher prices if the customer recognizes the higher value and really wants it. A customer who doesn't care about value or doesn't believe that it's there may balk at a higher price. You must prove to customers that your higher-priced item is worth more. Remember, it's the benefits to them that count, not the product features.

Why would a customer want to pay more for a drill that not only makes 1/4" holes but 1/8", 3/16", 3/4", and 1/2" holes if he or she would never need more than 1/4" holes? All the selling in the world is not going to convince that customer to pay more for that drill unless it's just to keep up with the Joneses. It's like selling ice cubes to an Eskimo; it may be possible, but it won't make you rich. Keep prices and products simple, as most people expect to eliminate price problems.

Your competitors are constantly trying to figure out ways to steal your customers, and pricing is one of their weapons. If they have no other tool in their box than beating your price, I think that makes it easier for you to fight back. And I don't mean fighting back with even lower prices; that only gets you lower profits. Fight back with value and show why your product or service is the better deal at a higher price. Use weapons like better quality, guarantee, selection, ease of use, and reliability to prove your point. But be sure your products can stand up to those standards, or your customer base will just ignore your claims in the future.

Once your reputation is tarnished, you might as well change your name and move to another town. Don't claim, advertise, or stress things that you can't provide or the tables will turn on you quickly. Be honest and present all your benefits as they really are. And remember to back up all sales with your ironclad guarantee.

If you can't find enough things that give your product a higher value, then you need to get busy and make some changes to stay competitive. If your competitors are showing that their products or services are a better value, then your sales and profits will start slipping. Your competitors want to beat you in your target market just as badly as you want to beat them. If you open the door, they are coming through and it will be difficult to get them out. Smart competitors only make you better at keeping your prices and value in line. You are also their competitor, and they are watching you even if you don't see them.

Ask Yourself

By setting your prices at levels that customers want to pay rather than what you want to profit will open many sales doors. Most of your clients and customers have a price range that feels comfortable to them. It's your job to price your goods and services in that price range. Look for ways to get your costs down rather than your prices up.

Pricing Headaches

Pricing your products and services can be a real challenge only because there is no real set of rules. Here are some things to consider when trying to set your prices:

> ➤ The price the market will bear

> ➤ Your actual cost

> ➤ Your profit goals

> ➤ Your sales volume goals

> ➤ The marketing cost

> ➤ What competitors are doing

> ➤ Seasonal changes and specials

> ➤ Service and maintenance costs

➤ Availability

➤ Large-quantity discounts

➤ Payment terms and discounts offered

➤ Your total overhead

➤ Prestige of ownership

➤ Big deals from suppliers

➤ Discontinued items or services

➤ Customer or business demand

➤ Display and promotion costs

➤ Advertising and selling costs

Do not change your prices too often or you will confuse customers and your staff, who will have to explain these changes. Sale prices are OK, but have a deadline and go back to your regular prices. Don't let competitors force you to make price changes that you don't want to make. Hold your ground and provide value.

State-of-the-Art Products

Do your customers want the latest products and services as soon as they are available? Will they be satisfied with the current technology and not be standing in line at midnight to get the new products as soon as they come out? Most people don't need or want the latest products and will continue buying the products they have been buying until they feel a need to change. But that's not a reason to avoid new ideas coming on the market, especially if you're part of the innovation. You still want to have the newest changes ready to go and use them in your marketing and promotion materials.

Twist and Shout!

If you have a new product or service that your target market has been looking for, don't just sit back like a proud parent and wait for everyone to congratulate you. Get the word out ASAP and start the sales coming in. Capture the new market before your competitors figure out a way to challenge you or undercut your price. Great new products and services only come along once in a while, and you have to capitalize on them right away or believe me, someone else will.

Plan your best marketing and promotion strategy and do it quickly. By being first in your target market, you will become the leader in your new innovative area. And the leader makes the most in sales and profits. So don't sit back and admire your new accomplishment;

be the town crier and get the word out fast. Get up and twist and shout until everyone knows about it!

Offer Silver, Gold, and Platinum Levels

Not everyone is interested in buying the top-of-the-line product or service. Some people use a hammer once or twice a year, so why should they buy the $25 model when the $6 model will suffice for their purpose? Offer choices. The professional who uses your product will usually want the best available, but the casual users don't need the best and would rather save the extra cost. Cater to the full spectrum of customers and make the sale comfortable for everyone.

When you offer products that vary in quality and cost, you get a bigger customer base because you can satisfy more levels of buyers. Consider supplying three levels of a product or service because the American mind usually thinks in terms of good, better, and best. Offer some type of sign or explanation of the different levels available. Be sure that your lowest-level product will still do an acceptable job and satisfy the customer.

Be able to explain the differences to your customers in easy-to-understand terminology. Don't try to sell more than the customer needs because he or she will know you're being insincere. Usually after a few questions, you can determine the level of product or service a customer needs. You never know, after using a product from your store, the customer may return to upgrade to the next level. Either way you will keep the customer happy and get the repeat business.

Follow Up on Large Sales

Making a large sale and getting consumers or another business to part with serious money is difficult in the first place. And if a new business is lucky and successful enough to get a large order, follow-up is necessary. You may ask why bother, you already have the payment and the product or service is in the hands of the buyer. Well, you could feel that way if you plan to be in business for only six months to a year. Here are a few reasons you should follow up after a large purchase:

> ➤ Avoid costly returns and exchanges

> ➤ Avoid arguments that result in credit card reversal

> ➤ Assure the buyer he or she bought the correct item

> ➤ Build a relationship for future referrals

> ➤ Show that you really care about your customers and clients

Business Knowledge

A follow-up after a large sale can be as simple as a phone call, e-mail note, or post card sent to the buyer. The customer will appreciate that you cared even after the sale was made. This simple step can make a big difference in getting repeat business and referrals.

What to Call About

Although you can send an e-mail or a postcard as a follow-up to a large sale, a phone call, even if you have to leave a message, is more personal. But either way, what do you say or write to a customer two or three days after the large sale? Here are a few suggestions:

➤ Are you using the product or service?

➤ Are you having any problems?

➤ Do you understand how it works?

➤ Are you happy with your purchase?

➤ Do you know who to call if problems arise?

➤ Do you have any friends who might be interested?

➤ Would you like me to call back in a month?

➤ Do you have any other questions?

Check Supplier Deals

Most businesses have suppliers they use to buy products for resale, parts for assembly, or for outsourcing on a regular basis. These suppliers will have special offers or deals from time to time and may or may not tell everyone. If a special deal has a limited quantity available, they may tell only their best customers or inner circle, so you may have to keep asking about specials to get part of the deal. Don't be afraid or ashamed to ask often and buy only when the offer is right for your business.

These special deals can be offered at any time and usually without notice. Excess product, open manufacturing time, or misprinted packaging can trigger a special deal at the option of the supplier, so you must stay in contact with all of your suppliers to take advantage of every opportunity. These are the deals that keep dollar stores all over the country in business. If you can get some of the same deals they're getting, you know it's worth the effort.

Overstocks, Deals, and Consignments

When buying for your store or distribution company, you'll occasionally be offered special merchandise at special prices. Your manufacturer or supplier may have overproduced or overstocked certain items and needs to turn its inventory into cash, so it offers some products at cost or below. To buy or not to buy, that's the question. You have to decide whether you can move the product to your customers quickly. The price will be tempting and the sales pitch will be strong, but don't let that sway your buying decision.

The product may be a great deal if you can offer it on a special display at a reduced price. If you advertise, can you highlight it in your ad? But you must decide if your customers and prospects want to own it. If you can't create interest or if there is no perceived need for the product, it doesn't matter how low the price is—it won't sell well. If at all possible, try to get a return clause that allows you to return any unsold product for a refund after sixty or ninety days. This may be hard to get because of the low price, but it never hurts to ask.

Another low-risk option for a retailer is selling products on consignment. The retailer receives a supply of products without paying for it up front. Some selling space is given up to display the product, but the retailer hopes to get a profitable return. There can be a prearranged time period after which the retailer pays only for the number of product sold and can return the rest or extend the time for the balance. If the product sells well, the retailer can restock or enlarge the display area. If it sells poorly, the retailer can return what's left and owes nothing. This is a good method of testing a new or unproven product with little risk.

The one risk the retailer takes is if a customer returns a product and the retailer no longer sells the item. The customer gets the refund, but now the retailer is stuck with product that it has already paid for and has to try to sell it again. If the product is damaged, the retailer should be able to get a refund from the original vendor, especially if that was part of their written agreement.

Always be on the lookout for special offers and deals that you can make quick or extra profits from. You never know when they will come along, so keep a little reserve available to take advantage of the opportunity. Sometimes the unexpected or unusual situations can really add to the bottom line and bring in new customers.

New Products and Services

As your business grows, you will become aware of other products that complement your current line. You'll also get requests from clients and customers for products and services that they would buy from you. Consider putting a suggestion box in your store or office and a link on your website for patrons to make special requests.

Business Alerts

Customers are always making special requests and expect the retailer to follow through. There should be something new at least quarterly that can keep your business fresh and up to date. Watch what your competitors are doing and stay one step ahead of them to keep your customers interested in your business.

You can be looking for new products and services as soon as you open your business. It's a task that never ends as long as you want to remain the seller of choice in your market.

Many of these new products can be found at industry trade shows and expos. And many manufacturers and vendors will find you shortly after you have opened. You will also get direct mail from other suppliers who have related products. Take the time to look at and investigate anything that can help your new company grow.

CHAPTER 16

Customer Service is King

In This Chapter

➤ Frontline people

➤ Owner contact

➤ Customer service don'ts

➤ Watch competition

➤ Outsource service?

➤ Be outstanding

In this chapter, I will show you what's necessary and expected from frontline employees and why the owner should always be accessible. You will learn how to monitor competitors and their websites and blogs. You'll also learn what you can outsource and how to evaluate the results. You'll see that outstanding service can grow your business more quickly.

The Importance of Customer Service

It's been said that customer service is the backbone of any business, and that without an exceptional level of customer service, the business will come tumbling down. As you start a new business, you must be committed to a high level of service if there is any chance of being a presence in your target market. This is not one of those

Business Knowledge

Without an exceptional level of service, you can't expect customer loyalty in today's marketplace. Competitors will offer great customer service and your patrons will be gone and very difficult to get back. Make outstanding service a top priority in your new business.

"I'll work on it later" tasks; it should be a front and center priority and in place before you turn on your Open sign.

Customer service in larger companies is part of training by the book, and employees come out of that training like robots following corporate controls. You can tell by their canned response and questions. They treat everyone the same regardless of what the customer wants, and they follow the rules to a tee. It's like the big corporate companies saying that customers must follow what their employees are telling them or they can take their business somewhere else. Well, now your new business will be the somewhere else where customers can shop and be treated better. Your new business can be the portal they can use to escape big business. As Jean-Luc Picard said in *Star Trek*, "Make it so."

Be Available for Customer Consultation

Of course, as discussed in Chapter 12, your frontline people have direct contact with customers, and their customer service will have a big impact on whether your customers return to your store or shop somewhere else.

Another part of customer service comes from behind the front lines, at the top of the company ladder. It's you, the owner, who customers want to have contact with on occasion. Don't be too busy to talk to customers, work your retail store, take incoming calls, read some of the website e-mails, and respond to customers. They know that you set the rules that make things happen. So be there for your customers when they need you.

This doesn't mean overruling a frontline employee in the presence of a customer; rather, it means advising the employee on any issues at hand. Even when there's no problem to solve, get out on the floor or on the phone and greet people who support your company. This is time well spent and starts to create a comfort zone for customers and prospects. They know that you make the rules, so they may like to give their input. That input can be very important to a new business that's trying to find the right method to satisfy customers.

Customer-Friendly Hours

I've seen a lot of stores and businesses suffer sales losses due to inadequate hours of operation. These businesses are open only when the owners feel it's convenient for them, not the customers. After all, they own the business, why shouldn't they set the rules? Well, you're certainly within your rights to do anything you want, but aren't you in business to make money and grow? You build a prosperous and profitable business by serving the customer, not yourself.

If you can't or don't want to keep the hours necessary to accommodate your customers, sell the business and get into a different one. If a customer wants to buy a product at a certain time and you're not open, he or she will find a business that is. Now your competitor has your customer's business and there's a good chance your competitor will get the customer's future business too.

Business Alerts

I have seen several businesses that are no longer around because they refused to serve customers when they wanted to shop. These owners chose to let their businesses suffer and eventually caused their demise. Business hours can determine success or failure in many businesses.

Are you willing to take the chance of losing customers just to satisfy yourself? What's the purpose of doing this? The only result will be lost business and lost customers. If you want to leave everyday at 5 p.m. but the business needs to be open until 9 p.m., you must find a reliable person or team to handle those extra hours. If technical or other special product knowledge is needed to serve customers, a trained person must be available. Just having the door or phone lines open isn't enough.

You need to consider your hours even before you open or purchase a business. But most new owners ignore the hours they need to be available for all of their customers. Check competitors and be open for business at least as long as they are, longer if possible. And if you're not there every day at closing time, make sure your employees aren't shutting down five to ten minutes early just to help them get out on time. Many times a customer will rush to a business right before it closes. Don't have the door locked or the voice mail on even one minute before your advertised closing time.

Make your hours customer friendly, not owner friendly, and it will add to your bottom line. Think of your average sale amount and multiply it out for a year. If you lost one or two sales a day, what would the lost revenue over a year be? Do the math, then wipe away the tears. A small business or start-up owner can't afford to lose even one sale.

Breaking Promises

One way to alienate customers and lose valuable trust is to say you'll do something, then you don't do it. It doesn't matter whether you intended to do it but forgot, or just promised something to get a sale. Customers who have had this experience with your business will not forget it and will lose faith in everything else you say or advertise. Why should they believe you? You've already demonstrated that you can't be trusted. About half of them will probably transfer their patronage to one of your competitors who can be trusted. This lost business will multiply if you keep breaking promises and frustrating customers.

How would you feel if a friend said he would meet you at the Italian restaurant at 7:00 p.m. and he still wasn't there at 7:30 p.m.? Or what if your car dealer said that your car would be ready at 3:00 p.m. and the total cost would be $89? Then when you showed up at 3:00 p.m. you found out it wouldn't be ready until 6:00 p.m. and now it's going to cost $265! You buy a health insurance policy that's supposed to cover everything, but your first claim is rejected because of a preexisting condition. Get the idea? Doesn't it make you want to run from that business as soon as you can?

Ask Yourself

If you want to build client and customer loyalty, you must exceed your promises. Without that complete feeling of trust, customer loyalty can waver and disappear.

These types of situations happen every day, and businesses do suffer lost customers because of it. Enough lost customers, and the entire company is in trouble. And all because promises were made and not kept—a situation that should not have happened in the first place and could have easily been prevented.

Customers will look at the promises you make to them as tests of your integrity and honesty. Passing those tests will reinforce their loyalty and put them more at ease in the future. They will begin to feel comfortable doing business with you, and it will be very difficult for competitors to lure them away. But failing the test will result in just the opposite.

If you break your promises, customers will wonder if they can ever believe anything you or your employees tell them. They will look at your products and your advertising and question whether you can be trusted. And don't think that you can only lose one customer because of broken promises. The negative word-of-mouth travels much faster than the positive. By not doing what you say you'll do will also cause you to lose prospects who hear that negative word-of-mouth. And if it happens often, your business will develop a reputation that turns people away.

Watch the Competition

A competitor could be defined as a person or business that wants the same target customer you want. Competitors want customers to buy products and services at their place of business instead of yours. These "evildoers" are after your sales, profits, and long-term loyal customers. They will not give up and are sometimes relentless in their pursuit of your, and everyone else's, customers and clients in their target market. You are also their competition and they protect their customers from your advances. It doesn't matter if you're a new business or not, there is no mercy from competitors who are seeking customers. That is why you need to know as much about your competitors as possible and monitor their marketing.

Questions about Competitors

It doesn't matter if you are a mature business, growing business, or new business, you will have competitors. These are other rival businesses that want to outsell you and outdo you in service, and take your customers. The secret to survival and growth is to know as much or more about them as they know about you. And don't think that because you haven't heard anything from them lately that they are not keeping an eye on you—they are. Your best chance of trumping them is to know what they are doing when or before they do it.

Business Alerts

Competitors are just as goal oriented as you are, and they want to see all their efforts produce results. Don't take their attacks and words personally; it's all business and that's the way you should run your company.

If you know the answers to the following questions, you might keep a step ahead of your competitors:

➤ Exactly who are your competitors? If you're not sure, check the phone book, directories, or the Internet. They are out there and you must find them.

➤ Are they big, small, or franchises? This will tell you the financial resources they have, and possibly the share of the market you're all going after.

➤ Are they expanding or growing? How quickly, and in what areas or regions, are they expanding? Do their websites give you this information?

➤ Where are they? Are they near or far from you, and if you're in retail, are their stores easily accessible? Is their presence felt locally or everywhere?

➤ How elaborate are their websites? Are they selling products or services online as well as from a retail location or through sales reps? Do they take orders 24/7, and how fast do they process those orders?

➤ What are their pricing strategies? Are their prices high-end, rock-bottom, or in the middle? Do they have different levels of pricing?

➤ How many employees do they have? Find out by visiting their stores or offices, and ask people who work for them or are their customers.

➤ How do they pay their employees? High, medium, or low—the quality of their work will be in proportion to their pay. Some may apply for a job with you, and then you will know.

➤ What are their strengths? Can you match or surpass them and compete? What do you need to do to stay in the same ballpark?

➤ How do they market? Through advertising, direct mail, signs, radio, coupons, or not much at all?

➤ Do they have any niche products? Are any of them patented, or can you offer something similar? Are these niche products priced high?

➤ Are the owners on-site? If they are absentee, it will take them longer to respond to your changes. If any of your competitors' stores is run by managers, go in and introduce yourself.

➤ How are customers treated? Be a customer and find out or send a friend to browse. Ask everyone if they have ever dealt with them.

➤ Are their open hours different from yours? Longer and more convenient customer hours can mean more business. Do you need to change your hours to compete?

➤ How do they react to you? When you make changes, do they counter quickly or do nothing? Do they ignore your new business and not consider you a threat?

➤ Why do you feel your new business can be better than your competitors'? Are you offering better products, service, or value, and how will customers know?

If you know the answers to most of these questions, you're a step ahead of most new business owners. And if you haven't shopped your competitors' companies, stores, or websites lately, do so for a bird's-eye view. Don't ignore your competition, because they are watching you. Know what's going on early so you can react in a positive way without panic.

Outsource and Monitor

Outsourcing is great for any business, especially a new one. It saves office or retail space, payroll costs, taxes, benefits, and a lot of time. But there are concerns that go with outsourcing that must be addressed. These great people will do all the work that you need them to do for less than you could do it yourself. The one thing you have to monitor is how they treat and handle your customers. They will be the first point of contact if you're going to use a call center, and you need to know how well they're doing their job. Customers may not know it's a call center and think they are your employees.

Business Vocab

Outsourcing is paying companies or individuals not employed by you to do routine tasks for your business. They must be checked out and monitored to be sure they are performing to the standards you expect.

Outsource companies will train and supervise their employees to give the best customer service they can, that little extra service edge might be missing. That is why you need to check and monitor them periodically. Call in to the response number, visit their offices, and listen to the way they deal with callers. Visit fulfillment centers that ship your products and inspect the packages going out the door. Don't hesitate to change companies if you feel they are not doing the job you expect and are paying for.

Make Your Service Outstanding

Customer service is a broad term with many aspects to it that have to be outstanding for customers and clients to really notice. Just being polite and helpful is not enough anymore because that's what is expected as a minimum. If you don't at least offer that minimum, your chances of survival is slim at most. People don't just want good customer service; they expect it. And if you're not offering it, there are many of your competitors who might be. At this point, price is not what determines where someone will shop.

Visit your competitors' businesses and websites and see what they're lacking in customer service. Do their employees smile, even on the phone, and speak in a pleasant tone that sounds helpful and sincere? Are customers leaving the business with a smile or demeanor that shows they were satisfied by how they were served and treated? Then go back to your business and find a way to step up the way you serve your customers. Since you're running a newer business, you can show that customer satisfaction is on the top of your priority list.

Business Knowledge

Some effects of customer service:

➤ A satisfied customer may tell five people

➤ An unsatisfied customer may tell twenty people

➤ The average company gets 70 percent of its business from existing customers

➤ 70 percent of lost customers say service was the reason

➤ Companies in the UInited States lose 20 to 30 percent of their customers each year

Make Them Say Wow!

In today's competitive marketplace, it's important to exceed your customers' expectations. Here're a few ideas that you can consider:

➤ Offer value plus: Customers expect a good value for the price they paid, but you should still try to offer a little more than they expect.

➤ Be quick: When people decide on a purchase, they want it right away. Don't miss a promised delivery date without offering something in return.

➤ Be friendly and helpful: Be so nice that it hurts—not them; you. People like to shop where they can count on help with a smile if they need it.

➤ Have informed staff: Frontline employees in retail or on the phone should know all pertinent information about every special offer.

➤ Be available: Have convenient business hours to accommodate all customers' needs.

➤ Reward regulars: Repeat customers are the backbone of any business; give them perks and thank them after every purchase.

➤ Refunds and exchanges: Go out of your way to make this process fast and pleasant, and always have a smile on your face.

➤ Find a unique way to make them say *wow!*

Use the Telephone

It may be over one hundred years old, but the telephone still works. Although a lot of people use e-mail these days, that personal *human-to-human* contact is missing. You can't feel that enthusiasm or lack of it without talking one-on-one with someone. The telephone is not exactly high-tech, but it's still the way to convey information with a little feeling attached. E-mail is great for short information transfers and is available twenty-four hours a day, but it can't seem to replace that personal touch. Each has its place in today's business world, so use them wisely and correctly.

Following are some good reasons to use the telephone in today's business environment:

➤ *Check on order satisfaction*: Just making the sale and forgetting about the customer won't lead to automatic reorders. Call customers to be sure they are satisfied, and correct any problems they bring up as quickly as you can.

➤ *Ask for suggestions*: Call customers for ideas on how to improve your products and services. While you're talking to them, thank them for their business.

➤ *Ask for referrals*: When customers are satisfied with their purchases, they should be open to recommending your business to friends and business associates. Don't forget to call your customers and ask them to refer you to others interested in what your business has to offer.

➤ *Offer specials*: Recent buyers may be open to additional purchases if the offer is right. Call customers to tell them about the specials you're offering. Try to gear your special offers to complement a customer's past purchases.

➤ *Customer surveys*: About sixty to ninety days after the sale, customers can be called and surveyed. Don't forget to ask for helpful suggestions.

➤ *Ask for testimonials*: Written or recorded verbal recommendations of your product or service can go a long way in helping to acquire new customers. Some can even be used in advertisements and commercials. Call your customers and ask for them.

➤ *Order processing*: The way to clear up issues with orders that are still in process is to speak directly to the person ordering. E-mail and faxing are fine for communicating facts and numbers, but personal phone contact works best when more in-depth conversations are needed.

➤ *Leave voice mail messages*: Even if you can't get your callee to answer in person, you can still leave a voice mail message. People do listen to their voice mail messages and will hear what you have to say, so be friendly and informative.

➤ *Offer a special discount*: Call customers who have ordered more than once or who have made a large purchase to offer them a special discount. This can build loyalty, which a new business needs to survive and grow. Let them know that only certain customers are receiving this special discount.

Great Customer Service Rules

If you want customers to have the best service experience, bring repeat business, and send referrals, use these guidelines now:

➤ Always listen to your customers

➤ Act on what they tell you

➤ Say thank-you after every purchase

➤ Handle complaints quickly and fairly

➤ Always keep your promises

➤ Don't make promises you can't keep

➤ Keep training and mentoring your staff

➤ Smile when talking to customers

➤ Give more than is expected

➤ Hire superstar employees

➤ Always be available when customers need you

➤ Read these rules again every month and use them

Business Knowledge

Make your own set of rules to follow for outstanding customer service right from the beginning. Read books, listen to speeches on youtube.com, and determine how you and your employees will treat the people who support your business. Put these rules on a sign and post it in your store or office. Bring the rules up at meetings and add to them when you can.

Create Loyalty

What has happened to customer service in the retail business? Big companies don't care; they just advertise low prices to draw customers for one-time purchases. But a small business needs loyalty to keep customers coming back. Common sense tells you to treat customers like royalty because they are. Following are some ways to create that loyalty and most are FREE!

➤ Don't forget to thank the customer every time a purchase is made

➤ Don't argue with a customer

➤ Don't ever try to fool a customer; the joke will be on you

➤ Don't set your business hours to suit yourself instead of the needs of your customers

➤ Don't chew gum or eat when talking to a customer

➤ Don't be too busy to talk to a customer

➤ Don't answer all phone calls with voice mail

➤ Don't forget to reward regular customers

➤ Don't make customers wait to pay you

➤ Don't ignore the long-term value of a customer

The Unresponsive Customer

Some people just want to get their business done and that's it. You and your staff should be able to pinpoint this type of customer right away. Always start with a friendly greeting, and if the customer's response is a mumble or nothing at all, get down to business immediately. You don't know, or need to know, what else is going on in his or her life, so make the sale quickly and professionally.

Be happy to accept your customers' business, their money, and, of course, say thank-you. If they are served and treated the way they want to be, they'll probably become long–term, repeat customers. Never force a customer or client to respond to small talk questions if they don't want to. Provide the sale and service that they contacted you for, and let them go on their way. Give customers the respect and service they want.

CHAPTER 17

Marketing and Publicity

In This Chapter

➤ Cheap marketing ideas

➤ How to get publicity

➤ Using promotions

➤ Careful advertising

➤ Direct mail ideas

➤ Cross promotion

This chapter will show you how to build your new business using all the marketing methods available. You'll learn that anyone can get free publicity, and I'll give you tips to find it. You will realize that you must keep doing some type of marketing during both the good and the slow periods.

Marketing and publicity may be the single most important part of making a new business successful. Without it there may be no business or very few customers or clients. Waiting for customers to come to you will not get you very far in today's competitive business world. You have to go out and get them and sometimes virtually drag them to your business. You know that they will

Business Knowledge

To get cash flow started in a new business you must have customers. And to have customers you need to do marketing, early and often. Start by using the least expensive marketing you can to see what works best for your business. Then expand on those that are producing the best results. But start early and continually keep doing some marketing to produce cash flow.

love your business and the way you treat them once they experience it. But they will never know that if you don't get them in the door or on your website for the first time. That's what marketing and publicity will do. After that first visit, it's up to you and your staff to make customers happy and keep them loyal to your business.

Cheap Marketing Ideas

Most of us start a new business and never budget enough for marketing. But we soon find out that we need to market our company if we want to survive and grow. So look for ways to keep marketing without spending much, if any, money in the process. There are ways to do this if you just look around you and take advantage of every chance you get. Here are a few ideas for cheap marketing:

> ➤ Speak and write articles for publications or media in your industry and offer them free. Put your contact information in your byline but not in the article. Send or e-mail them to publications that may be interested. Offer to speak at local nonprofit meetings.

> ➤ Network at least two to three times a month if you're a new business owner. If you think you're not good at it, keep networking and you'll get good real fast. Have a fifteen-second opening introduction describing yourself at the ready, then practice it. When you're networking, talk 40 percent of the time and listen 60 percent of the time. Don't ever be without business cards, not even at the beach. Attend meetings and events put on by the Chamber of Commerce, BBB, business groups, special interest groups, and networking clubs as often as you can, and join the ones you like.

> ➤ Treat customers like dogs. No, I'm not kidding. Think about how people treat their pets, sometimes better than we treat our relatives and neighbors. And what do we get back for all that wonderful treatment we give our pets? We get an unyielding level of loyalty, even from a cat! Wouldn't you like your customers, and especially your first ones, to feel this type of loyalty to your business? To do this, you must go over and above great customer service.

> ➤ Make a big impression. When you are a new or growing business, there are a few ways to look bigger and more established than you really are. Instead of starting your invoice numbers with 0001, try using five digits and a higher starting number like 22001. It makes you look like you have been in business for a while and had many previous customers or clients.

> ➤ Brainstorm with everyone. Meet with your customers, approach them in your store, talk to them on the phone or e-mail them and find out how they like your

new business and what improvements they would like to see; this is valuable information. Talk to employees, especially those who have contact with customers, ask for new ideas and reward them when you use one of their ideas.

➤ Stay in contact with your suppliers because they have information about your competitors that you don't have. Find out what's new and prepare for them. Offer to give your suppliers more business and get perks in return.

➤ Trade shows and expos on the national level are not cheap, but local expos or meetings are affordable. Showcase your best products and services and hand out literature and promo products. Some local events and meetings may let you exhibit free in return for you giving away a nice raffle prize. Take advantage of any of these opportunities that you can find.

➤ When you have an improvement that everyone should know about, be the town crier. Remember that you don't have to reinvent the light bulb; you just have to make it last longer, use less energy, or shine brighter. Little changes and advances can create big markets.

Free Publicity

When someone or a group says something about you or your business and doesn't send you an invoice, that's free publicity. Since a new business usually has a tight budget (or none at all), free publicity can be a great source of marketing. But since it's free, everyone wants it so you need to go after it whenever you can. It's not easy to get, but it's not impossible either. Make it part of your marketing plan.

Business Alerts

Always be prepared to get publicity wherever and whenever it's available. Have a ten- to fifteen-minute introduction of your business ready for spur-of-the-moment opportunities. Also have someone on your staff ready in case you're not available and don't want to pass up a good chance at publicity.

Following are some tips for using press releases and getting free publicity:

➤ Check the editorial policies and needs of each media outlet in the media directories at your library, and adjust your press release accordingly.

➤ Direct your material to a specific editor by name.

➤ Good timing for publicity on certain holidays or slow days will increase your chances of being used.

➤ Know who reads, watches, or listens to each media outlet to be sure you're hitting your target market.

➤ Follow up with a phone call or e-mail if your press release pertains to an event on a specific date.

➤ Take print media plant tours or studio tours to meet and get to know editors and reporters.

➤ Assume when calling the media that you may be taped, so consider everything you say is on the record.

➤ If you work with certain media on a regular basis, know when their deadlines are.

➤ Have some information available that's not in your release to entice editors and reporters to contact you.

➤ Always include your contact name and toll-free phone number or e-mail address in bold print at the beginning and end of your documents.

➤ Follow up to see who's using your press release.

➤ Request a copy of the publication or broadcast so you can be sure the information was used correctly.

➤ If your information and material concerns a national audience, send it to wire and news services.

➤ Timing for a publication's editorial calendar can greatly increase your chance of being used.

➤ Include some backup information in the press release to support your expertise in the field.

➤ Use double-space copy so the editors have room to make notes easily.

➤ Make sure you have interesting news copy and that it doesn't sound like an advertisement.

➤ If you're announcing a product, show how it's different and offer to send samples for media review.

➤ Offer to appear on radio or TV to be interviewed or to take audience questions free of charge.

➤ If your release relates to breaking news, send all materials via FedEx or UPS overnight.

➤ Before going on a live show, try to spend a few minutes with your host to get a feel for his or her personality.

➤ If your host is acting or asking hostile questions, respond in a cool, professional manner.

➤ Always demand a correction notice or retraction quickly for any print publicity that's inaccurate.

➤ Just because the media hasn't used your past press releases, doesn't mean you shouldn't keep sending them.

Advertise or Not?

A new business should use advertising selectively and look at other types of marketing in the beginning because advertising can be a drain on your marketing budget if you aren't careful. A lot of money is needed to keep advertising in front of a target audience long enough to pay off in sales. You will need to run a series of ads over a certain period of time targeting the same audiences. Don't expect to run an ad on Monday and your phone and e-mail to be going crazy by Friday. Advertising doesn't work that way.

Business Facts

According to Newsweek Media, 48 percent of TV viewers leave the room when commercials come on. Of those who remain, 82 percent do not really pay attention.

Advertise to Four Levels

When dividing up your available budget to spend on advertising for the quarter or year, you should consider looking at four levels. Here's an approach for using your money wisely and effectively:

➤ Existing customers: You're already making money from them and it's easier and more likely they will spend more or purchase new products. Keep them informed of all changes and innovations. Repeat business is the name of the game. Spend 40 to 50 percent of your budget targeting existing customers.

➤ Serious prospects: These people have not purchased from you yet but have come close. They've made several inquiries, browsed your store, or received a quote, and just need a nudge to be a buyer. Spend 25 percent of your budget targeting serious prospects.

➤ Casual prospects: These people have made an inquiry, sent back a postcard, and requested literature, but you never heard from them again—they need more prodding. Spend 15 to 20 percent of your budget targeting casual prospects.

➤ The rest of the world: These are people in your selling world who you have never heard from and who may never be a customer. Spend 10 to 12 percent of your budget targeting the rest of the world.

The part of the budget you're spending on levels two to four should be used to move people to the next highest level until they become customers. The part of your budget you're spending on level one, your customers, is to keep them as customers and attempt to sell them more.

Keep a separate list of prospects in each level and move them up the ladder, hopefully to level one. Be sure to delete those prospects that have moved up from the lower level list, or you'll be duplicating yourself and wasting valuable advertising dollars. If you see more results in one of the levels, continue mailing to that list every ninety days.

Business Facts

According to a survey, 69 percent of newspaper advertisers report little or no results from display ads. Many times a smaller ad or classified will draw response almost as effectively or more effectively than expensive display ads.

Phrases Not to Use in Advertising

The following words and phrases can do more harm than good if you use them in advertising. They will make you look either amateurish or wishy-washy and can have a negative effect on what you're trying to sell. Try to avoid them or reword them to sound more realistic.

➤ We won't be undersold (or underpriced)

➤ You will save big on…

➤ This is unbelievable

➤ But wait, there's more

➤ Remember this

➤ All the brand names you love

➤ We're easy to find at…

➤ Stretch your dollars

➤ Super-duper savings on…

➤ Prices now cut to the bone

➤ You'll love the way we do business

➤ Our friendly employees…

➤ Biggest selection anywhere

➤ We stand behind our products

➤ Check this out

➤ Don't miss this

➤ Special deals on everything

➤ Don't forget us

➤ It's sale time again

Direct Mail Works

For a new start-up business, direct mail may be the most cost-effective way of reaching new customers and clients. I have used it in almost all my businesses and it never failed to pay off. It can provide a faster response than advertising or publicity, although each of those has its place in your marketing mix.

Direct mail reaches more prospects than telemarketing or making sales calls do. Today, many potential customers have their phones on voice mail, so you don't get to make your sales pitch directly. There's an old saying: If you can't get your foot in the door, at least get your mail in there.

And if your headline is good enough to catch people's attention, the rest of the copy might even be read.

Why Direct Mail?

We all know what direct mail is because most of us find it in our mailbox every day. Sending advertisements through the mail has been around for decades and will probably continue for a long time. I've been sending direct mail for over thirty years and have not seen that many big changes. Most of the basics are still the same. The only improvements I've seen are better printing quality and more refined, corrected, and targeted lists.

No matter your business, there should be some direct mail in your marketing plan. No business can afford to get complacent and let attrition reduce its customer base. Customers stop patronizing a business for a number of different reasons; you must add new customers regularly.

The least expensive, street-smart way to do that is with direct mail. As much as we complain, postage in the United States is much less expensive than it is just about anywhere else in the world. And if you presort your outgoing mail, you can reduce the cost even more. The postal service would have a hard time existing without all the business mailers.

Business Facts

Some of the best response to advertising, which includes purchases from direct mail sent to general consumers, falls into four top categories of products and services:

➤ Groceries

➤ Auto services

➤ Apparel

➤ Cosmetics

People expect to receive direct mail and accept it as a fact of life. We grew up receiving it all of our lives. People who really don't want to receive direct mail can request to be taken off any general mailing list. But who wants to go through that much trouble; it's easier to toss out the unwanted mail. And taking your name off of all mailing lists is so final. What you're not interested in today, you may be in six months.

Some advertising mail goes to every address in a series of zip codes and is almost impossible to stop. Wouldn't you like everyone who is not going to respond to your direct mail taken off your list? Then you could mail only to the ones who are interested in your offer, and save all the money you would have wasted on the others. That's why it's important to have several lists to separate your priority targets.

Some form of direct mail can be used in almost any business, even if it's a postcard thanking your customers for their orders. And, of course, on the same postcard you can put another offer or product information. Regular contact with your customers and prospects is an essential part of staying in business, and the results should pay for themselves. Even the smallest business can afford some stationery and a few stamps. It's a minimal investment and worth the effort to see if it works for your new business.

Postcard Mailings

A fast and effective way to reach potential buyers at a reasonable cost is sending postcards. I didn't say cheap, but reasonable; any quality promotion requires an investment. Consider the cost of printing, lists, and postage an investment in your next group of orders rather than an expense. It keeps your company name, products or services, and latest offers in front of the people who are likely to buy them. The buying public, whether consumers or businesses, has a short memory and needs to be continually reminded that you exist. Sending postcards is one way that has been working for many years and is still effective.

Following are a few things to think about that can increase responses when preparing a postcard mailing:

➤ The list: This first and maybe most important factor in any successful mailing is the list. You must target the people who are most likely to purchase your products and services. Test several lists and watch the quantity and quality of the response. Selling snow shoes to people in Florida is probably a waste of time.

➤ The size: Many businesses have been using oversize postcards lately to *get in your face* and noticed. This may or may not work depending on the products. Larger postcards must go at the first class letter rate, which today is 45¢. To pay the postcard rate of 32¢, you must keep the size of the postcard between 3½" × 5" and 4¼" × 6". Use the size that will allow you to include as much information as you need and still be noticed.

➤ The timing: You will need to do your mailings when you feel that your target audience is thinking about buying your type of products or services. You can assume that a standard mailing will arrive in about five to seven days nationally and a couple of days sooner if you're doing a local mailing. Plan in advance and be ready to mail when the timing is best, and give your prospects enough time to order any special offers.

➤ The headline: People get a lot of ad mail in their mailboxes and at offices, so why would they spend time reading yours? A short two- to five-word headline that captures their interest can entice them to read further. Keep it large, short, and to the point, and make sure it can be easily seen. Recipients should want to read more. If they don't keep reading, you have no chance for a sale.

➤ The offer: Your copy must have a real purpose. You need to state why you are sending the postcard and why the recipients should call or visit your store or website. Something new and fresh will get the most response. Be exciting and different from your competitors.

➤ The printing: A commercial printer or broker will produce a professional-looking piece, but that can be expensive. It's best to check out the price and delivery time of several printers before you trust any one of them with your important postcard. Requesting you pay a deposit in advance is fine, but never, never pay in full before you see the finished product. And always request a final proof before the printing starts.

➤ The mailing: You can save on postage by sorting a mailing of two hundred pieces or more by zip code. But if you are sending one thousand or more postcards, consider using a professional mail house for best results. It can sort your list by computer, inkjet or laser print the addresses on your postcards, apply a postage indicia, and deliver them to the post office. And it will usually get your postcards out in twenty-four to forty-eight hours.

➤ The response: Once your mailing is on its way, you must prepare to handle any and all responses. Expect more inquiries or business when the mailing first arrives, and have enough staff ready to handle each response professionally. There should also be a way of tracking how much response you're getting and where it's coming from. Don't get frustrated with too many customer questions; this is why you sent the mailing in the first place.

Well-run postcard mailings can boost business and increase repeat purchases. With a postcard, your customers don't even have to open an envelope; your message is right there when they pick it up. Once you find that your mailing is working, expand it to other prospect lists and do repetitive mailings to your best lists. But each time make a few changes in the headline or the body copy. This type of direct marketing can be a less expensive way to give your start-up business some positive momentum. If it's working, use it often.

E-Mail Marketing

E-mail marketing is the great new way of promoting your business in the 2000s. The cost is minimal and with the right headline it gets read and maybe even acted upon. But the message and the offer must be of value to the receivers so it's not quickly deleted. If you waste their time once, you may not get another chance, so be sure of what you are e-mailing before you hit the send button.

Each time you e-mail the same list of people, the copy should be a little different, or at least the subject line should be changed. You should also give them a way to unsubscribe, because you don't want anyone unhappy with you, whether customer or not. You can find many articles on e-mail marketing and how to do it, but if you follow the advice above, you will always be more successful.

Using New Promotion Ideas

Having some type of promotion going on in your business from time to time can create interest and boost sales. Your grand opening was your first one, but don't stop there. Pique prospects', customers', and clients' interest several times a year.

A promotion can be anything from a new product introduction, special sale, or an ongoing offer to entice buyers. Promotions not only get people to buy, but they increase brand awareness for your business as well. People will remember you later if they are not ready to buy now. This brand awareness builds up over time and makes your business a *first choice* when customers are ready to buy. A new business especially needs this in its first few months to keep cash flow moving in the front door.

Eleven Marketing Mistakes

To keep you from making some common marketing mistakes, take heed of the following advice:

> ➤ Don't try to outsmart the market; you can't make customers buy, but you can change your offer.

> ➤ Don't lose focus; failure to pay attention to your customers' objectives is a big mistake.

> ➤ Don't ignore marketing; you must keep promoting your products and services in both good and bad times.

> ➤ Don't underestimate the need for repeat business; the only way to grow your business and survive in tough times is through repeat customers.

> ➤ Offer stellar customer service; treat customers with honesty, promptness, respect, and a smile.

> ➤ Don't overlook testing; whether it's direct mail or launching new product, monitor the early results before you make a big investment.

> ➤ Don't give up on publicity; free promotion for your business does not happen every time, so keep trying with new ideas.

> ➤ Don't take your eyes off of your competitors; know their changes and offers when or before they make them. Check their websites often.

> ➤ Don't remain stagnant; when the market changes, don't just sit there and watch; be on the cutting edge.

➤ Be street smart; not everything follows the textbook; learn and succeed by doing.

➤ Don't fail to change with the market; you will fall behind your competitors, and it will take a long time to catch up later.

Business Knowledge

Don't overlook marketing as you start your new business; it's more important than you may think. It's nice to have a great-looking store, office, or website, but if no one sees it, what does it matter? Start using all of the different marketing methods, and then decide which ones work best for your company. Marketing is a journey that takes many twists and turns and never ends.

CHAPTER 18

 **Promotions Work**

In This Chapter

➤ Promotion Ideas

➤ Retail Promotions

In this chapter you will learn why promotions can increase customer flow and contact if done correctly. You will see some inexpensive promotions you can use and how to do them effectively.

Ideas for Promotions

Promotions for your business can be anything from a special sale to something outrageous. Always try to be unique and different from your competitors so that people will remember your business. The only limit to the ideas you can use is your own imagination. Always be thinking about your next promotion and how it can help grow your new business.

Promotions don't have to be expensive; they can be inexpensive or even free. In slow times, you'll want to use the second two and spend as little as you can. Similar to free publicity, you want as much exposure from a promotion as you can that will generate sales. Promotions can be anything from coupons, contests, scratch offs, exhibits, games, or events.

Business Vocab

A promotion is anything that you initiate that creates interest in your business. It gets potential buyers to stop and look at what you're offering and enjoy the promotion at the same time.

A successful promotion gets the word out and is well received by the people you are trying to target. If few people know about what you are attempting to do, then few people will participate. Use any and all available ways to let people know about any of your promotions.

Business Knowledge

Putting your product in the hands of potential purchasers is still a great promotion idea. You wouldn't buy a car without driving it, a diamond ring without putting it on your finger, or a treadmill without trying it out in the store. Soap and detergent companies gave away samples years ago and built an entire industry from it, and you can too.

In Chapter 13, we discussed cross promotions with other businesses, scratch offs, mall-wide sales, and other events to promote your business and get customers excited to come into your store or use your services. But sometimes, just a good old-fashioned sale does the trick.

Business Alerts

Cross promotions are great, but be sure you are referring people to a reputable business that provides quality products or services.

Time for a Sale

Shoppers love sales; they're getting something they want and paying less for it. We all like the good feeling we get when we save money. It's the American way—a sale! People will buy things they don't really need or don't need at the time because of a lower price.

You don't want to have the same merchandise on sale all the time, or the regular price will mean nothing. You need to have enough margin in your regular price so that when you reduce it, you can still show some profit. Be sure your store is as full of products as possible during a sale. An empty store makes the sale look unimportant and will fail to attract passers-by. Here are some ideas for running a successful sale:

➤ Choose a name for your sale that will generate interest and curiosity. Don't copy a name that a competitor has used; be original.

➤ Make sure you have enough in stock to satisfy your anticipated demand. People will come to your sale expecting to leave with the product, not a rain check.

➤ Have the merchandise fit the type of sale you're putting on; don't try to sell your leftover swimsuits at a January ski sale.

➤ Your price reduction should be at least 25 percent and as much as 33 to 50 percent if possible. Marking items 10 percent off is not going to entice anyone to make the trip to your store.

➤ Put those items on sale that you've been selling at regular price before the sale and will be selling at regular price after the sale. Marking down popular items will draw people in to see the other marked-down merchandise you have for sale.

➤ Have a time limit; don't let the sale run forever. People will lose interest after a while.

➤ Have big displays of commodity items on sale; it makes it look like you're expecting a big crowd.

➤ Make sure there are a lot of signs in the store and in the windows touting the sale. Hire a costumed character to wave down passing motorists.

➤ Use newspaper advertising if you can afford it, or use an insert with coupons and a map to the store.

➤ Send an announcement to everyone on your mailing list about five to seven days prior to the sale.

➤ Display the related items together; if dresses are on sale, display accessories at regular price nearby.

➤ Let your customers know of an upcoming sale at the checkout prior to the sale. Hand them a flyer announcing the sale and give them coupons if available.

➤ If you have a VIP customer list, give them a two- or three-hour head start on the sale to offer them the best selection. Do this by invitation only, and they'll feel special.

➤ Talk to suppliers and see if they will give a better discount for the sale on larger quantities you may need to stock.

➤ Ask manufacturers of your sale items if they will lend you any display items they have to enhance your store's appearance during the sale.

➤ Tie a sale with something like a holiday or an event happening in your town. Making an event out of your sale may even get you news coverage.

➤ For end-of-the-season sales, see if your suppliers have any leftover related items you can get at a steal and add to your sale merchandise.

Sales are fun, profitable, and can bring new and old customers into your store. If your sale wasn't successful, it means customers didn't value the merchandise even at the sale price.

Learn from each sale, and the next one will be even better. Study your competitors' sales for ideas.

Business Alerts

An effective sale should have a start date and an end date. If you have too many sales too often your sale prices become your regular price. Sales are great cash flow boosters but should be used sparingly, or purchasers will lose interest and not pay much attention to the next one.

Gift Cards

How would you feel if a customer came to your place of business and said, "Mr. Merchant, please take this money from me now, because a friend of mine will come back later and buy something with it. But if she forgets about it, moves away, or doesn't use it at all, you can just keep the money." That would be a good deal, one of the best you can get. And it's exactly what's behind the concept of gift cards. If you're not using this concept to its fullest, you're missing out on easy profits.

Gift cards and certificates are an ongoing promotion and can be used by almost any business—your small business is no exception. Even if you sell big-ticket items, gift cards can be used for accessories or service. They are easy for the gift buyer who hates to shop or waits until the last minute. There is no worry about size, color, or availability because gift cards are always available. It's up to the recipient to do the shopping.

I've always been in favor of the card over the certificate. Cards make your business seem bigger, more professional, and more stable. And with the new small business gift card software that's available, every business can offer gift cards. The software allows you to keep track of the total amount outstanding with the click of a mouse and eliminates fraudulent copies.

Whether you use cards or certificates, don't overlook this profit-making opportunity. And if you decide to use certificates, number them and make them in colors other than black and white. Today's high-tech copiers can make forgeries too easily. And remember that every day is someone's birthday or anniversary—cash in on it!

Do Something Outrageous

One way to get free coverage for your business from newspapers, TV, radio, and other media is to stand out from the crowd. Plan an event or stunt that's not seen every day, and depending on the amount or seriousness of the local news that day, you may get free publicity. It takes research, planning, and a little luck, but it's worth a try. The least you can expect is to be noticed by passers-by.

The media is interested in subjects that are out of the ordinary and newsworthy. You must call, send e-mails, and even mail a flyer to them so they will know what and when the event is happening. What's newsworthy can be interpreted differently by each source. So if you don't appeal to one medium, it doesn't mean that you won't be of interest to others. Make it fun and outrageous, and get the word out!

Business Facts

Surveys show that a promotion can increase retail store traffic by up to 35 percent, but without a good offer when they get to the store, many shoppers don't make a purchase.

Retail Promotion Ideas

Promotions can come in any size, shape, or form and are limited only by your imagination and resources. Here are some ideas you can use or mold to your business objectives. But don't stop with these; try anything you think will work for your business.

➤ Hire a band to play outside of your store

➤ Hold an art exhibit

➤ Have an ice cream social

➤ Organize a parade

➤ Hire a balloon sculptor

➤ Hold free classes or seminars

➤ Sponsor a Guinness record-breaking contest

➤ Reward competitor clippings from yellow pages

➤ Do CD, DVD, and book exchanges

➤ Have a raffle drawing

➤ Hold a trivia contest

➤ Feature costumed characters

➤ Have a dance contest

➤ Celebrate unusual holidays

➤ Have a cutest baby contest

➤ Have a donut-eating contest

➤ Give away lottery tickets

➤ Have safe kids' games

➤ Hand out scratch offs

➤ Give a free gift with purchase

➤ Hire a storyteller or reader

➤ Host a radio station remote site

➤ Have a fill-the-bag sale

➤ Make window displays move

➤ Give away sports tickets

➤ Run a best-cake contest

➤ Give away free samples

➤ Hire a disc jockey

Use these ideas any way you feel they will benefit your business. And don't forget to alert the media for possible free publicity.

CHAPTER 19

First-Year Problems

> ## In This Chapter
>
> ➤ Unexpected happenings
> ➤ Owner attitude
> ➤ Excessive spending
> ➤ Early pitfalls
> ➤ Negative publicity

This chapter will explain and help you deal with many of the things that may occur in your first year of business. It may not be your favorite chapter, but it's necessary to make you aware of what can and will happen to most new businesses. And knowing how to solve, understand, and cope with these situations will help you get through them. You will learn that when unexpected things happen, you can keep a positive attitude, and that you should avoid excessive spending early during your new business growth.

The Unpredictable

Starting a new business is relatively easy, but staying in business is another thing. Owning a business means a lot more than buying a nice sign and ordering business cards. And not knowing what to expect and how to deal with whatever comes up will make the first year more difficult and challenging. That is when many new start-up companies disappear along with the owners' capital investment.

In a lot of these cases, the business can be saved and the problems solved effectively. It's the unknown that frightens new owners who run into situations that weren't in their game plan and catch them off guard. Instead of turning off the lights, locking the door, and escaping to South America, you can learn how to deal with unwanted potholes on the road to success. If you run away, the problems will still be there when you come back.

Business Alerts

Disasters usually come with no warning and no quick solution. They not only affect the owners, but the employees and customers as well. Keep a positive attitude, accept what has occurred, and start working on the way back to normal immediately. Keeping a cool head is the best way to proceed.

The Unexpected

Unexpected events or situations can hold you back or bring your business to a standstill. Having a contingency plan can get you back to normal faster. Following is an incomplete list of potential disasters. Take the time now to come up with some plans so these disasters don't catch you off guard.

➤ Weather related: Tornados, hurricanes, heavy rain or snow

➤ Natural disasters: Earthquakes, tsunamis, volcanoes, and floods

➤ Acts of violence: Terrorist attacks, wars, and military action

➤ Fires: Wildfires and building fires; prevention is the key

➤ The economy: Downturns can and will happen, so be ready to adjust and wait it out

➤ Accidents: Chemical spills, train wrecks, and plane crashes

➤ Crime scene and road construction: If close to your business, it can temporarily close you down

➤ Employee injury: Major job-related injuries can bring a business to a halt; make safety a priority

➤ Utility outages: They seem to happen when you are busiest

➤ Key employee leaves: Always cross train employees so this will not be a setback

➤ Your death: This will happen to all of us; have a transition plan

Some of these may seem a little far-fetched but they do happen somewhere, sometimes. It's certainly better to have some idea of what you might do if an occurrence like any of these catches you off guard.

Owner Attitude and Burnout

Your new business will have a personality and an attitude, and that will come from its owner or leader and filter down. If the owner is positive all the time, the employees and customers will also feel this way. But if the owner has a high and mighty attitude, the staff and customers will back off and business transactions will not be as pleasant as they could be. Customers may back off and look for other places to spend their money.

Ask your staff, customers, and friends to evaluate you in this area and be as honest as possible. You really want to know every negative thing; compliments are useless in this case. Make an effort to change any negatives ASAP, before they do any permanent damage to your business. The longer something goes on, the harder it is to reverse. But being a new business lets you make changes early and quickly.

First-Year Burnout

As I have said before, starting a new business is a little like having a new baby in the family: there's a lot to do and it needs to be done immediately. But working smart, instead of working hard and trying to do everything at the same time, will reap more benefits in the long run.

Many new owners and partners who try to do it all too fast may suffer burnout that can stifle a young business rather than support its growth. Keeping focused on your goals doesn't mean being involved in 100 percent of every activity. Too much constant multitasking will cause something to suffer, and it might be you, the owner. You might be able to do three or four tasks effectively, but try to do eight or ten at the same time and the burnout ogre starts creeping in. The human mind and body can only handle so much at one time, and then it starts to break down and rebel.

Business Alerts

Each person is different, and some can work fourteen hours a day without too much stress. But others will need a break and should take an hour or two off during the day to get away from the business. The business will be there when you get back, and you'll have renewed energy to tackle the tasks that need your attention.

To avoid this first-year burnout and stay on the road to growth and success, you will need to accept the fact that you must delegate some of the business responsibilities. What can't be delegated internally must be outsourced to competent companies that you have researched and approved.

A key employee on your staff can actually make you more money than he or she costs you by performing functions that are necessary and also time-consuming. For many routine tasks, hire part-time employees and use temps for peak periods and one-time projects. By freeing yourself from tasks that don't require serious or creative decisions, you'll have less pressure and more time to work on problem solving and marketing for growth.

For start-up and first-year businesses, problems always seem to arise when you don't have the time to solve them. But somehow they must be dealt with, and sometimes right away. Without some time in your busy schedule, these pitfalls can cause unnecessary stress and pressure on you to solve them and get all your other work done as well. Doing too much, too fast, and too often can cause burnout, and then no one benefits; this may even result in negative consequences.

Don't over-schedule yourself or accept work that you can't do productively while resolving problems and making other competent decisions. First-year business owners often want to try to do more than they can fit into an acceptable timetable. Even if you are willing to work twelve hours a day, don't try to fit in tasks that take eighteen hours.

You will need to block off some time to review how the business is doing and be aware of accounting reports and sales numbers. Some of this can actually be done away from your business location during meals or while exercising. Being involved and working in your business all of your waking hours is not going to make you more successful and may really do more harm than good.

Try to have at least one day a week off (really off) when you stay away from your office or store. Don't even bring work home so you can get involved in some nonbusiness activity. Work on a hobby, play golf or any sport, and spend time with family and friends. You might still think about your business and come up with ideas, but just make notes you can follow up on the next day. Don't let first-year burnout destroy your chance for success in a new or growing business. Give your mind and body the time it needs to regenerate.

Overspending

The title of this section is self-explanatory, or is it? If you don't think you are overspending, you won't make any efforts to curb it. If you see cash flowing out a larger number than it is flowing in, there is likely a problem that needs to be corrected. A new business may have more expenditures than sales or profits in the beginning, but it can't go on very long. You will be covering the shortfall with your start-up capital, but eventually that will dry up and then what do you do? It's best to get a handle on it early and start the adjustments when you see the opportunity to do so.

One area that can eat up cash flow and resources is hiring too many employees. This puts stress on payroll costs, taxes, supervision, and benefits. It is better to start with a minimum number of employees and train them to multitask and assume many duties. You will not only have better employees, but you'll also have people who can substitute for others if they are sick, leave, or are terminated. When tasks become too big for one person to handle, consider hiring a temp or part-time person to fill in. If the workload continues and looks like it will stay that way, then consider a full-time permanent person.

If you allow employees to make purchases for your business, have some limits as to what they can order. On large one-time purchases, ask for all of the information and a recommendation so you can sign off on it. Then you can decide if you really need the item now or if it can wait a week or a month. Don't put a strain on your resources by buying things before they are needed. Tell suppliers when you want something delivered, and don't accept it before that. Don't let excessive or overspending put you in a financial bind.

First-Year Pitfalls

Pitfalls occur in the beginning of many new businesses' growth cycle and must be dealt with. Let's look at some of the first-year headaches I've seen and experienced in over thirty years of starting and operating small businesses. They may not all happen to everyone, but it's likely that some will during your first year of business.

> ➤ Lost customers: It's difficult enough to get new customers. Don't lose them with poor customer service, low value for the money they are spending, inconvenient business hours, ignoring their requests, and failing to say thank-you after every purchase.

> ➤ Employees from hell: If you failed to interview and screen your first employees, they may not be treating your customers the way you expect them to. Either reassign them or replace them, because the overall well-being of the company is more important than any one employee.

> ➤ Excessive spending: If you are spending more money on expenses, equipment, and perks than there are profits coming in the front door, change course immediately. Consider buying or leasing used equipment, computers, and supplies. Don't hire unnecessary personnel that add to payroll and tax costs.

> ➤ No new customers: You should be spending any excess money you have on marketing to your target market. Find the resources to go to trade shows and use direct mail, advertising, and promotions to let potential customers know who you are, where you are, and what unique and special services you can provide for them.

➤ Big competition: Don't let the big guys scare you; they aren't there to put you out of business. They will draw more people into your selling area, and you can specialize in your niche products and services that they can't offer. Shop their stores and websites to find things you can do better, and then do it.

➤ Inadequate cash flow: This means that you have more bills to pay than there is money coming in the front door. Some ways to catch up are to increase marketing to get more sales, delay outgoing payments a few days, ask customers for a deposit if possible, make same-day deposits of cash and checks, and delay ordering supplies until the last minute. Watch spending until sales and profits catch up.

Business Vocab

Cash flow is the amount of money that goes through your business during a specific time period. It's what comes in from the customers and what goes out the back door to pay bills and expenses.

➤ Collection problems: If payments from other businesses are slow, you may need to change some of your invoicing procedures. Specify terms clearly and add finance charges for late payments. If the same customers are always late, consider asking for a deposit before taking their orders.

➤ Bad publicity: This can happen when you least expect it, so don't panic if it does. Find out all the facts and sources before responding. If your business is in the wrong, offer a remedy quickly to get it over with. Don't let unprepared employees talk to the media.

➤ Pricing dilemmas: Setting a fair price for your products and service is always a challenge for a new business. It's best not to be too high or too low until you see how the market responds to your entry.

➤ Suppliers want COD: This can happen if you're a new business or have been slow paying past invoices. Talk to someone higher than the accounts receivable person and make an agreement about getting the COD status lifted, if not right away, then gradually.

Ask Yourself

Instead of trying to decide how to set your prices, look at what you're selling from a value viewpoint. Customers are buying value and will pay what they think the item is worth to them. The more value, the more customers will pay because they can justify paying it. Think about ways that you can increase the value of what you are selling.

➤ Careless bookkeeping: If you're not keeping adequate records of sales, expenses, inventory, payroll, and taxes, you may be in for some unpleasant surprises. If you don't have time or don't want to do it yourself, hire a part-time person with experience in these areas. Paying taxes late causes unnecessary penalties and interest.

➤ Big-order errors: Regardless of who is to blame, a large order that's not quite right is a headache for everyone. Ask if the customer will accept it anyway or at a reduced price, or see if it can be fixed to make it right. Can you negotiate something on a future order, or would someone else buy it? As a last resort, try to sell it at an online auction or to a jobber.

➤ The unpredictable: Severe weather, fires, floods, crime scenes, accidents, earthquakes, and utility outages can close your business for a couple of hours to days or weeks. Rally your employees at an off-site location, plan your comeback, and contact your customers. These things will happen, and you'll never get advance notice.

These are just a few of the challenges that can make your first year in business a nightmare rather than a sweet dream. But don't think that you've been singled out and are the only one that has to deal with these problems. Everyone in business has experienced some of these and other pitfalls that require their immediate attention. Keeping a clear focus on what's happening and where you want your business to go will help you overcome the challenges. Don't be overwhelmed by problems; expect them and deal with them as they come up.

A Bad Publicity Story

This is a true story about a restaurant in a Chicago suburb a few years back. The name has been changed because it has no value to the lesson or the outcome. Watch how the owner used the bad publicity to his advantage and turned it around. This could happen to any business in any industry at any time so learn and remember it.

One spring evening at home, I was watching the ten o'clock news and a picture of a restaurant came on the screen. The announcer then said, "Have you eaten here lately?" I thought nothing of it until I looked closer and realized that I had lunch there two days ago. I had to listen to the rest of the story to find out what had happened there. I ate lunch there three or four times a month, so the story certainly had my curiosity and attention. The story went like this:

Earlier that day at the Kings Table restaurant in suburban Chicago, a lady was having lunch in a booth and a mouse ran across her foot then disappeared on the other side of the room. Well, she screamed and several other people saw the mouse running and got out of their chairs. Needless to say, there was near panic in the restaurant and the manager came out. He heard the story and told everyone there that the food was on the house whether they stayed or left.

Somehow, the health department got wind of the story and arrived a few hours later to do a full inspection of the premises. They found a hole that they thought the mouse resided in and several cockroaches in the kitchen as well as some other violations. They promptly closed the restaurant until everything was cleaned and fixed, which would take a day or two. The owner had obviously let cleanliness go for a while and the restaurant needed a complete work over.

Business Knowledge

When trying to reverse bad or negative publicity, go to the next level. The public will expect you to do certain things, so do much more than expected to rectify the situation. It will show that you are sincere and really care what people think and feel about you.

He could have just had everything cleaned, the equipment repaired, and reopened a couple of days later, but he had another idea. He hired a cleaning company with two trucks and asked them to park in front of the restaurant not just for two days but for two weeks. Everyone who drove by who had heard the story on the news saw those trucks in front of that restaurant every day for the two weeks. Whether they were inside cleaning or not, the sight of the trucks gave a feeling that the end result was going to be good.

The owner had planned to make some face-lift improvements in the near future and decided to do them now as long as the restaurant was temporarily closed anyway. A new façade outside and new floor and painting inside plus new equipment in the kitchen. A new look and a clean restaurant could turn the negative publicity he had received into a positive, he hoped.

When it was time to reopen, he invited the media and other important guests to a special lunch that was not open to the public yet. He needed some news coverage, but this news story was not as exciting as when he was closed down; he needed something to trigger a usable news story that would get him positive publicity.

When he opened the doors for the media lunch, he gave everyone a tour of the kitchen, food storage areas, and bathrooms, which were all spotless. Then everyone took a table in the restaurant area for lunch. After everyone ordered and food started to be delivered to the tables, he did an outrageous thing. He got everyone's attention in the middle of the dining room, got down on his hands and knees and licked the floor. Yes, he actually licked the floor to prove how clean it was. There were many pictures and video taken as he posed again in position. He now had his news story.

Well, many television stations used the story and video on that evening's news. Many newspapers used the photo of him licking the floor and the local paper put it on the front page. He wanted to show everyone that it was clean and safe to eat in his restaurant again, and he chose an outrageous way to do it.

He opened for business the next day and had a line waiting to get in for both lunch and dinner. I went back for lunch a few days later but got there early so I didn't have to wait. He had more business than he had before the negative publicity.

There are some lessons to be learned here that a new business can use not only about reversing bad publicity, but also about doing something outrageous. Your first year can have many sales peaks and valleys, so be prepared with something to attract customer attention. But don't use a mouse in your store—we already know that story.

CHAPTER 20

Trade Shows, Conventions & Conferences

> ## In This Chapter
>
> ➤ Keynote Speeches
> ➤ Attending
> ➤ Exhibiting
> ➤ Seminars
> ➤ Finding Shows

This chapter will stress the importance of attending at least one (preferably more) trade shows and expos in your industry every year. You will learn how you can do this without spending more money than you have in your budget. When to go and when to leave and how to get the most out of the show while you are there. Planning ahead will save you time and expense instead of doing it on the fly. You will want to see all important vendors, hear the seminars and presentations that will most benefit you while enjoying any free meals that are available. Don't skip this chapter because it's very important to your growing business.

General Sessions & Keynotes

These major speeches and informative industry gatherings will give you the latest on what's currently happening. They will have either well known personalities, government officials or association officers speaking for about an hour. They may conduct other business such as giving out awards, introducing prominent people or fundraising auctions for the association or charity. If you have signed up for the entire event and paid the convention or conference

Ask Yourself

Nothing is more exciting than hearing the opening keynote speech. It will prepare you for a great convention or show and make you happy you are there.

fee, you will be invited to these sessions. Some events don't check at the door for tickets and you may be able to walk in if you just have an expo or trade show badge on a lanyard. However, if you are able to get in, it's information you want to hear if at all possible.

Special Dinners & Luncheons

Many conferences, conventions and even trade shows have special dinners or luncheons to introduce a new concept or just entertainment. These are great for networking with people in your industry and exchanging ideas. They are worth attending if possible even if there is a fee or ticket price. The serious people and elite will usually be at these events and you may not be able to meet them elsewhere. This is your chance to exchange business cards and ask questions with key people in your industry.

Attending Shows and Conferences

You need to attend at least one industry trade show or convention every year just to keep up with the current trends and new changes. If there are several available you need to decide which one (or two if possible) will give you the most information for your specific business. You can also alternate each year to a different show if you feel you can't decide between all the shows available in your industry. You don't want any of your competitors getting all the new changes and innovations before you do so find a way to attend at least one. The knowledge you receive will keep you on the cutting edge in your industry and your customers will notice.

Getting the Most Out Of Attending

If your time is limited and the trade show is large you won't get to see everything so you will need a plan to make the most out of the time you have available. Here are some ideas to plan in advance:

➤ Study the show guide in advance and list must-see booths with their floor location

➤ Decide if you want to find new products, new suppliers or visit current suppliers

➤ Make a second list of booths you would like to visit if you have time left over

➤ If you see there is just too much to see for one person, bring a staff member and share the task

➤ Figure out how much time you can alot to each must-see booth so you visit all on your list

➤ Sign up early for seminars and presentations you want to attend before they sell out

➤ Always pre-register for the show so your badge will be waiting for you and you don't have to stand in any long lines

➤ If a booth is very crowded and there is no one to talk to consider coming back later in the day

➤ Contact the top 3 booth companies you want to see in advance of the show and let them know you're coming to see them

➤ If you are really getting behind on time, ask exhibitors to send the information to your office and contact them after the show

➤ Wear comfortable shoes, there's a lot of walking and standing at a trade show

➤ Have a lot of business cards with you and hand them out freely

➤ Have a pen (or two) to jot down notes about some of the exhibitors so you will remember after the show

➤ If you stop by a booth and find you have no interest in them, move on quickly

➤ Make appointments with those special exhibitors you saw to get further information

If you plan ahead and work that play, you will come out of the show with many ideas to use in your business. Be part of all the action; don't just sit on the side.

Exhibiting At Trade Shows and Expos

Some of the reasons you may want to be an exhibitor at a show are:

➤ Increase your sales and profits

- ➤ Announce new products and services
- ➤ Network with others in your industry
- ➤ Get new sales leads
- ➤ Meet and entertain current customers
- ➤ Pick up new distributors
- ➤ Offer show specials and discounts
- ➤ Increase brand awareness
- ➤ Build a new mailing list
- ➤ Find and hire sales reps
- ➤ Check out your competitors
- ➤ Conduct informative seminars
- ➤ Get media publicity

Business Knowledge

Select an exhibit space near an aisle end to get a better amount of people passing by. Being next to a larger booth will also make their visitors aware of your smaller space.

Tradeshow Exhibiting Expenses

Business Vocab

TRAFFIC at a trade show or expo means all the people traveling through the show aisles and visiting exhibit booths

Planning and saving in advance for the many expenses is a must for a new, small or growing business. There will be several different companies or people to pay to get your exhibit ready and installed at the show. Knowing these in advance will allow you to budget for some of them.

It's a good idea to budget about 20 to 25 percent extra for unexpected things that come up - and they will. For example, at tradeshows we've had our display light burn out, an extension cord that wasn't long enough, forgotten items that we had to ship Fed Ex overnight, and forgotten clothing. When you need something in a hurry at a show, you can forget discount-store prices; they've got you, and it's going to be expensive. Just pay it and forget it so you can have a great show.

Here are some expenses you should plan for:

➤ Your booth or space can cost from $1,000 to $4,000 for national shows and that's for the smallest size, usually 10x10.

➤ The exhibit display if you don't already have one. Custom designed ones are expensive but there are some used displays you can add you name and logo to.

➤ Shipping and freight charges from your location to the trade show hall. Ship at least 7-10 days before the setup date and always get insurance.

➤ Staff that will assist you in the booth and meet all the attendees who stop by.

➤ Travel and hotel for everyone who will be working your exhibit.

➤ Food for yourself and any of your staff that is there.

➤ Union charges to setup and take down your display. Most trade shows and convention centers have rules that don't allow you to set up displays or connect electric.

➤ Cleaning fees which need to be done to keep your booth looking good every day. This is usually not too expensive and should be done.

Working Your Exhibit Booth

This is the time all money you have spent will produce the results you expect and need. As they say in Vegas, "it's show time" and you get to participate. Here are some suggestions to get the best results from your exhibit booth:

➤ Keep the front area of your booth clear at all times

➤ Dress professionally and check your teeth in the restroom

➤ Don't sit behind a table, stand with a smile to greet passersby

➤ Have water and mints in your booth to refresh yourself and staff

➤ Don't eat food in your booth, it's bad manners and it looks terrible sitting there while you are talking to someone

➤ Greet visitors with a simple hello and give them time to look around

➤ Make sure you have enough staff in your booth to handle expected visitors or they will walk away

➤ Ask for a business card from visitors and make notes on them for future reference

➤ Consider a demo or video to attract attention and explain your products or services

> ➤ Never leave your booth unattended

> ➤ Ask visitors if they would like to take your literature with them or prefer you to send it later

> ➤ Have a contest drawing, for a novelty item that everyone will like or can use

> ➤ Take a short break every two hours if there is someone left to handle the booth

> ➤ Don't turn your back to the booth entrance, move to the side if talking to someone

> ➤ Have a last minute pep talk with any staff before the show opens every day

> ➤ Try to create some excitement in your booth to attract media attention

> ➤ Take photos and video of your booth in action!

After the Show

Make all the follow up calls that you promised quickly before interest is gone. Do a mailing to everyone who stopped by your booth thanking them and asking if you can contact them again. Get all the literature that people requested to them as soon as you can and follow up about 10 days later. Sort through the collected business cards and divide into groups by most important. Debrief your staff who was there to see if you know everything that happened. Meet with all your staff and relive the show for everyone so they will know how to handle anyone who contacts you. Lastly, decide if the show was worth exhibiting at and, if yes, start planning for the next one.

Seminars

Seminars and workshops can be divided into two groups; ones you attend and ones you lead. There are great reasons for being involved in both of them at conventions, conferences or trade shows.

Seminars by Others

Presentations and workshops that you can attend free or by paying for the conference are usually timely and informative. They can offer solutions, new ideas or teach you new methods of marketing and sales. Many events run concurrent seminars or breakout sessions where you can choose from two or three presented at the same time. Many of the speakers are paid and bring value that the show management believes can benefit all attendees. I have done many of these and research the industry so I can customize my presentation to be relevant. When these are available, it is wise to participate in as many as you can.

Seminars By You

One way you can speak or conduct a seminar at an event is being hired by the meeting planner to give a specific presentation and are paid a fee for doing it. If you are an expert in a field of interest to the industry, you will be worth being paid to share your expertise.

Another way is done at trade shows if you are an exhibitor with a booth. You may be able to give a 30 to 45 minute presentation on your products, services or what you can offer to the industry. These seminars are not paid because your reward will be any additional business that you get. You may have to solicit people to be at your seminar because some will know it's a live infomercial. Try to entice them by offering to show or explain something different or outrageous. Be sure to invite people to your booth where you have a one-on-one with them and find out what their needs are. Almost anyone attending the trade show or expo can go to these seminars without cost.

Finding The Right Shows

You need to select the best shows for attending and exhibiting. The shows you attend may be completely different from the ones where you want to exhibit. But always attend the shows that are within your industry, especially if you're not exhibiting. You need to know what's new, who's there, and what's happening. Other shows and conventions to attend are ones that you have an interest in, can learn from, or may find suppliers at.

There are many internet sites that list upcoming trade shows, expos, conventions and conferences. If there is an association in your industry, start there. They probably have a yearly event. Otherwise, search the internet using TRADESHOW followed by your industry name or description. You should have several choices from which you can select at least one to participate in.

CHAPTER 21

New Business Tips and Ideas

In This Chapter

- ➤ The slow times
- ➤ When times are good
- ➤ Advantages of being small
- ➤ Joining groups
- ➤ Other tips and ideas

This chapter will share some of the experiences needed to cope with opening a new business. What you read here did not fit into any other chapter but will help you plan and execute the operations necessary to get a business going. And when situations not previously discussed arise, this chapter will offer you some choices.

You may come back to this chapter often to reread some of the ideas and tips. They are not in any particular order, and I've included as many as I feel you can use in a new and growing business.

Business Slowdowns

Periods of slow business are a fact of business life and can happen for any number of reasons or maybe no reason at all. It's what you do that will get you through them to the next boom time. You could just give up and go hibernate somewhere, but that's silly and not what you started the business for in the first place. Slowdowns force you to come up with new ideas and ways of doing things. You may even keep these new procedures when the slowdown is over. Let's look at some ideas for slowdown periods that may help your young business get back on the path to growth.

Temporary Slow Periods

If your business will have cycles of slow months or periods, you should cut back on expenses rather than plan trips or vacations.

The owner of a small business can pitch in during slow times and even reduce the hours of some part-time people. Many times in my business with fewer than five employees, I would be the one who remained at the end of the day during those slow periods. I answered the few calls that came in and got firsthand exposure to callers' questions. I also tried to reply to most e-mails the same day. I was able to see what my staff was getting inquiries about.

Slow periods are also good times to analyze past performance and see if changes need to be made. They're also good times to look at reducing inventory, which you can build back up just before your busy period.

Take this opportunity to look for new products to sell during your slow times. If business is slow every summer, try to find something new that sells best during that time; something that will be of interest to your regular customers and get them to visit or call. Test several products and see what works best for your type of company. Then next year it may not be as slow in the summer, and you'll have a chance to make extra profits.

Business Knowledge

Almost every business has a slow time of year or days of the week. Plan to offer your best promotions for those periods. People may change their buying habits if the promotion has value to them.

So you really have two choices for slow periods. Either run away and hide until it's over, or do something about finding additional sales and profits. Obviously the second choice is the correct one. Finding products that sell during your slow times will add to cash flow rather than drain from it. You might just get lucky and find a new direction your company can pursue.

In our plastic card business, the summer months were the slowest time of the year, and I was always on the lookout for a compatible product to promote during that time. We came across the idea of scratch-off game cards that restaurants and fast-food places buy or order in the summer for fall promotions. As of this writing, we're getting a lot of response from a direct mailing that went to over 5,000 food establishments with three or more locations.

We're also looking into other customer groups with test mailings. Although we are getting new business this year, we hope it will really increase next summer with a little advance planning. So I think I'll hang around during the summer and monitor the results. It looks like scratch offs will turn into a year-round product that fits nicely with our other products. Slow periods are a good time to test new products and services to see if they can be added permanently.

A Serious Slowdown

A recession or business slowdown is not the end of the world, although it may seem like it. You can and will get through it if you make some adjustments and don't run and hide. Keep your business in a recession-prevention mode during and after an economic slowdown. Don't worry about what your competitors are doing; some may not even be around next year. Be smart, be cool, and you could come out of the slowdown stronger than ever. And don't give too much credit or concern to what the news sources are saying; they love disasters and can cause too much negative thinking. Don't panic and don't overcompensate for things that haven't happened yet. Here are some ideas to get you past the recession blues:

➤ Don't go price-reduction crazy: Lowering your prices too much won't always increase sales and cash flow. You must make profits to pay your expenses.

➤ Promote, promote, promote: Keep your name and offers in front of your target market even more. There are people buying and you want to be their destination.

➤ Outsource more: Find more services and products that can be performed by others. If payroll and health care costs are a burden, consider hiring temps and subcontractors.

➤ Cut costs slowly: Big, drastic cuts can also reduce services and delivery to customers. Be cautious and think each cut through carefully.

➤ Add related products and services: Think about what else your customers purchase and if you can offer it and make a profit. Ask your customers what they want, and then find it.

➤ Reduce inventory: But don't reduce inventory so much that you will inconvenience your customers. Keep fast-moving products at a level so they're always in supply and reduce the slow-moving ones.

➤ Keep marketing regularly: See if there are new or less expensive ways to entice new prospects. Test several first before you overcommit, and expand the ones that bring you new sales.

➤ Reduce travel expenses: Travel only when it's necessary. Use the phone or the computer for conference meetings. Skype is getting very popular and can be used for meetings.

➤ Focus on service: Customers will continue to buy from businesses that really care about them. Show your customers that you value their purchases and provide that little extra with a smile.

➤ Watch the news and industry publications: Have any of your competitors gone out of business? If so, go after their customers.

➤ If cash flow is slow: Try to negotiate longer terms with your suppliers. If you give them a good volume of orders over a long period, they will likely work out new terms.

➤ Keep your staff positive: When staff and owner keep a positive attitude, especially in front of customers, patrons will feel that this is where to spend their money.

A smile can go a long way to show you care, even if you're not in the mood.

Business Alerts

Paying employees who you don't need because of slow periods can be a serious drag on your cash flow. You must cut their hours or put them on furlough until business picks up.

Unnecessary Personnel

When the business slows down, you'll probably have people on your staff you really don't need. Keeping them on the payroll will be a drain on your cash flow and add expenses that you don't need. So you must do something to reduce this outflow of valuable cash. Most owners hate to let anyone go, especially if they're long-term employee and have been doing a good job. But you have to think of the health of the business first because without it, no one has a job. So sacrifices need to be made, and you, the owner, must decide what will be sacrificed. It's not the most pleasant part of your job, but it has to be done.

Before you open the door and point you, you, and you, stop and plan what you really need to do. Figure out how many total hours you need to cut, and see if you can accomplish it by taking a few hours from a lot of employees. This may be hard to do though, if they're not paid hourly. You can also hold a meeting and explain the situation to all employees as a group. Then ask for any volunteers to take extended time off and be called back when things pick up.

Also, be on the lookout for anyone you think may soon be leaving the company on his or her own. There's nothing worse than putting good people on furlough, then one of the remaining employees decides to leave. Before you lay off someone, listen to the grapevine; do you hear grumblings coming from someone? If so, sit down with that person and ask if he or she is planning to leave the company. Most people will admit their intentions and let you save someone else's job. Offer to write people in this situation a letter of recommendation, if they are worthy. They can carry this with them to future endeavors and will always remember you as being honest with them. You never know, some of them might end up in a position to be a customer of yours.

There's always a chance the people you let go will go to your competitors. You may want to remind those you lay off that certain information that would hamper your recovery and give unfair advantage to competitors is considered confidential and doesn't leave the company.

Let your exiting employees know that you appreciate their past work and under other circumstances you wouldn't want them to leave. You can ask each of them privately before they leave if you should call them back if business improves. The answer you get will give you an indication of how honest and loyal they will be when they leave. You can also inquire who would be available if you get surges in sales and need more people on a temporary basis. You can explain that they shouldn't just sit around and wait for you to call, but look for another position right away. Then if your turnaround takes longer than you expected or doesn't happen at all, you will have a clear conscience.

Buy Your Umbrella When the Sun Is Shining

Isn't it great when your business is doing well? You can't wait to get to work to see how much money you're going to make every day. If you worked hard and long for many years, you don't ever want to go back to those tough beginning times again. You want to just keep making money at a fast pace and increasing growth every year. That's the way it's going to be, so let's go on a cruise and have fun for two weeks.

This is why the small business person puts in all those hours at a low income to build a profitable business. If you stick to it and persevere, you finally reach the light at the end of the tunnel. But you don't really want to go back and travel that tunnel again, do you? So how do you keep from sliding back into the tough times when just staying in business was a real challenge? You have to plan for the difficult times ahead, whether you think they are coming or not. It's sort of like going to the dentist to get your teeth cleaned. You may not see its importance when you're doing it, but you will wish you had if problems arise later.

Plan and prepare when times are good and when the money is there because if and when things change, the money may not be available. Here are a few ideas you can use to be ready for any downturn:

➤ Pay down any credit lines you have so they are available when you may need to use them again. Also ask for credit limit increases, which you may need in the future.

➤ Reduce balances or pay off any company credit cards you have. This will release more available credit and save you that high interest you're paying.

➤ Put money away in a company mutual fund, especially if the market has been down lately. It may even appreciate before you need it. A money market fund is the next best choice.

➤ Prepay insurance premiums so they won't become a burden later. You may even get a small discount by paying in advance.

Business Vocab

Prepaying expenses is the practice of paying more than is required for fixed and variable expenses. This can be done to receive a discount or to prepare for a coming cash flow shortage.

➤ Stock up on stamps or fill your postage meter when excess funds are available. This is a necessary expense that won't creep up when funds are short. Stamps and postage are good any time and can be listed as an asset under prepaid postage.

➤ If you are paying your suppliers very well or early, you may be able to negotiate better terms or discounts. If you speed up their cash flow, you are going to move up on their favorite customer list.

➤ Buy miscellaneous items you know you'll need in the future when it's on sale. This is the time to take advantage of all those bargains you get offers about.

➤ Upgrade computers or buy software and features that you have delayed getting. The future of communication on computers may be Skype, and now is the time to install it.

➤ Do any needed manufacturing and office equipment maintenance. Breakdowns during tough times can be a real disaster. Review all warranties and get preventive service done.

➤ Stock up on expensive office supplies such as copier and laser toner. Buying other supplies and forms in larger quantities can also offer a savings.

➤ Do any research or product testing when you can easily afford to pay for it. The secret to reversing a downturn later may be offering a new product or service. Be ready to move ahead quickly.

➤ Test new mailings or direct mail pieces when you can easily pay the extra postage. You'll be ready if market conditions change and you need a quick influx of new customers.

➤ Test new advertising venues that you have been wanting to try. Check into print, broadcast, and Internet ads to see if they will help your business grow.

Don't wait until it starts raining to buy your umbrella; have several of them in the closet. Just like the weather, the sun can be shining one minute and shortly thereafter the storm can start. And remember, it even rains in the desert once in a while, so don't think it won't happen to you and your company. But if you're smart and prepared, you can dodge those puddles and survive until the sun comes out again.

Being Small

You may not feel that you get a lot of respect in the business world by being small, but think about it. There are over 15 million operating small businesses in America, and they create most of the new products and inventions. They also hire more employees and treat them better than most of the big guys do. They offer more job security because employees become a real part of the business. See, small business isn't so bad after all.

Small Can Be Great

Most small business owners never plan to get really big and become billionaires. They may have goals of becoming big small businesses, though, which is different. Entrepreneurs who built companies like Microsoft, Subway, Starbucks, and, more recently, Google, never had any intention of being small, let alone staying small. But your average business owner knows that those goals are out of reach for most of them. They are not willing to put the time and every penny they own into it over a long period, which is fine because success comes at all levels.

But growing a profitable small business doesn't mean you can't enjoy most of the luxuries of the good life. I know of quite a few owners whose income has reached the six-figure range. They enjoy their work and still have their ups and downs like the rest of us. They have many long-term key employees whom they can rely on and turn to for advice. The longest and most loyal people on their staff are most likely to be well paid and get perks they could never receive from a larger corporation.

A small business doesn't only mean a mom-and-pop store; it can also be a company with one hundred or more employees, or a retail operation with several locations. A profitable and well-run small business can provide everyone involved with a great place to work and a comfortable income. It's the feeling of security and being part of the action that will make the best employees stay. So be proud to own and operate your small business—there are many people in the world who would love to trade places with you.

Ask Yourself

Remember that being small but growing is a privilege that only a few people will experience in their lives. Many will work for large corporations and never be in control or get to use their ideas. Most of us can have a great life and live comfortably with our income from our small business. Smile every morning you open the door to a new day because you are in control.

Small Business Can Mean Big Business

When looking for new business for your company, the first place you may have a tendency to look is at the bigger corporations. Are all the best new orders only from big customers? Do you feel that smaller customers are not worth the effort or are too much trouble? Did you know that smaller clients and customers can build your business faster and let you sleep better at night? Don't overlook the profits from small business—they can be much bigger than you realize.

Once you know the value of small businesses, you then need to know how to serve them and keep them happy. Their needs and wants can be the same as large corporations but on a smaller scale. Or they may have completely different needs that you will have to address. If you're not sure what those are, you will have to contact some of them and ask. Don't try to force products or services that you previously supplied to larger companies on them—the response may be negative. Your best chance to capture and keep small business accounts will be by treating them with care, concern, and outstanding customer service.

Although small business owners want the same competitive prices that everyone else does, they can't expect the rock-bottom numbers that large corporations do. Keep prices fair and equal to the value you are providing to them. Don't deliberately overcharge them, or you may lose them forever. If they feel that they are getting fair prices and great service, they can become much more loyal than the larger companies. You can create an ongoing business relationship that can be beneficial to both parties. Smaller customers will have less personal transfer and turnovers in their buying positions, so you can get to know your contacts better. Many relationships between customers and suppliers can go on for years without interruption.

Another advantage of having small business customers is mistakes aren't so impactful. Let's face it, mistakes will happen, and they can jeopardize your customer relationship. With smaller orders, the cost or loss will be less to repair. And in the unfortunate case that you even lose a customer, it won't cripple your company. A major mistake on a large order with a major corporation can be a real disaster. It can cost more than you can afford and put your business in a serious hardship position.

Since most of you reading this are also small businesses, think about what you really want in a key supplier. What will keep you as a customer for the long run? Well, the people you sell to in other small companies want similar quality in their products, value, and service. Loyal customers should demand and receive more attention. Don't overlook the smaller accounts; they may be the ones that help you grow the most.

Join Up!

Joining associations, the local Chamber of Commerce, the Better Business Bureau, and other business groups will give you a lot of advantages over competitors. You will get to exchange ideas and learn from other businesses that want to help you succeed. It's best to attend a couple of meetings first to be sure it's advantageous and you enjoy them. Once you join, though, go to the meetings and contribute.

Join the Chamber of Commerce

If you're not already a member of your local or state Chamber of Commerce, consider joining. Valuable information is exchanged between business owners and representatives at Chamber of Commerce meetings. Where else can you find out what's going on business-wise in your town or state in a semi-social atmosphere? You'll meet and share ideas with people you would probably never approach otherwise.

Let's take it another step and say participate in your Chamber of Commerce's or business organization's functions. Be a part of the action and go on the golf outings, join a committee, or run for office. These activities don't take up as much of your time as you might think, and you may get out of it more than you put in. By participating, you'll have a say in what you want to see your organizations offer.

The more active members a Chamber of Commerce has, the more influence and power they will have when unfavorable legislation is introduced. They will work together as a team to keep the business community profitable and livable. The old adage that there's strength in numbers is certainly true. Most chambers of commerce and business organizations keep their dues reasonable so even the smallest stores and businesses can afford to join. Many times a smaller business owner can offer ideas that the bigger companies never thought of. Everyone should be equal and treated the same at a Chamber of Commerce meeting. You're all there to share information that will help your businesses.

The Chamber of Commerce is a great place for a new business owner to find out about a city or community and meet other business owners. There may be unique dos and don'ts that will assist a person new to the area. Chambers of commerce usually welcome new members with open arms, so don't be bashful. Many will let you attend a meeting without joining so you can see the organization in action. Don't operate your business with blinders on—join the crowd!

Business Knowledge

You may have heard the saying when the water rises, all boats rise with it. This is the objective of business groups and organizations. No one knows everything, and sharing ideas and information can only help everyone involved. Find one or two that you can join and participate in as many meetings as you can, and your business will prosper from it.

Toastmasters

When you own a business, manage a business, sell products or services, teach students, or want to be a professional speaker, you need to start at Toastmasters. It's a club or group in your home town that usually meets once a week at various times. You will easily conquer your fear of speaking in front of a group of 10 or 1,000. Once you start, you will anticipate each coming meeting and your next speech, which usually occurs every three or four meetings. You'll have a manual that will outline your objectives for each short speech in front of the group. Don't panic yet; everyone is there to encourage you, and you will get a standing ovation after your first speech of four to six minutes, which is called the icebreaker.

It's getting to that first meeting that is the step you need to take right away. Go to toastmasters.org, type in your zip code, and many clubs will come up. You can either call the president of the club at the number shown or just show up; you'll be welcomed with open arms. You may want to check out several different clubs in your area before selecting one to join. And you will decide to join after a couple of meetings because it becomes sort of addictive. Actually, some people join two clubs to go to more meetings and progress faster.

Each meeting lasts only seventy-five to ninety minutes, and it's fast paced. The person in charge of that week's meeting is called *the toastmaster* and will provide an agenda for that day. There will be two or three short speeches and each will have a person evaluating it. Then there are *table* him or her a subject or question to talk about. It's very short, but it makes you think quickly and improves your mental dexterity. All speeches and table topics are timed, and you see a stop light with green, yellow, and red lights so that you know when to stop speaking.

Business Knowledge

Toastmasters can help *anyone* from executives to bottom-level employees be better in their business position. You will learn to speak better, one-to-one, in meetings, for sales, and to groups.

When you join Toastmasters, you will receive your first *Competent Communicator* manual with ten speeches outlined in it. Each one advances you along a little more toward becoming a good speaker. When you finish the first ten speeches, you will receive a certificate from the Toastmasters' headquarters, which will be presented to you in front of your club. You then will select advanced manuals to continue your progress. By this time, your confidence and style is no longer a fear to you and future speeches show it. During each speech, the ah-counter will count any *ahs, ums, and so's, you knows, etc.*, but by the fifth or sixth speech, you won't have very many.

So how do I know all this about Toastmasters? Well, I've been a member for about four years now. And it took me only nine months to do my first ten speeches and get my certificate. I learned the correct mechanics of speaking in front of a group of two or ten or two hundred people. I anticipate every meeting and fill a role even if I'm not a speaker that day. It's great to see how quickly new members progress with all the help and encouragement from everyone there. But most of all, I enjoy the meetings because they are fun! There's a meeting waiting for you right now in your home town, so make that first step.

Other Ideas

When you get ideas for your new business and even as it grows, record them immediately. There's a good chance that you'll forget them if you don't. You will meet and talk to people everywhere, and you never know when a great idea will show itself. Keep a notepad and pen bedside in case you wake up with an idea you want to try. In my thirty years of owning many businesses, most of my ideas came from doing, seeing, and talking to people everywhere. Always keep your ears and eyes open and ready for the next idea that may be near.

Where Are Your Business Cards?

I can't believe all the professional people I meet who don't have extra business cards with them *at all times.* I assumed it was a no-brainer to always have some with you, but I guess I was wrong. When going on a sales call or entertaining clients in your office, business cards are part of the procedure, but what about nonworking hours? Do you refuse to discuss business and not meet a new prospect or client? Can a new customer only be found during working hours? Of course not; we meet all types of people during our everyday lives, all the time.

Our first line of offense is usually our business card. And if you don't have one, it makes the person you meet wonder how prepared and organized you are. If you can't even produce a business card, how can you be expected to do the job you represent? It doesn't matter whether or not you're in sales; you are your company when you are discussing business.

Business Knowledge

Business cards are an inexpensive way to promote your business and be remembered. They should be given away freely and left anywhere you can leave them. That one great call or e-mail you get will make it all worthwhile.

One evening when I was working at our ice cream store, a couple came in and sat in a booth. Being a cold weeknight in January, business was slow, so we started discussing small business. The man was telling me that he was a CPA and specialized in small business. Since I had a couple of businesses and felt neutral about my accountant, I thought it would be a good idea to save his business card. It's sometimes difficult to find a CPA who specializes in small business clients just by looking in the phone book.

I asked for his card and he fumbled around looking for one. When he didn't produce one, he asked for something to write his information on. I handed him one of my cards and he wrote his name and phone number on the back. His printing was a little sloppy, so one of the numbers was difficult to make out. And of course there was a small ice cream stain from the hot fudge sundae he was eating.

I took the card, put it in my pocket, and didn't really expect to call him or save it. If he didn't value his own service enough to have business cards with him, why should I? And by the way, he didn't even ask for one of my cards so he could follow up himself. He may be a good accountant but not too many people will find out. His business will likely grow slowly because he's not taking advantage of all the opportunities that are available. Why pass up a chance to acquire a new client or customer when the effort is so easy?

You should always have extra business cards in your pocket or purse, wallet and car for those unexpected meetings. Be ready when the opportunity presents itself and grow your business. Otherwise, you may be passing up an opportunity that won't come along again.

Give Discounts Cordially

If you are going to use coupons, loyalty rewards, or special discounts to boost sales, take them cheerfully. There's nothing worse than treating a new customer poorly because he or she is using a coupon and not paying regular price. You've enticed them to buy from you and made them feel guilty for getting a discount. What are the chances of them being a loyal customer? Probably not too high if they feel you're not happy about selling at a lower price.

You made the decision to use coupons or discounts, and they worked! They brought new customers to your business, so make them feel welcome. This is the time to put on your professional friendly face. They are new customers who if treated well can help you build your business for a long time. They might not have found you without the coupon, but now they're here. It's foolish not to take advantage of it.

Don't skimp on quantity or quality in an effort to recoup the discount. It will surely show through and the customers will feel uneasy and slighted. And that type of feeling will not be a stepping stone to getting long-term loyal customers. Make them happy that they chose your business and were able to try your product or service and save money too.

A good approach to take is after a customer uses a coupon or discount, completely forget about it. In your mind he or she is just like anyone else who called or came in your door. After all, you hope the customer comes back and purchases at the regular price next time, so treat him or her that way.

Home Business Meetings

If you have a home-based business and need to meet with a client, what are your choices? Most likely, you don't want them coming to your small in-home office, so you need other options. Your first thought might be their office or place of business and that's great, if it's available. But what if they are in the same situation as you or just want to get out of the office? You need to find places that will give you the privacy, quiet, and room necessary for the meeting at hand. Selecting the incorrect site can put a damper on an otherwise successful plan.

Ask Yourself

You want to go to a quiet and professional place to meet your clients and customers. But what if there's a problem when you get there? Always have a backup location in mind.

Here're a few suggestions for off-site meeting places where you can get down to business:

> Go to a restaurant during the off-hours. Select the type of restaurant that most fits your type of client and that you know offers great food and service. Request a table away from other guests and not too close to the kitchen door.

> For shorter meetings or when a lot of table space is not needed, try a hotel lobby. Most nice hotels have comfortable chairs and coffee tables that aren't being used often. Be sure to purchase coffee, orange juice, or a soft beverage so you're then a customer of the hotel. A light snack or a hors d'oeuvre tray is another option. Don't go during happy hour when it's noisy and there are too many other people.

> If you're a taxpayer (aren't we all?) you can sign up for free use of a small meeting room at your local library. Your library card number will be the key, and there should be no limit to how many times you can do this. Just plan enough in advance because the rooms get booked often and quickly.

> If you live in an apartment complex, gated community, or large condo building, it may have a meeting room or club house. During normal working hours, such rooms are not used very much and should be available on short notice. If you don't live where these are available, ask a friend who does if he or she can set it up for you as a guest. Most management companies won't object if the room is left clean and the meeting is short.

> For short, informal meetings, the local park or river walk could be the answer. Specify a favorite bench or attraction area and be there a little early. This is fine for brief discussions or to hand over literature and quotations. But have an alternate choice ready if the weather turns bad.

Meetings with clients are important when going after that first contract or sale. Find a place that best suits your business and type of customer. Get that face-to-face exposure that can be the start of a long-term business relationship, and don't forget your smile.

High Rollers

High rollers, meaning customers who buy a lot of your products or services, can be a plus or a minus. Of course you want the sales, but at what cost? Most of your big customers will be happy with great products, service, and competitive prices. But others will demand more and push you to your limits or into a corner. These are the ones that will make you question if they're really worth it. Is the gain you receive worth the cost and aggravation that is needed to keep that customer?

The first consideration is obvious: are the troublesome high rollers profitable? Do you make money from them, and can you serve them without additional expense? Most businesses offer some type of discount or reduced price for large purchases, and that is fine. The larger sale allows you to purchase or manufacture at a lower cost and increases profits across the board. But what, if anything, do you have to give up to get those sales? Normally a little recognition of the high rollers' importance to your company and calling them by name will satisfy them. Remember, they need to make this large purchase somewhere, and if you make it easy, affordable, and friendly for them to buy from you, why should they change?

These high rollers are usually very busy and the purchase or order from you is just one of many things on their to do list. So the easier you make it for them, the more likely they are to return. Even assigning a special person or account number can reduce any stress or confusion during repeat business. Your employees should know who these high rollers are and how to handle them correctly. Don't let a novice or trainee get involved and frustrate them. Have a plan or special procedure in place for them.

Don't allow high rollers to tell you how to run your business. Suggestions are great, but demands are not. Offer a competitive price and VIP service, but don't let *them tell you* what they are going to pay. Several big discount stores have tried to do this to smaller suppliers and backed them into a corner. If their demands put your company in trouble, and you end up unable to meet them, they'll be the first to walk away and go to your competitor. Don't ever put your company in this position; you may not survive. And don't beg for their business—just offer your best products, service, and price.

Once you have a high roller on your customer list, a few perks and extras are OK. Birthday, anniversary, and holiday gifts are always a nice touch. But don't make any gift or extra look like you are buying their business; you just want to thank them for it. And never offer gifts before a sale is made; it looks like a bribe, and you don't want to give that impression. A personal acknowledgement or note from the owner goes a long way toward showing them that their business is appreciated.

Profitable high rollers are always in demand, so don't take the good ones for granted. Your competitors are always out there trying to lure them away from you. Don't let long-time, regular high-roller customers get lost in the shuffle; give them the recognition and service they deserve. They will keep you happy with increased sales and profits.

Be a Radio Guest

Being on the radio as a guest is a great way to promote your company. It can give you a lot of exposure that you can't get any other way. If you do it right, people will listen and remember what you had to say. Practice makes you better, and rehearsing with a friend or associate before you're on the air will get some of the bugs out. Here are a few other ideas to be a success on the radio as a guest:

Business Knowledge

Participating on a television or radio program is one of the best types of promotion you can get for your business. Send e-mail, stop by, or mail to stations at least twice a year and let them know you are available. The cost is either minimal or free, and you invest just an hour or two of your time. The exposure will reach people who you won't reach any other way, and it will pay off for your business.

➤ Don't be nervous: If the thought of thousands of people listening to you makes you nervous, forget about them and concentrate on the one-to-one conversation with the host. Have water nearby to keep your throat clear.

➤ Be entertaining: The host always wants to entertain his or her audience and selects guest with unique opinions, views, or humorous things to say. Don't disappoint, or your on-air time may be cut short.

➤ Be interesting: Tell the audience something useful that they didn't already know. Use creative phrases.

➤ Prepare an opening and closing statement: Make your opening and closing statements short but memorable so that your time and comments will stay in the listeners' minds. Add the plug for your book or company briefly in the closing.

➤ Thank the host: Don't forget to thank the host for inviting you to be on the air and giving you the opportunity to present your story and answer questions. Always remember that it's the host's show and you are just the guest.

➤ Be ready for questions: Answer questions, whether from the host or from call-ins, in short sound bites rather than drawn-out explanations. Prepare a list of FAQs so you can be ready with quick responses to any of those.

➤ Keep it moving: Your host will want to cover as much as possible in a short time, so don't go on and on about any one subject. Boring dialog will lose listeners or put them to sleep.

➤ Stand up: Whether in the studio or on the phone, your voice will project better, sound more confident, and be more authoritative if you're standing. Standing also keeps you ready to think on your feet and give excitement to your message.

➤ Listen well: It's hard to answer a question or respond to a comment if you don't hear it clearly. Give the host or caller to the station enough time to speak and hear everything they are saying.

➤ Use vocal variety: Don't say everything at a monotone voice level. Emphasize phrases and get excited when you can. It keeps the audience's attention and makes your host stay awake.

There are some things that will make you a better radio show guest and maybe even get you invited back. If your "appearance" is over the telephone, never use the speaker, hold the handset or use a hands-free microphone.

Obsolete Products

The dictionary defines obsolete as *out of date, old-fashioned, antiquated,* and *of less use.* Does this sound like anything you're trying to sell? If you have become too comfortable with selling the same products and services, it's time to wake up and smell the market. Very few, if any, products last for decades without improvements or upgrades.

Look at automobiles; they have been selling for a hundred years now, but how much of the original are in today's models? The concept is the same but the structure changes regularly. In fact, most cars become obsolete every five to ten years and offer changes in *each* year's models. When you see an older car, say one that's fifteen years old, driving on the street, don't you wonder who would ever buy one like that? Although fifteen years ago it was the hot new model, now it's become obsolete. Would a car dealer stay in business if it only sold fifteen-year-old cars, even if they were new?

Many business owners become too comfortable marketing what has always sold well. But if you're running your business with blinders on, you may get broadsided. Sure, you can keep offering the same products and services year after year until three things happen:

➤ Major improvements in your product become available

➤ Your competitors offer alternative products and start making encroachments on your customer base

➤ The market for your products dies completely

Following are some classic examples of obsolete products that would seriously harm your business if you didn't weed them out:

➤ 8-track tapes

➤ Black-and-white TV

➤ Record player needles

➤ Tires with tubes

➤ Manual typewriters

➤ Leisure suit

➤ Outhouses

➤ Flash cubes

➤ Manual pinsetters

➤ Straight razors

➤ Coal furnaces

Some of these may sound a little silly today, but they all were popular in their own time. Companies stopped selling them because people stopped buying them. Don't make the decision to stop selling something when it's already too late.

CHAPTER 22

Sell Out or Bail Out

In This Chapter

➤ Growing too big

➤ Stress and long hours

➤ When to retire

➤ Time to sell or close up

Once your new business is open for a while, you may come to a crossroads. This chapter gives you several options for when the time arises. It's your business and you will decide what and which way to go.

Are You Getting Too Big?

When you started your business, all you wanted to do was grow and get bigger and bigger; that's everyone's goal. But after a while, successful growth may actually make your business larger than you expected. This is both good and bad news, depending on how you feel about it. It goes back to that old maxim "be careful what you wish for." You have more paperwork, more employees to manage, more benefits to pay, and more problems to solve. Plus you will have to sustain those sales and profits to pay for your expenses at this higher level.

Will you open more physical locations or do more business on your website through the Internet? One or more physical location additions will require build-out costs, furniture, equipment, and more employees. This is OK if it's how you do business and will not cannibalize the original location. Also remember that you will have to sign a several-year lease on the space unless you plan to buy it. It's always nice to say you have two or three locations until the first of the month when the rent and utility bills are due, not to mention the paydays for the new employees. I'm not trying to discourage you, but I want you to think through expanding your business before you make a final decision.

Business Alerts

Many owners who expand too quickly put a strain on cash flow and any reserve they may have. I have seen owners who opened additional locations almost go out of business because they didn't realize the cost and time involved. It's best to have a credit line already established before opening a second location so the new location doesn't hurt the cash flow of the first location.

One way to decide if you should open another location is to make a pros and cons list. Give two points for every con and one point for every pro. You have to have more pros than cons, and the pros need to score higher than the cons before you go ahead and open an additional location. If the pros don't score more points than the cons, wait a few months and go through this exercise again. You can still be scouting out locations and getting cost information, but don't make any commitments yet. If you're going to do this, you want a 100 percent positive attitude that it will work for you.

Too Many Nuisance Sales

Are you getting a lot of sales that are small and take so much to handle or process that you're not sure if you're making a profit on them? You don't have to continue doing business as you did when you first opened; you can change your rules and policies as you grow.

The price or minimum order you set when you started the business may now be too low. By raising your minimum order level, you may get less business, but you may do the same volume of business. By setting the small order price a little higher, you may or may not get the same volume of business but profits will be higher. Either or both adjustments will likely solve your problem.

These nuisance sales (and I don't mean bad sales) can cause your cost per sale to increase and reduce your profit. In many cases, it takes just as much time and effort to fill or process a small sale as a larger one. So you need to make adjustments and try to keep as much of this business as you can, but at a higher net profit level. These small sale situations may start to show up in the first three to six months after you open. Don't ignore them but work out a solution and implement it.

Stress and Long Hours

Some people can handle stress better than others. In business, it's a given that there will be stress, often especially for the owners and leaders. Like Harry Truman said, "the buck stops here," and the people at the top of the organization have to deal with "the buck" on a regular basis. There is no place to run or hide if you want your business to be prosperous and grow. The stress that comes with business problems must be accepted and must not affect decisions. The business and everyone else in it are expecting rational and positive decisions from the leader, regardless of the stress he or she feels at the time.

One way to handle stress in business situations is to prioritize tasks, expecially unpleasant ones, from the most important to those that can wait. Dealing with your state revenue department knocking on your door for unpaid sales tax and threatening to close you down tomorrow would be a high priority. But dealing with a delayed delivery of a hot-selling product that's out of stock can wait or be delegated to a trusted person on your staff. All problems are important and must be dealt with, but they may not require your immediate attention. Some may need to be put a little farther down on your list of priorities.

Business Vocab

Stress is what we define as personal pressure, anxiety, and the feeling you don't have complete control of the situation. Step back, move slower, and don't let stress influence your decision-making process.

When stress gets the best of you in your business environment, it's a good idea to get out of your store, office, or home business room for fifteen to thirty minutes. Take a walk around the block, get in your car, and go for an ice cream cone or just start talking to someone about a nonbusiness subject. When you get back to your business tasks, you may be able to think more clearly. It's well worth the short interruption to relieve a little stress and get back on track. Some stress is good and makes you more apt to come up with the right solution or decision. Use stress to your advantage, but manage it well.

Long Working Hours

I'm sure you're aware that when you start a business, it's not a 9 to 5 job; it's more like summertime's dawn to dusk. But that's not a surprise to most people. If you really love what you're doing, the long hours go fast. Your body may be tired daily, but your mind is ready to keep going. As your business grows, you expect to hire and delegate some of the more routine management tasks. Some owners do this and some won't let go of anything. Don't be the second type, because it will make you lose interest in the business.

Business Knowledge

There are many people who just love the long hours they spend in their businesses. They actually consider it their career and their hobby at the same time. We may call them workaholics, but to them it's just routine and they enjoy the work.

When owners get stuck with too many routine management tasks, they start to feel resentful toward the business. Long hours no longer go fast, and the work stops being fun and challenging. Working extended hours when you don't enjoy what you're doing can start to cause health problems. Family and friends will notice changes in your dispostion and some will shy away. It doesn't matter whether you've been with the business one year or twenty years—this is the time to make a decision to plan your exit.

Retire or Move On

As I said earlier, exiting a business can come early or late in your tenure, even if you are the founder. Few people start a business and stay with it for twenty years or more, but that certainly is an option. From my own personal observation, an owner is ready for a change of some type in about eight to ten years on average. At this point, an owner needs a way of disposing of the business. The three options are: selling it, closing it down, or handing it over to a family member.

Selling the Business

Selling the business may be the most profitable way to go. But if the business is not doing well or in a dying industry, selling it may be difficult or almost impossible.

Another option in a business-to-business company might be to just sell the repeat customers to a competitor. When you are officially closing, send a letter on your letterhead to your customers telling them that you've transferred all of their records to the competitor and you advise them to call or e-mail them for reorders. The company you sell them to should pay you a flat rate for each customer based on the order profit or a base amount right away, and about 20 to 30 percent of each customer's first order. A competitor would be foolish to turn this down because there's no risk.

Business Alerts

When preparing a business to sell to nonrelatives, look at the total sales first. The wise buyer will see that higher sales can be made into higher profits with some adjustments in expenses. Even if profits are low or nonexistent, large sales totals can entice a buyer who has ideas and past experience.

If you have high-profit customers, you can mail or e-mail a feeler letter to several competitors and see if they would bid offers for these customers. Then you can select the best offer combined with the best service for these customers. Most of the customers (80 to 90 percent) will follow your suggestion and call the buyer of their business when they order next. You may have to offer the company that is buying your high-profit customer a guarantee or refund offer.

You will still have to pay off your suppliers and other expenses, but this is a much faster way to sell your business than having it listed on the market for a year or two. Plus, you don't have to show any past company financial information, just the profits made on the customers' orders.

Giving the Business to a Family Member

Were you building a business to give to a son, daughter, or other member of your family? If this was your intention, that person who will own the business and be in charge should have worked in the business for at least a year or more. He or she should have seen all parts of the business, how it works, and the methods used to solve problems. Without this hands-on exposure before taking over the business, the chances of success are low.

You can encourage your relative to try new ideas, but not too quickly and nothing major at first. Advise him or her to learn everything about how to run the business successfully before implementing big changes.

Ask Yourself

Do you want the business you started and built to go on after you leave? Consider who you are turning it over to—new owner, relatives, friends, or employees—and be available to assist the new owner for the first several months.

Even before you hand down your business to a relative, a serious question needs to be answered: Does the person(s) who you are giving the business to really want it? Are they just going through the motions so they will get a decent paycheck, or do they really care about the business?

You will be able to see the answer over time while observing their attitude and work habits. If they are clock watchers or need a lot of time off, that's a negative sign. Many business owners have handed down their business to their children, who didn't really want it. They suffered greatly and some actually closed their business within two years. If you have spent a long time building the business from scratch, you don't want to see that happen.

Close the Business

There may be a situation when you're not able to sell the business within a reasonable time or for a reasonable price and you just want to get out now. Your option, then, is to close the business.

One way to close the business is to sell off all inventory and/or equipment at super-low prices. Pay off any open invoices and expenses and pocket whatever is left, if any.

You should consult your accountant and lawyer (Chapter 4) when declaring that income or return of funds originally invested. Be sure that all taxes are paid, and have your accountant submit all the correct forms to federal, state, and local government tax offices as well as notify them that you are closing. They must be notified of your final day or they will pursue you for estimated taxes after you close.

If your bills or liabilities greatly exceed your cash and assets, you might want to consider declaring bankruptcy. But if you want to get out of the business, don't consider Chapter 11 because it keeps the business open and reorganizes debt through the court. Taking the Chapter 7 or 13 route will close the business completely.

Whether you have any personal liability for unpaid bills and loans will depend on your business entity. All your personal guarantees will be due unless you are filing personally. Most corporations and LLCs will not hold you personally responsible, but you will lose any investment you put into the business.

Business Facts

According to www.bankruptcyaction.com, the number of filings for 2010 were as follows:

➤ Businesses: 58,322

➤ Non-Businesses: 1,538,033

Both of these statistics are more than double the filings for 2007.

Financially Unstable

When a business has trouble paying its bills and profits from sales can't cover the expenses, a company can be difficult to operate. If you are buying products for resale and you don't pay the suppliers on time, there could be a delay in future shipments. If you don't pay the electric and gas company bills, it could become very dark and cold in your office. At this point, you need to decide if you stay and work out these problems or leave the business in some way. This is not the fun part of owning a business, but it does happen to many of us and we need to make a decision about which direction we want to go.

If you want to try to work things out, you may be able to sell the business at a higher price after you stabilize your financial situation, which could take from a few months to several years to accomplish. If you want to just shut down and leave, consider one of the methods previously mentioned. Either way, financial problems create a crossroads, and choices have to be made, sooner rather than later.

INDEX

A

Accepting Credit Cards and Giving Credit 107–115
  customer credit 113–115
    credit policy 114–115
    deposits 114
    large corporations 114
    lease to buy 115
    progress payments 114
    repeat customers 114
    selling for resale 115
  merchant service provider 107–110
    application 107
      batch settlement 108
      processing fee 108
      shopping cart software 108
      transaction fees 108
    credit card machine 109
      point-of-service (POS) register 109
      www.merchantwarehouse.com 109
      www.usamerchantsolutions.com 109
    processing software 109–110
      credit and debit cards 110
  PayPal 110–111
  scams and excessive fees 111–113
    batch-out fees 113
    card decline fees 113
    chargeback fees 113
    customer support charges 112
    hidden setup charges 112
    report charges 113
    statement fees 113
    tech support fees 113
    termination charges 112
    training charges 113
    voice authorization fees 113
Accountants, Lawyers, and Bankers 41–50
  accountants 42–46
    account assignment 43–44
    changing accountants 45–46
    federal tax ID 42
    relationship 43
    state tax ID 42
    tax reports 44
    what to expect 44–45
      accounting records 45
      government agencies 44
      IRS 44–45
      letters 44–45
      power of attorney 45
  bankers 49–50
    business loan 49
    changing banks 50
    Dun & Bradstreet report 50
    line of credit 49
    loan officer 49
    relationship 49
  lawyers 46–48
    after-hours number 48
    availability 48
    Better Business Bureau 48
    business entity selection 48
    fees 46
    finding a good lawyer 47
      bar association 47
      business organization meeting 47
      business people 47
      Chamber of Commerce 47
      personal referral 47
    office hours 48
    prepaid legal services 48
    We The People 48
  need for professionals 41–42
Ask Yourself v, 2, 4, 21, 36, 45, 50, 66, 71, 89, 103, 108, 120, 121, 136, 149, 150, 167, 172, 182, 215, 220, 234, 240, 250

B

Business Alerts 8, 13, 26, 32, 39, 43, 51, 58, 60, 61, 83, 86, 93, 97, 100, 105, 112, 131, 134, 137, 148, 153, 164, 177, 181, 183, 193, 204, 206, 210, 211, 230, 246, 249

Business Facts 3, 17, 50, 52, 53, 56, 64, 67, 68, 70, 74, 110, 119, 125, 154, 158, 195, 196, 198, 207, 251

Business Knowledge 5, 9, 11, 23, 36, 38, 44, 45, 47, 57, 59, 67, 75, 77, 82, 88, 93, 102, 118, 124, 129, 132, 143, 146, 158, 161, 162, 175, 179, 186, 188, 191, 202, 204, 216, 222, 228, 236, 237, 238, 242, 248

Business Vocab 2, 19, 31, 42, 64, 65, 77, 104, 108, 114, 125, 139, 165, 170, 185, 203, 214, 222, 232, 247

Buying a Business 73–83
  due diligence 76
    answers to problems 76
    brand 78
    business age 76
    business broker 77
    business neighbors 79
    buyout option 79
    cash flow 77
    copyrights 78
    corporation or business 78
    customer demographics 76
    customer lists 78
    customer loyalty 79
    customer mailing list 76
    debt 77
    employee relations 78
    employee retention 76
    equipment 76
    equipment upgrade 79
    financial statements 76–78
    inventory 76
    key employees 78
    lawsuits 79
    learning the business 76
    lease transfer 76
    licenses 78
    location 76
    long-term obligations 78
    noncompete clause 76, 78
    office/store lease 78
    patents 78
    payroll/benefits 76
    phone directory ads 78
    products/services 76
    profitability 76
    reason for selling 76
    renovations 78
    security deposits 78
    supplier accounts 78
    target market 76
    training 76
    transfer suppliers 76
  employees and training 79–81
    break-in period 79–80
    retraining the employees 80–81
    training the new owner 80
  lease issues 79
    equipment currency 79
    payments 79
    vehicles 79
  retraining the employees
    customers 80
    employee brainstorm 80
    suppliers and vendors 81
  seller financing 81–83
    buy-sell negotiation 82
    cash down payment 82
    company unemployment
      State Department of Labor 83
    key man insurance 83
    letter of intent 82
    life insurance policy 83
    pending legal issues 83
    personal guaranty 83
    promissory note 83
    proof of funds 82
  training the new owner
    on-call period 80

on-site training 80
where to find an existing business 74–75
  advertisements 74–75
  business brokers 75
  referrals 75
    banks 75
    Chamber of Commerce 75
    networking groups 75
    Rotary 75
    sales rep groups 75
    SCORE 75
why buy an existing business? 73–74

C

Chamber of Commerce xii, 10, 34, 47, 75, 105,
    119, 162, 192, 235–236
Customer Service 179–189
  available for customer consultation 180–182
    customer-friendly hours 180–181
    promises 182
  competition 183–184
    business hours 184
    customer treatment 184
    employee pay 184
    expansion 184
    financial resources 183
    identify competitors 183
    location 184
    market strategies 184
    niche products 184
    on-site vs. absentee owners 184
    pricing strategies 184
    staffing level 184
    strengths 184
    website 184
  importance of customer service 179–180
  outsource and monitor 185
  outstanding service 185–187
    create loyalty 188–189
    customer service rules 188
    effects of customer service 186
    exceeding expectations 186–187
    telephone

    customer survey 187
    order processing 187
    order satisfaction 187
    referrals 187
    special discounts 187
    suggestions 187
    testimonials 187
    voice mail messages 187
  telephone service 186–187
  unresponsive customers 189

D

Defining Your Target Market 85–97
  business customer profile 87
    competitive advantage 87
    competitors 87
    customer loyalty 87
    custom products 87
    industry stability 87
    order frequency 87
    product innovation 87
    product match 87
    service 87
  competitors 89–91
    company type 90
    customer service 90
    employee wages 90
    identify competitors 90
    marketing 91
    new locations 90
    niche products 90
    ownership activity 90
    pricing strategy 90
    strong points 90
    trade magazines 89
    weaknesses 91
  consumer demographics 86–87
    age range 86
    education level 86
    ethnic background 86
    family size 86
    gender 86
    income range 86

neighborhood age 86
  work profile 86
cp
  location 91
  site visit 91
finding customers 92–93
  business customers 92
  online customers 93
  retail customers 92
jump-start business 93–95
  advance orders 96
  advertising 95
  cash discounts 96
  contest 95
  direct mail 94
  free consultation 95
  free literature 94
  free seminar 96
  free trial 95
  gifts 95
  guarantee 96
  introductory offers 94–95
  networking 96
  press releases 95
  sales appointments 94
  teach a class 96
  telemarketing 94
  toll-free number 94
  website 96
reasons to buy 87–89
  added value 88
  business hours 89
  customer education 88
  customer service 88
  delivery/availability 88
  frontline experts 89
  loyalty rewards 88
  returns/exchanges 89
  selection 88
  signage 88
  special orders 88
  unique selling proposition (USP) 88
staffing levels

employees 90
target markets 85–86

E

Employees 127–144
  building trust 144
  frontline authority
    customer satisfaction 140
    monthly resolution fund 140
    team players 140–141
      duties and goals 140
  interview process 128–134
    hiring hourly employees 128–129
  interview with care
    employment application form 131
    hiring hourly employees
      Employee's Withholding Allowance Certifi-
        cate 129
      Form W-4 129
      income tax withholding 129
      red flags 128–129
    hiring telemarketing employees 130–131
      script trial run 131
      skill set 130–131
    in-store sales people 131–132
      skill set 131–132
    interview questions 133–134
    outside sales people 132–133
  superstar employees 142–144
    traits 143–144
  supervise, mentor, and delegate 135–142
    bully employees 141–142
      bullying other employees 142
      bullying the boss 142
      bullying the customer 141
    delegate and oversee 137–138
    employee assets 136
    frontline authority 139–140
    guidelines 135–136
    negative attitude 136
    open-door policy 138–139
    positive attitude 136
    team players

after-work sports team 141
autonomy 140
bonuses 141
employee recognition 141
employee retention 141
employee rewards 140
employees suggestions 140
follow through 141
open-door policy 141
promotions 141
secondary positions 140
trust and respect 141
temps 132
train, retrain, and cross train 134–135
cross training manual 135
scheduled retraining sessions 135

F

First-Year Problems 209–217
first-year pitfalls 213–217
bad publicity 214–217
big competition 214
big-order errors 215
careless bookkeeping 215
collection problems 214
employees from hell 213
excessive spending 213
inadequate cash flow 214
lost customers 213
no new customers 213
pricing dilemmas 214
suppliers want COD 214
unpredictable events 215
overspending 212–213
cash flow 213
overstaffing 213
part-time employees 213
staff multitasking 213
temps 213
purchase limits 213
owner attitude and burnout 211–212
first-year burnout 211–212

day off 212
delegate 212
key employee 212
unpredictable events 209–210
accidents 210
acts of violence 210
crime scene 210
death 210
economy 210
employee injury 210
fires 210
key employee departure 210
natural disasters 210
road construction 210
utility outages 210
weather 210
Franchises 63–71
business hours 65
due diligence 68–70
additional locations 69
approved products 69
Better Business Bureau 69
company hot line 69
corporate-owned stores 69
Dun & Bradstreet 69
equipment ordering help 69
franchisee references 69
franchisor financing 69
location help 69
normal business hours 69
on-site training 69
product prices 69
protected territory 69
quality of products/services 69
reputation in industry 69
store design plans 69
expertise 63–64
attitude 64–65
focus 64
risk 65
franchise dos and don'ts 70–71
franchise fee 66
proprietary information 66

rent a franchise 65
trademark 65
where to find a franchise 66–68
  bookstore 66
  start-up capital 67
  start-up literature 68
  www.everyfranchise.com 67
  www.franchise.com 67
  www.franchiseleader.com (resales) 67
  www.franchiseopportunities.com 67
  www.franchiseresales.com (resales) 67
  www.franchisesolutions.com 67

L

Location 51–62
  distribution/industrial space 54–55
    considerations 55
      24/7 availability 55
      delivery dock 55
      electric 55
      floor material 55
      hazardous materials 55
      heating and AC 55
      lighting 55
      major roads 55
      noise restrictions 55
      office space 55
      parking 55
      raw materials 55
      signage 55
      storage space 55
      ventilation 55
      waste space 55
      water pressure 55
      zoning restrictions 55
    leasing agent 54
    office-warehouse unit 54–55
  home-based business setup 52–54
    air purifier 53
    closed-circuit television 53
    CO detector 53
    cushioned chair 53
    dedicated fax line 53

    deliveries 54
    delivery vehicle 54
    fire extinguisher 53
    large waste basket 53
    locked file cabinets 53
    refrigerator 53
    separate landline 53
    smoke alarm 53
    tax deduction 52
    water cooler 53
    zoning laws 54
  Internet business 60
    backup files 60
    executive site 60
    physical office 60
  leases and options 60–61
    free rent period 61
    lease 60–61
    lease dos and don'ts 61–62
    renewal clause 61
    rental agreement 60
  retail space 55–59
    central location 56–57
      commercial real estate agent 57
    due diligence 57–58
      neighboring businesses 58
      property management 58
      site visit 58
    landlord 58
    remodel 58
    reorganize merchandise 58
    shopping mall 58–59
      customer traffic 59
      mall events 59
      signage 59
      store design 59
    triple net charges 58
  space 51–52

M

Making the Commitment 1–15
  business assistance 10–11
    SCORE 10–11

Success Story Archives 11
www.score.org 11
business plan 14–15
know your industry 4–7
  observe the business 6–7
  work in the industry 5–6
learn how a business works 7–9
  continuing education 8–9
    community college 8
    seminar 8
  read and listen 9–10
    Amazon.com 9
    Barnesandnoble.com 9
starting a small business 1–4
  case study 3–4
  your goals 2–3
Marketing and Publicity 191–202
  advertising 195–197
    advertise to four levels 195–196
      casual prospects 196
      existing customers 195
      rest of the world 196
      serious prospects 196
    advertising don'ts 196–197
  cheap marketing ideas 192–193
    brainstorm 192–193
    Chamber of Commerce 192
    customer service 192
    networking 192
    speaking engagements 192
    supplier contact 193
    trade shows 193
    write articles 192
  direct mail 197–200
    e-mail marketing 200
    postcard mailings

headline 199
mailing 200
mailing list 199
offer 199
postcard size 199
printing 199
response 200
timing 199
free publicity 193–195
  broadcast interviews 195
  correction notices 195
  editorial calendar 194
  follow up 194
  interesting news copy 194
  media demographics 194
  media tours 194
  news services 194
  press release 194
  review samples 194
  timing 194
  wire services 194
marketing mistakes 201–202
new promotion ideas 201

N

New Business Tips and Ideas 219–236, 227–244
  business associations 235–237
  business cards 238–239
  business slowdowns 227–231
    serious slowdown 229–230
      ideas 229–230
    temporary slow periods 228–229
    unnecessary personnel 230–231
  discounts 239
  high rollers 241–242
  home-based business meetings 239–240
  obsolete products 243–244
  prepare for slowdown 231–233
  radio guest 242–243
  small business advantage 233–235
  Toastmasters 236–237

P

Planning Your Grand Opening 157–168
  budget 158
  events and celebrations 166–168
    anniversary celebration 167–168
    birthdays 167
    clothing drive 166
    food drive 166
    sales 166
  giveaways and deals 161–162
    www.americas-cards.com 161
  ideas 158
  jump-start your business 158–160
    advance order specials 159
    advertising 159
    cash discounts 159
    contest 159
    direct mail 159–160
    free consultations 159
    free literature 159
    free trial 159
    gifts 159
    guarantee 159
    introductory offers 159
    press releases 159
    promotions 160
    sales appointments 159
    seminar 159
    sense of urgency 160
    telemarketing 159
  opening day 157–158
  partner with other businesses 162–163
    BNI 162
    cross promotions 162–163
    Sales Pros 162
  radio and television 165–166
    follow up 166
    national talk shows 166
    publicity 165
    regional talk shows 166
    show producer 166
    target audience 166
  soft opening 162
  the media 164–165
    articles 165
      Bacon's Magazine Directory 165
      Bacon's Newspaper Directory 165
    expert in your field
      presentations 165
    interview 164
    newspapers 164
    radio stations 164
  website celebration 161
Products, Services, Guarantees 169–177
  new products and services 176–177
  one-stop shop 169–170
  post-sale follow up 174–175
    contact suggestions 175
  pricing 171–173
    competitors 171–172
    incorrect pricing 171–172
    pricing challenges 172–173
    reputation 172
    value 171–172
  sales guarantee 170
    refund 170
    repair 170
    replacement 170
  state-of-the-art products 173–174
    marketing and promotion 173
    silver, gold, and platinum levels 174
  supplier deals 175–176
    consignment 176
    overstock 176
    reduced price 176
Promotions 203–208
  cross promotion 204
  ideas for promotions 203–207
    contests 203
    coupons 203
    events 203
    exhibits 203
    games 203
    gift cards 206–207
    sale ideas 204–206

costumed characters 205
coupons 205
displays 205
end-of-the-season sale 205
event name 204
mailing list announcement 205
newspaper advertising 205
newspaper insert 205
popular items 205
price reduction 205
signage 205
sufficient stock 204
supplier discounts 205
time limit 205
VIP customer list 205
scratch offs 203
stunts 207
retail promotion ideas 207–208

S

Sell Out or Bail Out 245–251
financial instability 251
growing too big 245–246
nuisance sales 246–247
retire or move on 248–251
close the business 250–251
giving the business to family member 249–250
selling the business 248–249
stress and long hours 247–248
Setting Up Suppliers 99–106
finding suppliers 99–101
Million Dollar Directory 100
product samples 100
testimonials 100
Thomas Industrial Directory 100
open credit 104
deposits 104
discount 104
prepayment terms 104
outsourcing 105–106
find outsourcers 105–106
quality control 106
partner with suppliers 101–102

free sales literature 101
supplier loyalty 102
supplier relationship 102
quantity pricing 103
shipping costs 103
Start-Up Capital 31–40
angels 33–34
accountant 34
angel headhunters 34
annual meetings 34
attorney 34
business plan 34
entrepreneurs 34
high-level angels 33–34
low-level angels 33–34
online pledge funds 34
private clubs 34
referrals 34
successful professionals 34
bank and credit union loans 34–36
bankers' questions 34–35
accounts payable 35
accounts receivable 35
business plan 35
cash flow 35
competitors 35
expense control 35
industry outlook 35
inventory controls 35
owner/officer commitment 35
payroll 35
profit history 35
repayment scenarios 35
sales and gross profits 35
use of loan proceeds 35
reasons for rejection 35–36
credit cards and lines of credit 36–37
business credit cards 36
equity line of credit 37
personal credit cards 36–37
revolving line of credit 37
friends
investment agreement 32–33

grants
   Small Business Investment Company (SBIC) 40
home equity financing 37–38
  appraisal 37
  credit score 37
  equity credit line 38
  HELOC (home equity line of credit) 38
  income verification 37
  loan to value 37
  tax deduction 38
needed funds 31–32
other capital sources 38–40
  bootstrapping 39
    Apple Computer 39
    Domino's Pizza 39
    Nike 39
    UPS 39
  business incubators 39
  grants 40
    AOL 40
    Callaway Golf 40
    FedEx 40
    National Association of Small Business In-
      vestment Companies (NASBIC) 40
    SBA 40
    Staples 40
  venture capital firms 39
relatives
  business plans 33
  investment agreement 33
SBA loan 38
Small Business Administration (SBA) 36
www.sba.gov 36

W

Website and Blog 117–126
  blogs 124–126
    content updates 126
    cross-promotion 126
    Facebook 126
    starting your blog 125
    Twitter 126
  business goals 118

  frequently asked questions (FAQ) 118
  home page copy 118
  home page design 118–119
  Internet service provider (ISP) 119
  purpose 121
  purpose of website 117–118
  Royal.Pingdom.com 119
  shopping cart software 119
  site promotion 123–124
    affiliate marketing 124
      pay per click 124
      pay per sale 124
  site updates 121–122
  suggestion box link 122–123
    comments and questions
      posting the results 123
  update site
    background colors 122
    content 122
    promotional e-mails 122
  URL 119
  website address 119
  website design
    software package 120
  website don'ts 120
  www.godaddy.com 119
  www.infoplease.com 125

Y

Your Business Structure 17–29
  business entity 19
  C corporation
    general corporation 21–22
    pros and cons 22–23
  general partnership 19–20
    pros and cons 20
  Limited Liability Company (LLC) 24–25
    pros and cons 24–25
  naming your business 26–28
    naming dos and don'ts 27–28
    unique name 26–27
  protect your business name 28–29
    service mark (SM) 28

  trademark (TM) 28
S corporation 23–24
  IRS form 2553 23
  pros and cons 24
sole proprietorship 18–19
  doing business as (dba) 18
  pros and cons 18–19
United States Patent and Trademark Office
  www.uspto.gov 26
U.S. Census Bureau 17

ABOUT THE AUTHOR

Barry is the author of 6 business books (2 International) and is a speaker at many conventions. conferences. trade shows and corporate meetings. He has assisted and coached other entrepreneurs on starting a business, customer service and inexpensive marketing methods.

He began his entrepreneurial career when he was only five years old. He decided that he wasn't going to sit for hours in front of his house and try to sell a pitcher of lemonade. He loaded two pitchers in his wagon and took them to nearby construction sites and sold out in fifteen minutes. When he got back home, his friend's pitchers were still almost full. At age ten, he was given the worst paper route because he was the youngest but he tripled the number of subscribers within one year to one of the largest paper routes in Chicago.

Barry has started, operated and survived in 20 businesses over the past 30 years, several at the same time. He has become an expert and created lucrative markets for computer supplies, business forms, Norman Rockwell lithographs. collector cookie jars, old casino chips and a couple of franchise retail stores.

He has over 100 published articles in business journals, Chamber and Association newsletters and featured articles for Home Business and Opportunity World magazines. His business success articles have been used on the American Management Association website for members only. His BLOG (www.barrysbusinessbooster.blogspot.com) is visited every day by many small business owners and entrepreneurs.

Barry is available as a speaker for your next event, conference or company meeting. www.idealetter.com or email: idealetter@aol.com.

36584796R00160

10 December 2014